Praise for *Home Field Advantage*

"I think any new homeschool family should have *Home Field Advantage* when they begin their journey. But why wait for when school starts? Give this book as a baby gift and get the family off to the right start!"

– Gena Jones, *parent*

"As a mother of soon-to-be school-age children, I find *Home Field Advantage* to be just the resource I'll need to inform my homeschooling decisions. After reading it, I feel much more knowledgeable about the most common teaching methods and how to choose the methods that will work best for my family. I am confident that with the help of the resources in this book, I will be able to make a great homeschooling plan and adapt it as needed. I am looking forward to the journey ahead."

– Eva Mayfield, *parent*

"I am definitely adding *Home Field Advantage* to my reference books for homeschooling my four children. Not only does the book give me more tools to craft a better education for my kids and makes implementation so doable, but reading it has also deepened and enriched my understanding of my children! It's so refreshing to get the *Cliff Notes* on education methods and philosophies from an expert who isn't selling any one of them! Why hasn't such a useful tool for parents come along before?! If you have ever hesitated to homeschool and to take education out of the hands of the trained experts, here is one book saying you can! After reading it, you'll be certain the education experts shouldn't be the only ones having all the fun with your kids!"

– Steffanie Casperson, *parent*

D0874810

HOME FIELD ADVANTAGE

A Guide to Choosing Teaching Methods for

Your Homeschooling Champions

SKYLA KING-CHRISTISON

Night Owls Press

Published by Night Owls Press LLC, San Francisco, CA, 94119, U.S.A.,
www.nightowlspress.com.

Editor: Genevieve DeGuzman
Production Editor: Andrew Tang
Cover photo by Skyla King-Christison
Cover and book design: Night Owls Press

Library of Congress Cataloging-in-Publication Data:
King-Christison, Skyla.
Home field advantage: a guide to choosing teaching methods for your homeschooling champions/ Skyla King-Christison
p. cm.
Includes bibliographic references.

Paperback ISBN-13: 9781937645076
E-book ISBN-13: 9781937645069

1. Education. 2. Homeschooling - Methods.

2013930773

For Joe and the kids: You are my everything, and I wouldn't trade you for anything!

CONTENTS

HOME FIELD ADVANTAGE

A Guide to Choosing Teaching Methods for

Your Homeschooling Champions

INTRODUCTION:
The Adventure Starts

Successful teaching takes experience and knowledge. One comes with time, and the other comes with study.

IT'S six in the morning. The alarm on my cell phone begins to play a cello suite, a carefully selected alarm tone that wakes me without alerting the kids still sleeping in the next room that someone tall enough to cook breakfast is already awake. I sneak into the living room for some prayer time and morning meditation before ironing Joe's work clothes and peeling some vegetables for my breakfast juice. I cherish those fleeting morning moments before the high-energy day begins to unfold. There's no time quite so calm and reassuring as that hour or so before the rest of the world wakes up.

Soon I hear Joe's alarm, loud enough to wake the dead and signaling the end of the peaceful morning quiet and the beginning of the day. I can hear the kids beginning to stir, milling around their rooms, and the rustling of Joe readying himself for another day at the office. The boys, Hunter and Haven, don't get up right away, but spend a few minutes in their side-by-side beds reading books to each other, giggling over a story about a lap dog who hates having to wear a bow because the other dogs make fun of him. My eldest, Hannah Jane, is already making her bed and choosing the day's fashion statement.

Almost every day starts off the same way. As part of their chores, the kids must make their beds and feed their animals: Hannah Jane takes care of the dogs because no one else wants to deal with them. Haven is on cat duty and waits for Hannah Jane in the garage, so that she doesn't get scared being alone. Hunter feeds his beta fish, Fin McMissile, on the kitchen counter.

Soon they're all lined up at the breakfast bar, Hunter and Haven with their bowls of oatmeal sprinkled with cinnamon, and Hannah Jane with her wheat toast and butter. I sit with them, perched beside my Jack LaLanne juicer, gulping down my breakfast of juiced greens as we form a plan for the day.

We all talk about what's on the day's agenda, whether it's a field trip day, a co-op day, or whether there are some errands to be run. Then the kids all tell me what super special thing they have planned for the day: Today, Hunter says he wants to ride his bike. Haven wants to play his favorite games on Starfall (more.starfall.com), an online collection of math and language arts activities. Hannah Jane remarks that we really need to spend more time painting and that she wants to lead us all in a painting class in the afternoon. This makes me laugh because this is typical Hannah Jane confidence on display. She's led classes for her dolls before, and she's sure she's awesome at everything she does—so, naturally, we all need to take her class.

Once the breakfast dishes are put away, we scurry down to the schoolroom where we start off class with "circle time." First, we read a story from a collection of Baha'i children stories and work on memorizing a prayer. Then, we get out the rhythm sticks and clack them together as we sing out a poem about a little bird that is afraid to fly. Hannah Jane and Hunter roll on the floor with giggles because their 4-year-old brother, Haven, gets such a serious look on his face when he recites poetry. Haven loves the attention so he keeps going, louder and more serious than ever, before breaking out of character and joining them in wild laughter. We then move to singing skip-counting songs while we pass bean bags around in a circle and sing our way through all of the 50 states and their capitals. Finally, we do a little Montessori-style grammar lesson on a circular chalkboard that I made from an old tabletop and some chalkboard paint.

Once we've worked our way through the energetic, lighthearted subjects that we can all do as a family, the kids head off to their desks. Their three little desks, purchased from a city school liquidation sale, are clustered together so that the kids all face each other. Hannah Jane, age 8, works at her own pace and without much guidance. She starts on her spelling assignments and Latin work before heading upstairs to the family desktop computer to do her online lessons where she writes reports and posts them to her blog. Today's report is about tsunamis. Her other assignments for the day are all bookmarked in her textbooks and follow a similar course each week, so she can seamlessly move from one activity to the next on her own without much prompting from me.

The boys, just 18 months apart in age, now 6- and 4-years-old, work mostly on the same things and need much more of my attention to get through their day. Hunter likes to have his own space, so he sets up paper folders, standing open around the perimeter of his desk, marking his learning territory in case it's ever in question. During our spelling lesson, I call out words that we've been working on, and the boys take a stab at each one on their own white boards. Hunter's work is mostly right and Haven's work mostly isn't, but Haven is just 4-years-old, so I don't worry too much. Haven can spell "say" but not "says" even when I announce, "The next word is *says*. It is spelled like "say" with an "s" on the end." I figure he's doing a pretty fantastic job for his age and that he'll pick it up eventually just by being there.

As we push through Hunter's class work, Haven loses interest and asks permission to work on playdough at his desk instead. Hunter moves on to math, and as he puzzles aloud over a story problem, Haven sits nearby, silently recreating the problem in dough sculptures to tease out the solution. When Haven blurts out the correct answer to a problem, Hunter sulks for a moment; Haven has beat him to the punch when he's supposed to be playing with playdough. But Hunter manages to compliment his younger brother. "Good job, Haven. That was pretty hard and you got it." And he adds, "I could have gotten it, too, if I'd had playdough, you know."

By noon we're all ready for lunch. The kids make their own lunches and a giant mess to go with it. The boys both make peanut butter and jelly sandwiches. Hannah Jane makes a cheese quesadilla, and as soon as Haven sees it, he wishes he'd made that instead. They strike a deal, each giving the other half of their food so that each gets a little of both. I ask the boys to clean the jelly mess on the floor, and bless their hearts, they do try. But true to form, the gooey mess manages to get more gooey. I resist the urge to clean it up right after them because I want them to feel like their efforts are appreciated. As soon as they're gone, I attack the now giant sticky swirl on the floor with a wet rag.

After lunch, Hannah Jane practices playing the flute in her bedroom, while Haven perfects his two-handed rendition of *Twinkle, Twinkle* on the piano. Hunter still insists that he doesn't like to play music and so he hangs out on the stairs whining about how boring it is when everyone else is practicing an instrument while he wants to play outside in the field.

As soon as the music session is over, the three of them race off into the goat field to wile away a few hours having some grand adventure under the remotest tree, just where the little irrigation canal crosses with a trickle of water on to the neighbor's property. Their voices are faint from where I watch them in the sunroom window, but I can see them across the acreage, crouching in the high grass together, chasing a chicken, and then sitting and talking seriously for a long, long while.

It's during these afternoon stretches of outdoor playtime that I write, reply to e-mails, and blog about the latest and greatest homeschool activities we've discovered or invented. I make phone calls, schedule the roofer to come give an estimate, and call my friend, Steff, to see if she's up for a Mom's Night Out at the Crepery. It's also during this time that I plan for the week ahead and search the Web for just the right art project to accentuate next week's lessons. Afternoon's recess is a time for deep breaths, for reflecting on what we've done, where we started, and new goals we need to be moving towards as a homeschooling family.

It's also during that priceless hour or so in the glow of the afternoon sun that I reflect on just how good life is and how lucky we are to be home, learning together as a family. I think back on my time in the classroom, about my friends who feel like they never get enough time with their kids. Then I look out the window at my three little ones imping around the field with their pants rolled high, shin deep in cold, running water that's diverted from the river that overflows with the snowmelt, and I think, *We've had our challenges, but we've done well.*

From Teacher to Homeschooling Mom

In college, I was often asked by professors, prospective employers, and others why I wanted to be a teacher. My answers were well rehearsed: I had always had a fascination with the way our brains absorb information, and I had a desire to help guide the next generation down a path of excellence. For those inclined to teach, these are the idealistic if not the usual motivations.

But I harbored another reason why I wanted to become a teacher, one that I rarely shared with others at the time: I had my heart set on homeschooling.

I kept this a secret from my colleagues and classmates. No one pursued a degree in education with homeschooling in mind. It just wasn't done. To my peers who were passionate about the service of teaching, my decision to pursue a college degree with homeschooling as the end game would have seemed unusual, even downright scandalous. Looking back, I now know it was the best choice I ever made.

Despite these secret motivations, up through graduation I was a teacher in training in the very conventional sense. I won prestigious teaching awards and accolades for my course work aimed at teaching middle school math and science, and I felt ready to tackle the classroom. Like most teachers, I worked for an unpaid year in the public schools and then set out to find my first paid position, passionate to put my ideals and skills to the test.

We arrived in our new home state of Oregon after the school year had begun, so all of the positions in my area were already filled. This meant applying for a job outside my training in a special education classroom. During an interview for my first teaching job, I was asked the usual questions about my background, but then the interview shifted into startling territory. I was asked how I felt about putting kids in a padded closet.

My eyes widened. "A padded closet?" I repeated.

The interviewer didn't blink. Kids exhibiting behavioral problems in class were occasionally confined, he explained, until someone stronger and trained in behavioral management could come and haul them off. I'd simply have to press my foot to the door for the duration of their confinement (obviously it would be against the law to put a lock on that door).

Welcome to the institutional environment of the public school system.

Looking back, I knew this was a red flag, a harbinger of what I could expect in the classroom, but I was young, desperate to be employed, and certain that once I was on the "inside" I could fix the system. Surely, with my sunny disposition and desire to help, I would never need this dreadful padded closet. I would be responsive to the needs of my students and all would be well.

I was wrong.

Without any background or training in special education, I found myself working in a classroom with eight third, fourth, and fifth graders who were considered too violent to be integrated into a mainstream classroom, two autistic students, three other teachers, and the padded closet. Disruptions were the rule of law during the day. The children who were so out of control that they were a risk to other students were routinely kept in the closet until they either calmed down or had to be removed by strong-armed behavioral specialists. I still remember the peephole on the closet door, a tiny window into that dreaded confined space. The days were long and emotionally draining. Tense moments in the classroom were often mirrored outside the classroom during meetings with defensive and irate parents.

Despite my best intentions going in, I never did fix the system.

The experience did whet my interest in behavioral research. After just one year, I applied to a doctoral program in school psychology and looked forward to working under researchers committed to demystifying and treating anti-social behavior among students. I thought if I learned from the best and armed myself with an understanding of psychology instead of just a smile, I would stand a better chance of making a difference in the classroom. As a school psychologist with credentials, I would be able to return to the classroom that I had left and show that these kids were capable of learning.

Then the unexpected happened. A few days after my interviews for the school psychology program, my husband and I found out that we were expecting our first child. This changed everything and life priorities and career ambitions were shuffled around. I politely turned down my acceptance to the graduate program, notified my employer that I wouldn't be returning after summer break, and got ready for the next big challenge: being a career mom.

Thinking back to my studies in the field of education, I realized I wasn't just preparing to become a great teacher inside a classroom. I also wanted teaching to inform my role as a parent and to be a great teacher inside the home.

Everyone was sure I would change my mind. The university offered a deferral to the program, and the public school discussed maternity leave as an option. But the prospect of raising a family fundamentally changed something inside me. Now the children I would be responsible for were my own. I had a real chance to provide an education in a way I thought best. Previously uncontrollable factors such as a child's home life were in my control. I would have the prerogative to use a "whole child" framework, where I could value every moment and filter out outside expectations and negativity. I could observe changes in a child's thinking around the clock and over a span of an entire education, tweaking lessons to make things click for each individual in a perfectly natural way without regard for a roomful of students and their needs.

This was what I'd been waiting for.

The final decision to homeschool our children came when Hannah Jane was finishing up her second year of preschool. Because of her October birthday, she didn't make the age cut-off for kindergarten and had to be held back a year. Rather than do another year of preschool we decided it was the opportune time to test out homeschooling. We would just try it on and see how it felt. If it didn't work, she could start kindergarten the following year and not fall behind. If our homeschooling experiment went well, then we would proceed at home, with a fair understanding of the lifestyle we would be adopting.

We endured our share of doubts. My husband often asked, "Are you sure about this?" We had long talks into the night. Would I get burnt out with my days being endless stretches of the same thing, with no breaks or transitions between work and home? Would I even be able to teach three different grades at once when the kids got older and subjects became more varied and intense? What would our families think? Were we ready to be labeled hippies, fanatics, helicopter parents, or the endless number of other monikers that get stamped on your forehead like a scarlet letter when you tell people you homeschool? Being as sensitive as I am, would I be able to stand up to the scrutiny of a world that has embraced public education, staring me in the eye and saying, "So you think you can do better? Prove it."

But then I would think for a second about teaching a classroom of someone else's kids or my own, and it seemed pretty clear that this was the way to go. The idea of sending my own children to the institutions I had just peeked inside of was scarier than the scrutiny of the world. All of those fears faded in comparison with the very real and exciting idea that I could give my children more at home than the schools ever could.

FAST FORWARD TO the present. Since starting with Hannah Jane, our other two children, Hunter and Haven, are now completely homeschooled. In those five years, we have loved almost every minute of the experience and still dream of homeschooling our way through middle school and high school!

Over time, as I have met more and more homeschooling families through co-ops and play groups, I found that I was constantly being asked about how we were schooling at home, or what was being taught in public schools. While many homeschooling parents are confident that homeschooling was the right choice, they are also constantly second guessing themselves and their own skills. At the playground, parents picked each others' brains over curriculum and scheduling, trying desperately to get a feel for what other families were doing and trying to make sure that they weren't missing out on any critical content or activities.

Then a light bulb went off in my head.

Echoes of the professional teacher I trained to be got me thinking about ways to reach out to other parents and share what I had learned over the years in my training on educational methods that could be adapted for the home. I started looking around. I searched our local library, canvassed friends for recommendations, and paged through the bookstore at Amazon and other retailers. I couldn't find a single book that parents could turn to for a crash course in teacher's education. What resources were available to parents that would provide an overview of all the educational and teaching method options out there?

The ideal book would outline a variety of theories and methodologies and lay it all out, giving parents the "big picture" of education. Wouldn't it be fabulous if parents didn't have to rely on fortuitous conversations at the playground to get advice on how to tailor their lessons to their needs?

Since the ideal book didn't yet exist, I decided to write one. The book in your hands is the result of that thinking and research.

About the Book

Home Field Advantage is an easy-to-use guide to some of the major approaches to education and the overarching theories on how children learn. It is the result of many years asking myself what the average parent needs to know in order to find success and peace while educating their children at home.

Sure, parents and families can do their own research on education theory and practice, but it can be time-consuming. Finding all of the right information is difficult if you don't already have a background in education. Let's face it...how do you know what concepts to search for online or in library catalogs if you don't already possess an understanding of the basic concepts in the field? It's hard to Google "Trivium" if you've never even heard of the word. In *Home Field Advantage*, I walk you through several schools of thought on teaching, and give you a crash course on concepts that your average education major studies before receiving a teaching license.

You might be wondering, *Well, I'm not studying to be teacher. I just want to learn a way to better homeschool my children. Why should I care about teaching methodologies?* That's a good question. Many families decide to homeschool their children because they want flexibility and to move away from the one-size-fits-all system often used at institutional schools. Knowing your teaching options can help you be less rigid and even more creative in how and what you teach at home. My goal is to present the education basics on the most fundamental and practical level so that you can decide for yourself what will work for your family and what you feel you want to research further. I won't exhaust every topic I present, but I'll help you get grounded in the basics.

Reading *Home Field Advantage*, you'll learn how to:

- Individualize every lesson, drawing from different schools of thought, mixing and matching methods to create a *more personalized* educational experience for your children.

- Implement methods that don't go against your own beliefs and practices, but also don't simply mimic your natural teaching style (and I'll go over why that's important).

- Meet the distinct needs of your children with a confidence that can revolutionize their homeschooling experience.

- Pick and choose the elements of education that best meet your educational goals.

- Create the academic environment that you envisioned when you took that first, brave step towards educating your family at home.

There are 12 chapters in this book. Chapter 1 examines how homeschooling is changing and why it may be a better option for your family. In Chapter 2, we look at the important aspects to understand when evaluating educational methods. These include the history, guiding principals, and defining characteristics of each method, as well as how each method can be adapted for homeschoolers. Finally, we also consider "fit" and whether a method would work for you and your family, or if you might want to look elsewhere.

Chapters 3-7 go through several formal educational methodologies in detail, evaluating each one using the criteria we set forth in Chapter 2. The methods we'll focus on are:

- Montessori method
- Waldorf education
- Trivium
- Charlotte Mason education
- unschooling

In Chapters 8-10, we shift gears from looking at formal methods to examining broader concepts in educational theory that don't necessarily form an entire methodology, but instead can assist you in assessing the needs of your students regardless of the method being implemented. These broad, educational concepts are:

- Whole and part instruction
- Theory of multiple intelligences
- Learning styles
- Child temperament

Think of the formal educational methods we discuss as being analogous to a house with its own distinct architectural style and layout. The educational concepts, on the other hand, are the minutiae in that house: the wallpaper, fixtures, or artwork that make the house your own. Without these personal touches, you may have a house that meets the basic needs of your family, but it won't be the warm and inviting home of your dreams. To really make an educational framework work, we'll also need to focus on these details—such as the nuances in your child's temperament or learning style—to help you structure school time in the best way.

Finally, in Chapters 11-12, we'll tie everything together. First, we'll go over how to plan your homeschooling journey with a step-by-step educational plan, where you'll get to: figure out your financial situation for homeschooling and plan a homeschooling budget that works for you and your family; customize a school day schedule for each of your children; personalize your lesson plans with a focused teaching style; and choose the best curriculum for each subject from a range of options. You'll also learn how to shop smart and to invest wisely.

Next, we'll discuss how you can design your learning environment. I'll offer tips on the type of furniture, equipment, and color and lighting that will minimize distractions yet also provide a vibrant space for learning.

Self-education is the key to becoming a confident homeschooler. You don't need a fancy degree to find this confidence—just a desire to learn about your options and the schools of thought on how children learn. Use *Home Field Advantage* as your quick reference and easy-to-read guide to help you embark on the not-so-average adventure called homeschooling.

Each chapter in this book is as practical and hands-on as possible, with home-tested tips and strategies you can actually use with your family. You'll also get recommendations for activities and hear about real-life experiences with a particular teaching style. A resources section packed with recommended books, websites, and my own worksheets for designing your home educational plan is also included. There's even a glossary to help you learn the educational terminology used throughout the book.

And while my personal experiences inspired me to share my expertise with you, I didn't stop there: I interviewed 15 families who homeschool their children. I found these families through local homeschool activity groups and online forums, and asked parents questions about how they chose their method of homeschooling, what has worked and what hasn't, and how they figured it all out. They shared some of their favorite resources with me to pass on to you.

> Self-education is the key to becoming a confident homeschooler. Use *Home Field Advantage* as your quick reference and easy-to-read guide to help you embark on the not-so-average adventure called homeschooling.

In addition to interviews, I also visited the homes of a few families that use the methods discussed in Chapters 3-7. You'll get a glimpse into the lives of several very different homeschooling families and begin to see the tangible and intangible benefits of home education in action.

NOW THAT YOU'VE got a feel for where we're heading with this book, let's get started. But before we dive into the methodologies, I'd like to go through some of the reasons and motivations for exploring homeschooling, and why it's becoming an increasingly popular option for families.

ONE:
The Case for Homeschooling

Knowing why you are homeschooling and what you want to offer your child is the first step.

WHY do families choose to homeschool their children?

It's a simple question, yet there are as many answers to that question as there are homeschooling families. If you're interested, here's my family's answer. In the Introduction, I told you a bit about my background in teaching. Within just a few months teaching in the public schools in Oregon, I realized a fundamental truth: There really is no single best way to teach all students.

My daughter who's bookish by nature might appear to do just fine in an institutional setting, but we would never see what she could really do unless the entire class were at the same level, because there's little room, even in gifted classes, for kids to really work as intensely as they want on any given topic.

What if Hunter, my kinesthetic learner, were in a traditional classroom where the teacher was tasked to get as many kids as possible to pass a standardized test (a test based completely on reading and writing to be taken by kids sitting quietly at their desks)? Most likely Hunter would fall behind because there would be no time to teach him concepts in the way that he learns best—by moving and doing rather than by passive reading and listening.

At home with just my three kids I can make sure that my book-loving daughter gets a steady supply of written material on the topics that interest her most. I can make sure my hands-on learner is exposed to the right environment filled with physical activity and action-based learning. This personalized approach to education simply couldn't be replicated in a typical institutional classroom where the primary objective is passing the year-end written exams.

I've always believed that parents are actually in a better position to provide their children a tailor-made schooling experience that public schools simply can't offer. That's why you're doing this, isn't it? For that chance to inject a little bit of magic and creativity in your children's learning experience?

Moving Away from One-Size Fits All Education

Studies have long proved that children learn in a variety of ways. Some children are fairly flexible in their learning and can absorb material delivered in almost any format. Most children, however, have an innate learning style or disposition that works best with one or two teaching methods or information delivery strategies.

In a traditional classroom setting where the average classroom size is typically between 20 to 30 students, there is no conceivable way for a teacher to individualize lessons for every student. Even with the best efforts (and many teachers are the hardest working people out there), it's nearly impossible to personalize the learning experience. It's not the fault of the schools or the individual teachers. It's just the reality of the institutionalized system. In this system teachers inherit a curriculum chosen years before by a committee of parents and educational specialists. Teachers have to follow the designated curriculum until they can sit in on the next committee to offer their own ideas. Teachers also face limits set by state curriculum standards. Classroom management issues and parental conflicts also distract from the focus on teaching.

> Most children have an innate learning style or disposition that works best with one or two teaching methods or information delivery strategies.

Those methods drilled into pre-professional teachers in their university programs rarely get a chance to be applied in the classroom as teachers are often encouraged to "stick to the script." Sure, teachers can try to pepper their teaching in the classroom with different methods, but the fact is the school has generally chosen one course and teachers are expected to shuttle all children who pass through their doors down that same path. It's enough to make you wonder why we send our teachers through all of that training in the first place.

In my teaching days working in a special education classroom, as I struggled with a slew of behavioral issues, I frequently found myself thinking, "He would really thrive in a Montessori environment..." or "The Paideia schools might really help her." But even in a class of 10 students and four adults, I wasn't in a position to provide each child with the lesson format that I thought would work best because the deck was stacked against me, so to speak. I had limited "plays" and no wiggle room. Even if I could get the other teachers in the class on board, when was I going to plan all of these different lessons with different delivery styles? As a typical classroom-based teacher, the clock isn't on your side. The institutional classroom format simply doesn't allow for individual strategizing, even with classes as small as the one I taught.

Can Homeschooling Do Any Better?

When you make the bold choice to homeschool your children, the dilemma of which method to practice doesn't magically disappear. In fact, it becomes even more complicated. By removing your child from the school system or keeping them home from the beginning, you're effectively saying, "I can do better." That bold assertion brings with it more than a little pressure to at least look like you know what you're doing while you're figuring it all out. And most parents do figure it out.

In 1990, the National Home Education Research Institute issued a seminal report that found that homeschoolers were scoring significantly higher than their same-age peers who were traditionally schooled.[1] It's not too surprising when you consider that home education allows for the luxury of individualization and comes with teachers who have real stakes in their students' lives. But what was interesting was that "only 13.9 percent of the mothers (who are the primary teachers) had ever been certified teachers." Teaching certification didn't seem to have an impact. The study found "no difference in the students' total reading, total math and total language scores based on the teacher certification status of their parents." The study concluded that the "[findings] did not support the idea that parents need to be trained and certified teachers to assure successful academic achievement of their children."

An Uphill Battle

In the checkout line, the woman behind the register peered over the pile of clothes on the counter to be rung up, smiled at Hannah Jane and said, "School clothes, huh? Well, these sure are cute! You'll be the star of the class!"

The kids giggled at the cheerful comment. They had been taught not to correct adults, but they couldn't contain their reactions to the thought of being the "star of the class" in our basement classroom with their siblings for classmates. Heck, half of their class comes to school in pajamas, so it doesn't take much to out style one another.

The woman looked a bit perturbed at the reaction to her compliment, so I explained, "We homeschool so the idea of school clothes gives them the giggles. I'm sorry."

"Oh, well, there's nothing wrong with homeschooling," she responded. She was struggling to feign supportive approval, but I could see her expression changing. "I mean, you can send them to school later when they will need someone more trained and the high tech equipment that schools have and all that."

Oh no, here it comes, I thought, the public scorning that you're always expecting but rarely get confronted with head-on. Generally, it's just disapproving looks that you can't counter with an informed discussion because no discussion ever takes place, but now I could sense one was coming. I braced myself.

"Well, I'm actually a licensed teacher, but I think any—"

"Well, that's different then," she countered, cutting me off. "If you're a real teacher, then your children will probably do okay at home. But don't they miss their friends?"

"Actually, what I was going to say is that *any* motivated parent can be a great teacher."

I could feel a speech coming on, but it felt good. "Even without a teaching license, parents have access to textbooks, if they choose to use them, and all the tools to teach kids everything they would learn in school. It pays off, too. Homeschooled kids generally outscore public school kids on standardized tests."

I kept going. "And my kids have tons of friends. Sitting silently next to 20 other kids your age isn't a recipe for friendship. My kids get to choose their own friends without having to be in the same class with them. And they don't have to deal with bullies or brats. They can choose to only spend their time with kids they feel drawn to. It's pretty great."

My heart was thumping, but it felt good to say all of those things out loud to a naysayer with my posse of smart, short people behind me nodding in agreement.

The woman stared wide-eyed and her forehead crinkled. I could see I wasn't going to change her mind. But I also didn't want to just nod and say, "You're right. I've made a horrible choice for my kids."

Despite research showing better achievement scores among children homeschooled by parents without any teaching certification, many families still harbor doubts. One problem is the strong bias against homeschooling that still persists. All it takes to send a homeschooler into a self-doubting tailspin is an encounter at the grocery store or the park with someone who questions whether the average parent can provide the same caliber of education at home as public schools with their highly trained educators, facilities, and equipment.

I understand why the doubts persist. The ante is upped. You realize that you don't have the numbers excuse, limitations, and worries that the average teacher faces. Sweat drips from your brow as you consider your odds and what limited resources you may have. You look around at other homeschoolers and their families and you might wonder: *Am I giving my child the best learning opportunities possible? What are other parents with kids that seem so well-adjusted and brilliant doing right? Are those same outcomes within my reach? Am I gambling with my children's future by homeschooling?*

Changing Attitudes

Public opinion about homeschooling is changing gradually. I remember a trip we made to Salt Lake City to visit a new museum of natural history that the University of Utah had just opened. Hannah Jane wanted to take the architectural tour. Spurred on by a sense of adventure and need for some mother-daughter bonding, we ditched her brothers and father in the dinosaur area and headed to the meeting place for the tour.

While we were waiting for our tour guide, a trainee remarked on Hannah Jane's interest in architecture and asked her what grade she was in at school. I caught my breath. My kids dread the grade question because the truth is often difficult to explain. At the time, Hannah Jane was in fourth grade math, second grade language arts, and third grade science.

My daughter stood there, looking uncharacteristically dumbfounded and stumbled for an articulate answer to the woman's seemingly simple question. I finally stepped in and explained why this was a tricky question for her. I expected a look of confusion, or worse, of pity, but the trainee just lit up!

"How wonderful!" she exclaimed. "I was just watching a special on CNN the other day where they looked at other countries' education systems and some of them let kids be in different levels for different subjects, and I just thought, 'Well that makes so much sense!' And here I meet you and you're doing that at home!" With a hint of envy in her voice she smiled at Hannah Jane and said, "You may not realize how lucky you are. As a kid, I was always so much better at reading than everything else, but I was stuck reading baby books just because I was born in a certain year."

Homeschooling has become more accepted in the public consciousness over the past few decades, but there was a time when homeschooling was less the norm, and the perception of homeschooled kids was that they may or may not be properly educated. Parents that homeschooled their kids were pegged as either religious zealots or hippies who shunned society's conventions. There were even lingering concerns as to whether or not homeschooling was considered legal.

Today, with the right to homeschool firmly established in all 50 states, you would think that the legal battles would be behind us. For the most part, this is true. I personally know hundreds of homeschooling families in the various states we've lived in, and I only know of one family who has ever had legal trouble. In that case, the teenage child was at the mall during school hours and was hauled in by a truancy officer. The mother was asked in court to show proof that she was actually educating her son and not simply excusing him from the burden of school. She panicked. Some homeschoolers like this family don't keep strict attendance records or major projects to show off. Fortunately, they were able to pull enough papers with dates and names on them together to prove that they were indeed doing something at home that was school-related.

This is a scenario that every homeschooling parent wants to avoid. Since I was told about the incident, our family now keeps strict attendance records even though I've never been asked to show proof or documentation. We also use the Homeschool Buyer's co-op website (homeschoolbuyersco-op.org/homeschool-id) to generate free homeschool ID cards that the kids can have on hand if ever they are out and about during school hours and their right to be there is challenged by authorities.

When a neighboring town proposed extremely strict truancy laws in response to a major incident of vandalism, our local homeschooling community was abuzz with fears that their kids would be accosted by police officers for riding their bikes during the day or running to the market for science experiment supplies. Homeschoolers turned out en masse to the public hearings when those laws were proposed and, at least for the time being, they haven't been passed.

Though your odds of facing legal trouble are slim, sadly there are cases that come up from time to time when a family's right to educate at home is still challenged by the very officials who should understand the law. For this reason, many families choose to pay dues to the Homeschool Legal Defense Association (HSLDA), which provides free legal services in defense of homeschooling rights to members, among other services.[2] (*Note:* Members and outsiders alike have criticized HSLDA of being closely tied to the conservative right. Still, even those who disagree with HSLDA's political leanings often pay dues to ensure legal protection if their own right to homeschool is ever challenged.)

Homeschooling Legal Battles

Since the beginning of state-sponsored education in the U.S. there have been several significant challenges to the legality of educating at home. After the turn of the 20th century, however, the bulk of legal disputes shifted to the area of funding responsibilities: Is it lawful for homeschooled children to receive services from public schools? Can groups of homeschoolers lay claim to education funds from the state? Can they use school facilities? The answer to the question of access to public school facilities and services isn't cut and dry and the battle isn't over yet.

According to Chris Klicka, attorney and prominent voice for the Home School Legal Defense Association (HSLDA), only 10 states have passed equal access laws for homeschoolers as of 2000, and the remaining states have the liberty to allow or deny access to publicly funded activities at their own discretion. This issue differs from the issue of whether or not it's legal to homeschool because, in Klicka's words, "This [the right to educate at home] is a right guaranteed by the First and Fourteenth Amendments of the U.S. Constitution. The right to homeschool is not a state-granted privilege."[3] Unfortunately, there is no clear-cut protection on the right to have access to publically funded education in either the U.S. Constitution or any of the state constitutions. This has made access to funding and funded services central issues in recent homeschooling legal battles.

Within those states that have enacted equal access laws, students may still be required to meet certain requirements, such as prove that they are homeschooling legally and that they have passing grades in all of their core subjects.[4] An even larger and more important question has focused on the extent that the state can regulate what a homeschooler does at home.

In the 1976 Runyon v. McCrary case, the court stated that "...parents have a constitutional right to send their children to private schools and a constitutional right to select private schools that offer specialized instruction, [but] they have no constitutional right to provide their children with private school education unfettered by reasonable government regulation."[5] This ruling appeared to rely heavily on statements made during the Wisconsin v. Yoder case where it gave "no support to the contention that parents may replace state educational requirements with their own idiosyncratic views of what knowledge a child needs to be a productive and happy member of society" but rather "held simply that while a State may posit standards, it may not pre-empt the educational process by requiring children to attend public schools.[6]

As recently as 2008, the state of California made an apparent effort to make homeschooling illegal. In February 2008, the Second District Court of Appeals in Los Angeles released a ruling that all children must be taught only by credentialed teachers.[7] This was followed by a highly publicized statement from Justice H. Walter Croskey, stating: "California courts have held that under provisions in the Education Code, parents do not have a constitutional right to homeschool their children."[8] This sent parents of the estimated 200,000 homeschooled students in the state into an uproar. The California Supreme Court was asked to reexamine the ruling. Eventually, clear rights to homeschooling (under the ever-watchful eye of the state) were restored just months after the right to homeschool was challenged.

As a result of these and other cases, it was made clear that states remained in control of schooling standards to varying degrees across the country. While some states have very strict requirements about testing, content, and scope of lessons, others simply require that you declare your intentions to homeschool and say no more.

Why Homeschooling May Be a Better Option

While interviewing the homeschoolers who use the various methods we'll discuss in this book, I was intrigued by the varied responses to the question of "why homeschooling?" From one I got a hearty chuckle followed by, "because I got sick of being called into the office every week and it seemed easier to deal with [my child's] behavior issues at home." Another parent was homeschooled herself and was also formally trained as a teacher, so she said she never even considered anything else. I've known moms who wanted to homeschool to be more involved in their children's lives, and some who simply live in a bad school district and are homeschooling as a way to productively mark time until they can move or win the charter school lottery. Every family makes the decision to homeschool for very personal reasons.

In this section, we'll focus on several big reasons many families choose homeschooling for their children:

1. Families find standardized education limiting.

2. Families want a more challenging and dynamic environment for their children.

3. Homeschooling provides a way to promote core values and healthier social attitudes.

4. Homeschooling provides better ways to manage special needs and developmental issues.

Reason 1: Families find standardized education limiting.

Part of the resurgence of homeschooling can be attributed to the fact that our public school system is under fire. Not surprisingly, parents are starting to ask the hard questions, no longer willing to just go with the norm when it means placing their child's future in the hands of a system that seems to be undergoing an upheaval. Faced with low-quality options, more people are opening up to the idea of homeschooling. It's no longer a fringe idea but a real, viable option for all kinds of families.

The criticism of standardized education is plentiful and varied:

Educational quality is falling short. In the U.S., we've been falling behind other developed countries in terms of proficiency standards. Our dropout rates are startlingly high, especially in large urban areas and many students aren't receiving the community and family support they need. Furthermore, public school enrollment is expected to increase by six percent between 2009 and 2018; increased enrollment means more strain on an already malfunctioning education system.[9]

With further overcrowding of classrooms looming on the horizon, more and more research is going into studying the negative effects of cramming too many students into a classroom. One study finds that both students and teachers in overcrowded classrooms report distraction from the elevated noise levels.[10] Students who actually want to hear and learn can't focus over the buzz. The teacher, sometimes outnumbered 40 to one, can do little to control noise levels. The same study also reported that "over crowdedness diminishes the quantity and quality of teaching and learning with serious implications for attainment of educational goals." It recommends that governments put more resources toward the building of additional classrooms.

These recommendations often fall on deaf ears as many states face massive budget cuts and dwindling public coffers. A look at Quality Counts, an annual report card published by *Education Week* on the condition of education state by state, shows that "21 states had a class-size reduction policy in place for the 2007-2008 school year" with all but fifteen states with "laws restricting the number of students that may be included in a general education classroom, in some or all grades."[11] However, after the economic downturn in 2008, "19 states relaxed or eliminated their class-size laws or policies, usually as a cost-saving measure."[12]

What does this mean for public schools? As the economy slowly recovers, we can expect class size to soar upward. Cutting educational resources is often a simple way to cut costs. Some teachers report now having class sizes up to 40 kids strong. For middle and high school teachers, 200 students may pass through their classrooms each and every day. It simply isn't possible for teachers to have meaningful interaction with that many students.

The curriculum has become too standardized. The 1983 National Commission on Excellence in Education report called for a more structured academic plan in high school. Schools encouraged students to take more core courses, creating a uniform learning environment. After the No Child Left Behind Act was enacted in 2001, states started focusing more on test scores, again streamlining classroom education to fit one, specific model, and leaving little room for different types of learners or intelligences.[13]

In this setting, students with special needs or learning preferences, who don't quite fit into the education system in place, don't get a chance to fully thrive. As Sir Ken Robinson, a respected supporter of creativity in schools explains, "Current systems of education are based on the manufacturing principles of linearity, conformity and standardization."[14]

There's little room for learning outside of reading and math. In recent years, states have shifted the focus to reading and math, stunting the development of other subjects.[15] Schools have also shifted toward standardized testing, with many high schools now requiring exit exams. Non-tested subjects like art, music, and physical education have been cut to make room, and time in other academic subjects, like science and social studies, has been reduced.[16]

The consequence of this standardized way of teaching and learning is that, as Robinson puts it, "many brilliant people think they are not, because they've been judged against a particular view of the mind."[17] Students who fall behind are left behind if they don't score well on the standardized tests in reading and math. It becomes a downward spiral for many students as they progress through the system that can't recognize other latent abilities or talents.

We'll explore this idea of being judged against a cookie-cutter standard further in Chapter 9 when we discuss multiple intelligences.

Reason 2: Families want a more challenging and dynamic environment for their children.

We assume that most schools meet our child's basic needs—meaning that our child leaves school each day still breathing and hopefully knowing a bit more than they did the day before. But human beings have needs that go beyond basic survival.

You may have heard of Abraham Maslow's Hierarchy of Needs theory.[18] Maslow posited that people have five categories of needs that can be visualized on a pyramid array (see next page). At the base of the pyramid are the basic, physical needs; higher up on the pyramid are interpersonal and psychological needs related to emotional well-being, fulfillment, and self-actualization. In Maslow's hierarchy, each lower category of needs must be met before an individual can achieve the higher needs. For example, we must have the survival basics before we can even concern ourselves with job security; before we can cultivate self-esteem and a sense of belonging, one must have be in good health and feel safe and secure.

In the homeschool environment, parents are in a better position to help their kids attain those more complex needs closer to the top of the pyramid, such as security, love, self-respect, justice, truth, and wisdom. By nurturing those needs in an individualized way for each child, homeschoolers can open doors of personal fulfillment and development beyond what can be achieved in the conventional classroom.

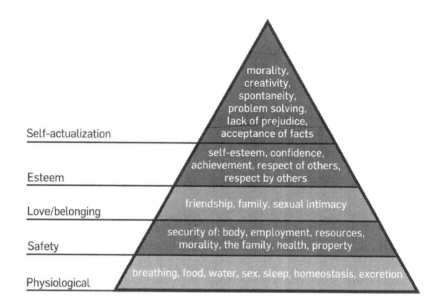

Image source: Maslow's Hierarchy of Needs, Wikimedia Commons[19]

Here are several ways homeschooling environments can fulfill your child's broader needs:

It's much more than mass-produced education. Most homeschooling parents want more. We should expect more from the educational experience, right? We want our children to be nurtured and to thrive. We want them to follow their interests and become the unique individuals they were born to be. We want them to fulfill their individual capacities rather than to meet expectations from a standardized framework.

As mentioned before, the rising student-to-teacher ratio simply makes individualizing the educational experience impossible. In fact, overcrowded classrooms are at the core of the growing discontent with the public school system. It's not to say that there aren't school districts and teachers doing the absolute best job that they can; rather, the very nature of the institution can't, no matter how refined, meet the unique, individual needs of every child.

It enables students to excel and advance beyond their grade level. Take Raecale, a prospective homeschooler with two older children in public school and two younger children that she hopes to keep home when they reach school age. A big reason for wanting to keep her younger boys home was seeing how her older girls' capabilities had been marginalized in classrooms. Speaking about her daughter, Raecale recounted how the system set a ceiling for achievement: "The teacher pointed out her above-average scores on the DIBLES (Dynamic Indicators of Basic Early Literacy Skills) test. She tested at 4.5, which is half-way through 4th grade in reading and comprehension."

Raecale shook her head in disbelief. "The teacher then told us, with a wrinkle of her nose, as if to say, 'This is best,' and that she would only let my daughter check out books in the library from the second grade level."

Raecale told me another story about her other daughter who excels in math: "In fourth grade, her teacher pointed out how well she was doing in math. I then told the teacher that she scored 100% on her previous year-end core test. She flipped through the papers and said, 'Yep, I guess she did,' as if she had no idea or concern. I then asked her if there were any extra programs she could get into in her grade that would encourage her interest in the subject. The teacher said no. I asked what I could do at home to help her. She told me I could probably search online for something."

Raecale's frustration at the inane rules and indifference from teachers was tangible. We discussed the futility of testing without any way to measure an improvement beyond a certain threshold, or ability to adapt lesson content based on outcomes (e.g., what happens after your child aces the test?). Raecale wants her younger boys to have a different experience from that of their older sisters. She wants them to be able to learn at their own pace from the beginning and not have to be held back for the group.

An update: Since I last spoke to Raecale, she has removed one of her daughters from public school to homeschooling full-time, and her other daughter is half timing it in public school for the duration of the year and will be at home full-time the following year. Raecale is making bold choices to safeguard and encourage her children's brilliant minds.

Reason 3: Homeschooling provides a way to promote core values and healthier social attitudes.

During my interviews I fully expected that many parents would cite religion as being the major reason for homeschooling. Yet after talking to countless families over the course of this project, I found that not a single family gave religion as their main reason for homeschooling. How silly to be a homeschooler myself and still buy into the stereotype.

While families didn't cite religion as a major reason they chose to homeschool, they did speak of the importance of core values. Homeschoolers I spoke to expressed a general desire to teach children to value human life and experience, to practice kindness toward everyone instead of pleasing social cliques, and to carve out time in their day to pray or meditate. It's no wonder that these humanistic values are a central part of the philosophy to choose homeschooling. With its emphasis on learning and development beyond just academics, homeschooling's educational foundations center on teaching children how to be fully human. This is a goal any parent would want.

One area where I think homeschooling excels on the values front is in how it imparts lessons on socialization and good behavior. Many people worry that kids who don't go to school are going to become socially dysfunctional, either inappropriately spewing facts in casual social settings, worrying about their pocket protectors, or being so debilitated by the mere presence of non-family members that they retreat into a shell and hide until they can get back home. Scenarios like these are far-fetched and absurd. Where does this concern about socialization come from? Is this because kids who go to traditional schools and often face cliques and queen bees, bullies, drugs, and early sexual pressures without proper adult oversight or intervention are so properly socialized? Do people really think that kids who spend seven hours a day confronted with these issues are better socialized than their homeschooled counterparts?

Having worked in the public schools and been a part of the homeschooling community for years, I can tell you that concerns about your children's socialization are largely unfounded. Gone are the days of the isolated, shut-in homeschoolers who never leave the home, and hear no opinions on the world other than Mom's. Today's homeschooling world is comprised of co-ops, social clubs, group field trips, science fairs, and even part-time public schooling. Days buzz with activity and interaction. In fact, I'll argue that kids who don't go to an institutional school have more diverse and positive social interactions than any other kids.

Here's how a typical week works for my kids: On Mondays, my boys both go to a speech class at the public school for an hour where they play in small groups of same-age peers. Tuesdays are choir and music days. After choir, a few students come over to our house where I teach flute lessons, and the girls work on trios to perform during concert season. After music sessions, there is almost always a play date where my kids visit someone else's home or other kids come stay at ours until dinner time. This year, about 30 homeschooled kids ages 4 to 14 put on an elaborate production of *Les Misérables* complete with singing, dancing, costumes, and stage props.

On Wednesdays, we take a break, stay home, and buckle down academically. Thursdays are club and co-op days. One Thursday a month is Culture Club, where a group of about five families each study a new culture, and on club day they present to the other members on what they learned. Everyone shows up in different costumes, with neat visuals to show and pass around, and the meeting always closes with food brought from all of the different cultures we heard about that day. Generally, after the official club meeting ends, the moms sit around upstairs and chat, while the kids write

> Today's homeschooling world is comprised of co-ops, social clubs, group field trips, science fairs, and even part-time public schooling. Days buzz with activity and interaction.

and rehearse an impromptu play to perform for the moms right before everyone goes home. Next year, Thursdays will be a co-op day where the kids will attend selected classes taught by other parents with several dozen other homeschooled kids for about half the day in a rented church building. On Fridays, we usually have school time until lunch, and then there always seems to be some sort of play date, park date, or field trip that fills the afternoon.

On a less regular basis there are "park days" when moms on the homeschooling forum post, "We need a break! Who wants to hit the park?" and several families show up to hang out. There are also special interest clubs that we've done from time to time, like poetry club, American Girl book club, chess club, and Latin club. And because my kids each take a class or two through an online public school, we have all sorts of holiday parties at the bowling alley or roller rink with their "classmates," as well as organized field trips for things like bakery tours or rock and gem shows.

With this whirlwind of activity, how could homeschooling be considered anything but wonderfully social? At the very least, you can't argue that homeschooling stunts social development. Making a connection between shyness and homeschooling is all too common but easily discredited. We hear it all the time: "I knew this kid who was homeschooled and he was just weird. Totally shy. Wouldn't talk to anyone." Are there are no shy kids in institutional settings? Can shyness simply be corrected through proper socialization like crooked teeth with braces? And what's wrong with being shy? What about the role of innate temperament that is independent of the environment? The assumption that homeschooled kids who are shy are shy *because* they were homeschooled is simply misguided.

To properly examine the socialization issue, let's start by defining what role schools play in the development of our children. Most people would say that the purpose of school is, above all else, to educate our children. Then, of course we would like for our children's school experience to assist them in becoming confident individuals who are kind and cooperative members of a functioning society. Peripherally, most parents will admit that they hope their children's school experience helps hone their skills to such a degree that they have no trouble getting into a good college if they so choose and that they develop the social skills that lead to career success.

Looking at each of the expectations that we place on the "institutional school experience," we see that homeschooling demonstrates a clear advantage over institutional schooling in several ways:

Homeschooling eliminates distractions and social pressures.
First, let's examine the expectation of getting a quality education: Can a child who's worried about this week's "it girl" teasing her about her clothes focus on her subjects? Can the boy who has been tossed against a locker for a week straight by bullies be fit enough to absorb class lectures? Even something as innocent as sitting behind the cutest boy or girl in school during math class can distract the most studious of kids from hearing the teacher's lesson on logarithmic functions. A battery of distractions constantly competes for your child's attention at school, taking the focus off of learning and placing your child in "self-preservation mode" where social pressures take precedence.

During my time teaching in public schools, I often saw packs of children rally around the least appealing, most bratty kid in the group. It was upsetting to see very sweet, caring young people feel bad about themselves and wish to be more like the mean kid, even occasionally making awkward attempts at showing attitude that was obviously unnatural for them.

Scenes like this had a great deal of influence over our choice as a family to homeschool. I wanted my children to be inspired and guided by those who had developed the capacity to engage in mature social interactions rather than mimic the immature social interactions of their same-age peers. Yes, we still deal with the pack mentality that rolls off the neighborhood school bus every day at 4 p.m. But having interacted with fellow homeschooled kids who don't rely on age or status, my kids can participate in the neighborhood social groups without being hugely influenced by the negative aspects. The pressure to "fit in" isn't as much a factor when they are around friends and peers.

It teaches self-confidence and positive behavior. Those stressors that can interfere with your children's education can also rob them of learning how to be confident, genial individuals. Real world interactions rarely reflect the petty tensions or dramas we often see at play in elementary or high school. We all feel a little mortified when we see grown-ups behaving badly. If kids spent their initial years in the presence of courteous and enthusiastic adults and peers, rather than in the midst of stressed teachers and packs of ill-socialized, surly peers, would their frame of reference for acceptable behavior shift?

Kids who learn at home are rarely, if ever, grouped by their "date of manufacture" and thus develop the ability to interact with and value people of all ages. I hear this most commonly talked about with regards to how well homeschooled children interact with and relate to adults. To me, the difference is most charming when I watch homeschooled kids interact with those younger than themselves. The idea of someone being a peon simply because they are younger is completely absent. In large social groups of homeschoolers, young ones are nurtured and guided by older peers, aided rather than ridiculed, and more meaningful and nuanced interactions take place across the spectrum of age and intellect.

I can remember clearly the first time I was smacked in the face with this beautiful multi-age dynamic. My daughter was part of an all-girls book club that was having their monthly meeting to do Nancy Drew activities in a member's home. The host mom had sent out an e-mail that they had a river running through their property and that the girls should bring their swimsuits for some play time after the meeting was over.

My Hannah Jane, 6-years-old at the time, was not a swimmer but longed to be a part of the action. She fretted and worried for a week about the possibility of being the only non-swimmer in a group of almost entirely older girls who ranged in age from 7- to 12-years-old. When the day came, she asked me not to come in but to stay on the property in the van in case she needed me. She hadn't decided how to approach swim time yet, so she wanted me nearby in case people made fun of her and she needed to flee the scene.

After an hour or so had passed, I thought they must certainly be done with their meeting and playing by now, but she still hadn't come to the van. I headed out to investigate. Taking a path behind the house and following the voices, I walked down a wooden boardwalk that weaved through a sprawling, reedy marshland toward the river. At the end of the walkway I saw the most angelic, charming scene I had ever set eyes on.

The older girls had split into groups: half were in the river, half were on the banks. They were taking turns helping their younger, shakier swimmer, Hannah Jane, now clad in a bulky life vest, swing out on a rope swing and plop into the water filled with a group of cheering girls. It was like a scene from a team-building camp where participants had just sat through hours of lectures on how to show support and cooperation. But no: These were just girls who liked the same books and who knew how to be friends regardless of their age differences.

I snapped a thousand pictures of my little non-swimmer, beaming ear-to-ear in the river with her new best friends, twice her age. It was a red-letter day for this homeschooling mother.

It provides an environment that discourages bullies and bullying. Some may argue that the drama of school life is developmentally important, a kind of trial-by-fire that all children can benefit from. I find that the people who believe that were generally the bullies or queen bees in school. On the other hand, people who were bullied in school almost always say that having been bullied not only wasn't a skill-builder that allowed them to tackle adult life with greater ease, but that it created life-long emotional scars.

A friend of mine once told me about her experiences of exclusion in school. She was frequently subjected to cruel words that diminished her self-worth on account of her weight. While she admits that most of the time it was just silent exclusion rather than outright bullying, there were instances when boys called her horrific names, girls giggled when she walked into the bathroom, and cruel, anonymous notes were left in her locker. Does she feel like she's tougher for having lived through the mean halls of high school? The question makes her laugh. The idea of bullying as a confidence-builder is the stuff of Hollywood movies in her opinion.

Is this what we want for our kids? Of course not. Do some people make it out of school unscathed? Sure, I did. I was neither popular nor an outcast. I had a comfortable band of friends who blurred the line between nerdy and edgy. I was never in the homecoming court, but I was never bullied. I wasn't the star of any sport or theatrical production, but I had close friends that I could confide in. Yet I have several dear friends who attended the same school and felt like their existence was miserable, and that the cruelty they perceived continues to follow them. We even had a suicide in our small school; despite the sheltered world of a private Church of Christ school, there were issues that, to some, felt dire.

Homeschooling offers real-world experience. Since not everyone deals with bullies, there are other points to consider like the reality of how school socialization may or may not prepare us for the "real world." Whom do children interact with in school? Probably only with kids who share their birth year. But when else in life are individuals grouped by age?

Beginning in college, we have classes with students of all ages and backgrounds. We are expected to interact with professors in a more natural, democratic manner than we did with teachers in elementary and high school. We probably spend more time in the workforce during college than we did in high school, with work-study or part-time jobs to make ends meet. Will we have co-workers who were all born in the same year? No. This world of same-age cohorts ends when we reach adulthood.

Children who have only ever interacted with teachers that are considered infallible authority figures and with students who are of the same age and maturity level may find it difficult to interact in meaningful ways with peers who have different life experiences and interests. Homeschooled kids, who have far more diverse social interactions, have a distinct advantage in this respect. They won't find that 40-year-old freshman in their college class a difficult person to talk to simply because he has kids and responsibilities. They won't have trouble challenging an ambiguous grading choice from a professor. If children do have trouble interacting with others, it won't be because they were homeschooled.

Homeschooling and Harvard: The College Question

The issue of whether homeschooled kids can get into college is a common concern and one that is not completely unfounded. In the past, when homeschooling was less pervasive, college entrance officers were somewhat unsure of whether they could enroll a student who had no transcripts or proof of prior education. There were application forms with blank spaces for which a homeschooling student had no information to enter. While not unattainable, college entrance was difficult at best with lingering biases and the uncertainty of the legality of homeschooling.

Thankfully those days are behind us, and homeschoolers generally now stand on equal footing with institutionally educated kids as they prepare to enter college. Homeschoolers have also become savvier. Aware of future hurdles, they have begun taking the necessary steps, like getting a GED or taking AP (Advanced Placement) classes to have some proof of knowledge and ability, as well as taking the SAT and ACT so that they can showcase "hard numbers" in their college applications. Statistics are now available to prove that, in general, homeschoolers are outshining their institutionally educated counterparts. You can be sure that the college entrance officials have taken notice.

Here are several other reasons why homeschoolers shouldn't worry about whether their children will get into college:

Homeschooled kids are more than just prepared. In our home, we've always allowed the kids flexibility to take their interests as far as they desire. This has resulted in my daughter at age 7 unofficially taking a University of California at Berkeley biology class by watching all of the video webcast lectures and pausing here and there to discuss the concepts with me. Other than at home, where can a 7-year-old take college biology? She's not a savant and wouldn't last a second in any other college-level course, but she had an intense interest in the inner workings of DNA. Determined to feed her curiosity, she decided to listen in on that course to build up some foundational knowledge on her own. She understood about three quarters of what she heard and could accurately discuss and absorb another 10 percent of what she didn't already understand.

At institutional settings, students are expected to be ahead in every single subject area if they're going to be allowed to progress beyond the norm in any one of them. At home, students have more flexibility. No doubt, when Hannah Jane gets to college biology, she'll shine.

Researcher Brian D. Ray found that "over 74% of home-educated adults ages 18-24 have taken college-level courses, compared to 46% of the general United States population."[20] This could mean either that homeschoolers took AP courses within the walls of their high school, that they actually had dual enrollment in both college and high school during their last year of K-12 education, or that they took college classes at the traditional time and place. It's worth noting that AP courses are still unavailable within the homeschool setting in most, if not all, states and many advanced homeschoolers often take public school part-time in order to attend these classes while they're free in high school, rather than pay to take them in college. Clearly, homeschoolers are prepared for the rigors of university education and many admission boards know this.

Attitudes are changing among college admissions committees and college counselors. In fact, according to the Homeschool Legal Defense Association, homeschooled kids are doing better than just getting into college. "Admissions personnel who used to view homeschooled applicants with skepticism are now scrambling to recruit and enroll students who collectively score better on the SAT than their peers," says one expert.[21]

In 2000, *The Wall Street Journal* featured some stats about these high achieving homeschoolers on its opening page: "...self-identified home-schoolers have bettered the national averages on the ACT for the past three years running, scoring an average 22.7 last year, compared with 21 for their more traditional peers, on a scale of one to 36. Home-schoolers scored 23.4 in English, well above the 20.5 national average; and 24.4 in reading, compared with a mean of 21.4. The gap was closer in science (21.9 vs. 21.0), and home-schoolers scored below the national average in math, 20.4 to 20.7."[22]

Homeschoolers are outperforming their institutionally schooled peers, and college admission officers are taking notice. In 1997, Dr. Irene Prue, Assistant Director of Admission of Georgia Southern University, released a nationwide survey of admissions personnel's knowledge, attitudes, and experiences with home-educated applicants. In general, a total of 210 respondents in the study reported that homeschoolers are academically, emotionally, and socially prepared to succeed in college.[23]

In 2008, *The New York Times* held a Q&A on college admissions in which parents wrote in inquiring about biases against homeschoolers among college admissions boards.[24] The four admissions deans that participated (from Yale University, Pomona College, Lawrence University, and the University of Texas at Austin) were evenly split in the overall tone of their responses, but all four stated that their universities welcome homeschoolers.

Jeff Brenzel, the Dean of Undergraduate Admissions at Yale University, stated, "We see only a few homeschooled applicants, and we do occasionally admit a homeschooled student. Evaluation is usually difficult, however. It helps if the applicant has taken some college level courses, and we can get evaluations from those teachers. We are not keen on homeschooled students where the only evaluations come from parents and the only other information available consists of test scores." With more optimism, Bruce Walker, the Vice Provost and Director of Admissions at the University of Texas at Austin, said, "We probably provide better service and a more complete and personal evaluation of our homeschooled children than we do to our more traditional applicants. While homeschooled children present slightly different application materials, the differences are shrinking. We are seeing parents become more entrepreneurial in finding good educational experiences for their children, and more parents are pooling resources to provide the more specialized subjects in the sciences."[25]

The Wall Street Journal also reported that many colleges are adjusting their admissions policies to homeschoolers: "Many colleges now routinely accept homeschooled students, who typically present 'portfolios' of their work instead of transcripts. Each year, Harvard University takes up to 10 applicants who have had some homeschooling. And how are they performing alongside their traditionally schooled peers?"[26] They do fine, says David Illingsworth, senior admissions officer at Harvard. He adds that the number of applications and inquiries from homeschoolers is "definitely increasing."

When a subset of the population consistently scores in the 75th-80th percentile on standardized tests, naysayers pay attention. Maybe that's why many colleges no longer require a GED from homeschooled students; fantastic SAT scores are enough to get a foot in the door. In fact, many college counselors, such as those that run Homeschool College Counselor, even advise against getting the GED, prompting parents instead to create diplomas for their children upon "graduation" so that they aren't immediately stereotyped by the GED. "When a student is applying for admission and doesn't have a high school diploma, it says to the admissions office that this student flunked out, dropped out, was kicked out, or wasn't dedicated enough to graduate high school. The last thing you should want for your student is to be lumped in with this group!"[27]

I've consistently read anecdotal accounts from homeschooling parents about how colleges were either impressed enough with a student's portfolio and test scores to not worry about a student's official transcripts, or simply requested that a GED be taken in time for the admissions board to review it.

Reason 4: Homeschooling provides better ways to manage special needs and developmental issues.

The choice to homeschool is often related to how families want to deal with their children's special needs—ADD (attention deficit disorder) and ADHD (attention deficit hyperactivity disorder), in particular. At home, parents feel more confident that they can creatively circumvent medical interventions and can access outside help without it interfering with their children's academics, social life, or self-identity. Many families want to use therapy instead of medication, or simply cater to the immediate needs of their children themselves. They also don't want their children to be singled out or ostracized for developmental differences, which parents fear will be the case in institutional settings.

I encountered this reason to varying degrees with about a quarter of the homeschoolers that I spoke to for this book, and while I certainly don't want to focus too much attention on medical issues that I'm not qualified to address, I think it's important not to disregard or gloss over the number of homeschoolers who choose this path to help manage their children's behavioral or attention issues.

Among many in the homeschooling community, it's often thought that educators can be too quick to recommend medical intervention to treat disruptive children because it's convenient and better for classroom dynamics. Do we live in a society that favors fast solutions? One can make the case. In the 2009 documentary *Fresh*, a man observes that the only thing Americans fear is inconvenience. That observation struck me as relevant. What could be more inconvenient in a classroom of 30 kids than one student who needs constant special attention and care?

During congressional testimony in 2000, the Deputy Director of the Drug Enforcement Agency, Terrance Woodworth, drew a stark comparison between the use of stimulants to treat attention disorders in the U.S. and in the rest of the developed world. He cited that the U.S. produces and consumes about 85 percent of the world's production of methylphenidate.[28] Suggesting that we're a culture of quick fixes, behavioral-developmental pediatrician Lawrence H. Diller in *Running on Ritalin*, writes, "How we deal with our kids' problems reflects our thinking and a much larger problem in our culture."[29]

During my time teaching in public schools, I observed some creative ways to deal with students who were difficult and whose parents were unwilling to subject them to medication, and tried a few strategies in my own classes. I remember one boy in a first grade class I taught who was off-task almost 80 percent of the time. And not just a little off-task. This young boy would wander around the room, sometimes even crawling around between my legs as I taught, while the other 18 or so kids listened quietly from their desks.

A particularly memorable moment came during a lesson on planets. Earlier that morning I had arrived at the school and carefully measured to scale an exhibit of the solar system. Throughout the building, I had taped up very small paper cutouts of the planets along the walls. When it was time to go exploring, I gathered all of the children into an imaginary space shuttle, and walking down the hallway we quietly rocketed through space in search of the planets. As we journeyed to each planet, we would climb out of our shuttle for a short, lively lesson on each one.

We had already made our way past Saturn and were heading for Uranus—only to discover that Uranus wasn't there. The spot on the wall where I had taped up the planet was nowhere to be found. I stood staring at the blank space, puzzled for a moment. It's a dreaded teacher moment when you've got a class of kids all excited about the lesson, and suddenly you find yourself stumped.

I was about to retrace my steps to check another area in case I had overlooked the planet when the young boy blurted out, "I ate it!"

I looked at the wall and looked back at him.

"I'm sorry!" he said. "I was out in the hall and I saw it and ate it." It turned out to be the truth. Earlier in the day, when he had been especially disruptive, I had sent him into the hall for a break. He had seen a colorful circle of paper the size of a nickel and had promptly eaten it.

This kid was as sweet as can be, but it was exhausting to have him in class because I had to put so much energy into keeping his head in the game during class time. With so much effort devoted to keeping him

> Dealing with special physical or mental health needs is often as much a part of homeschooling as it is a part of mainstream schooling. As a homeschooler, however, you have many more options.

on task, I often had little energy left for any creative strategizing for the rest of the class. Teachers and administrators recommended medical intervention, but at that time his mother was firmly against it. As a parent, I admire her stance to keep her son off of medication and in mainstream classrooms, but as a teacher I realize just how much her son took away from the other kids. It's a catch-22.

Dealing with special physical or mental health needs is often as much a part of homeschooling as it is a part of mainstream schooling. As a homeschooler, however, you have many more options. If you're adamant against medication to treat behavioral problems, for example, homeschooling can be ideal. You often have more flexibility to meet the specific needs of all your children at home.

Still, parents with children who have special needs may worry that they don't have the skills or the patience to tackle behavioral issues at home. That's understandable. In an institutional school setting, a team of professionals, from teachers to school aides and counselors, interact with your child every day. Any behavior that deviates from the age group norm is more likely to be identified. A teacher or other school professional can then recommend testing or outside assistance for your child. At home, a parent may feel inclined to assume that disruptive behavior is simply what kids that age do and shrug it off until it becomes overwhelming. It's easy to be blind to potential problems when we're talking about our own children.

Despite these difficulties, there are several advantages that homeschooling has over traditional settings for kids with special needs:

Parents develop a better understanding of their children's behavior. At the home of Heidi and Jason, the sense of warmth and calm was undeniable. The physical environment was tidy and uncluttered without being in any way cold or sterile. Homemade garlands made out of felt adorned the hearth in the kitchen, celebrating a recently bygone holiday, and the savory scent of dinner wafted from the crock-pot. I could feel the perfect harmony between order and warmth. As my kids ran off to play with hers, Heidi and I settled down in the living room, just a room away from the play area, to talk about their daughter, E., and their homeschooling adventures.

Jason, Heidi's husband, had been diagnosed with ADD late in life when he was in college. After all those difficult school years, he had been relieved to finally understand the roots of his personal struggles and began to develop strategies to deal with them. When their daughter E. began displaying behaviors similar to those that Jason had grappled with, they first laughed it off as E. being "so Jason." It wasn't until half way through their first year of homeschooling that they took E. to a specialist and learned that she had ADD, too.

By homeschooling, Heidi and Jason became more confident about identifying and dealing with their daughter's behavior. Like many parents, Heidi had originally thought E.'s behavior was normal for kids her age. Now that E. has a younger brother, Heidi has seen the behavioral differences more clearly. "E. gets these grandiose ideas and sets these crazy goals," Heidi recounted. "For example, she had this coloring book and she said, 'Mom, I am going to color every single page in this coloring book beautifully, and I'm going to do it all today!' After a few perfect pictures, she was tired of coloring but didn't quit because she had set this pie-in-the-sky goal. By the end, each picture just had a line of crayon across it. I told her she didn't have to finish all of the pictures that day and maybe it would be better to wait and make them nice when she felt like it. But she didn't stop. One mark was better than waiting and coloring pretty pictures later."

Rather than the sense of panic that many parents might have felt, Heidi was surprisingly unruffled. "I now know that the setting of huge goals and either not following through or giving half effort is a big ADD personality thing," she explained. "So we work on setting more reasonable goals and following through when we can. I have to learn to choose my battles."

Parents have more room to explore non-traditional strategies to managing ADD. Even though the ADD diagnosis wasn't the sole reason why Heidi and Jason decided to homeschool, being at home allowed them to develop non-traditional strategies for helping E. get through her studies that group schooling simply couldn't accommodate.

"When E. looks at a worksheet, she is just overwhelmed by the sight of all of the blanks she has to fill in," Heidi explained. After trying a worksheet-based math program with E. and realizing that she wasn't well suited for paper-based curricula, Heidi and Jason began to invent games that allowed E. to demonstrate her knowledge in a way that worked for her. Making use of E.'s boundless energy, they ditched the confines of the classroom and went outside. "We'll go out on the driveway and use sidewalk chalk to draw big numbers all over the driveway," Heidi said. "I'll call out a math problem, and E. will run around and find the answer and stand on it."

Near the end of our visit, the kids scrambled into the room where Heidi and I were chatting. E. started running back and forth across the room, literally bouncing off of one wall and then the next, her wild energy no doubt exacerbated by the presence of my own exuberant and cheering crew of shorties. To quell the mounting chaos, Heidi gave a quiet verbal cue to her daughter to calm down. As E. persisted in slamming into the walls, Heidi called her over for a "quiet minute" of serious hugging. E. peered over her mom's shoulder at me, a huge smile on her face. "This is my hug tank!" she exclaimed.

Throughout this tender intervention, Heidi calmly asked E. a few times if she felt better or if she needed another quiet minute. E. would have stayed in her hug tank for a lot longer, I think, if my own daughter hadn't been eagerly calling her back to the play area. As E. skipped back to the playroom, she looked markedly calmer than when she had burst in. Only a minute or two had passed but the hug tank had worked its magic.

Parents can turn to alternatives to medication. Fear of medication seems to loom large over many homeschoolers; with all of the media talk about America's overmedicated children, this seems like a reasonable fear. Several of the families I spoke to for this book felt strongly that if their child were in school, the teacher would push for their child to take a pill as a solution to behavioral problems or to be sent to a special classroom with kids who had more extreme needs. Some families even said that they avoid seeking medical advice because they worry that doctors would insist on a medication regimen.

Having watched her own sisters and her husband explore medication for their ADD conditions and suffer the side effects, Heidi felt that managing E.'s unique temperament with strategies like the "quiet minute" and physical games has been the best course of action. "Jason lost his appetite and lost fifteen pounds when he first tried medication." After subsequent bouts with medications, "his focus became too much and he cared too much about small details. If this is what medication does, is it actually better than no medication?"

While Heidi said she would support her husband trying medication again if he felt he needed to, with E. she said it would be different. She pointed out that her life is so intertwined with E.'s that it would be harder for her to accept medication to treat E.'s behavior. Jason is at his job as an engineer for the better part of the day, but E. is right there with Heidi all day everyday. Heidi and E. struggle and win daily battles—together. With E.'s infectious laughter and genuine smile, it's safe to say that Heidi found something that works for her whole family.

Professional Treatment: Medication, Counseling, and Coaching

Homeschooling families have decided to take their children's education into their own hands and have made the bold choice to step out of the mainstream. That D-I-Y attitude fosters strong inclinations to "do everything themselves," and this often includes helping their kids develop coping strategies for behavioral and emotional problems. While I agree that some of the best intervention happens at home under the loving care of family, it's clear that there are special situations when even fiercely independent homeschoolers need to ask for help—professional help.

When doing my research for this book I spoke to child psychologist Ted K. Taylor, Ph.D. I asked Dr. Taylor about families struggling with children exhibiting disruptive behavior. He acknowledged that parents have several fears about seeking professional assistance.

First, they have hope that the problems their children are experiencing will disappear or fade over time, or that their children will mature and eventually change their behavior. "Sometimes parents think their child will just outgrow the problems, even though their child's behavior is very different than most children and is causing problems in multiple settings. Frankly, this is one of my biggest concerns," Dr. Taylor admitted. "Disruptive behavior, especially defiance and aggressive behavior, is very stable over time. Additionally, reputation with peers becomes highly stable if [parents] don't intervene early to change it."

Parents should embrace early intervention. According to Dr. Taylor, "if appropriate psychological interventions are offered when children are young (e.g., ages 3 to 8) large treatment changes can be achieved that tend to last into the future." In other words, early intervention can make a difference. "If we wait until children are older to get help, interventions are less effective," Dr. Taylor cautioned.

Second, parents are worried that seeking help will automatically lead to medication as a quick, easy solution. "They fear that schools or doctors will simply want to put their child on medication—something they don't want."

For children that may be diagnosed with Attention Deficit Hyperactivity Disorder (ADHD), medication can be helpful—but medication alone doesn't constitute treatment. According to Dr. Taylor, "for some problems, such as aggressive or oppositional and defiant behavior, the best treatments don't even involve medication. A comprehensive treatment plan for a child diagnosed with ADHD should include the option of medication combined with psychological treatments."

What do these psychological treatments for ADHD look like? "The most effective interventions for these problems involve a psychologist or other therapist trained in behavioral and cognitive-behavioral therapy who works closely with the family," explained Dr. Taylor. "[These professionals] coach parents on how to understand their child's temperament, prevent problems effectively, promote the development of self-control skills in their child, set up effective routines, and bring out the best in their children. Some coaching for the child includes strategies to improve focus, organization and study skills. The goal of all of this is to develop positive habits to replace the ineffective ones."

Another fear that Dr. Taylor acknowledged some parents have is that getting professional help will label their child, or that others will treat their child differently, as a result. For significant behavioral issues, though, this may be a moot point. "Children who show high levels of disruptive behavior are already being singled out." He recounted this heart-wrenching story: "I remember watching a video of a group of boys about 6- to 7-years-old in a social skills group," he said. "These kids really wanted to be good. But it was hard for them, given their temperament and personalities. I remember one boy was saying how in his school he was the 'baddest.' He then paused and reconsidered his answer. 'No, I'm the second baddest.' He knew the rank order of the 'baddest' kids, and I'm pretty sure his classmates did too. Getting treatment wasn't singling him out. In fact, other kids rarely know anything about who is getting treatment. But getting help can help change that reputation with others. If we do nothing, those habits, those reputations with others, those beliefs about themselves, just bake in and become harder to change," said Dr. Taylor.

When it comes to deciding the treatment approach for their children, parents are encouraged to try a balanced approach. "Some parents sometimes choose to first try these psychological treatments before making a decision about medications," said Dr. Taylor. "Other parents decide to try medication and psychological treatments together. Both are reasonable choices."

Homeschooling allows the flexibility to teach different subjects at different grade levels. Homeschooling also gave Heidi and Jason the flexibility to advance E.'s level of education in areas in which she excelled. Institutional schools often take a blanket approach to education where kids who have special needs are uniformly held back even if their educational proficiency is more nuanced. For example, while math was a challenge for E., she happened to be an exceptional reader. "She was reading on a fourth grade level when she was old enough to go into kindergarten. The school she would have gone to was overcrowded, and I had heard horror stories about how outnumbered the teachers were. So we kept her home for kindergarten so she could work at her own level in different subjects," explained Heidi. "By the time they built a larger school, homeschooling was working for us, and we didn't see the need to send her to the bigger school where she wouldn't be able to do her own thing."

Homeschooling can circumvent the social stigma at institutional settings. I've always appreciated the fact that my son, who needs speech therapy, has never had to walk out of a mainstream classroom alone to go to the special class for his services, while everyone looks on. He's never had a teacher assume that he's less brilliant than his same-age peers simply because he has an "articulation delay," a condition where there are some sounds his mouth hasn't figured out how to form yet, so he replaces them with other, less accurate sounds.

As a student teacher, I recall observing how a special education child struggled with the attention he got every time he had to leave the classroom for his special classes. He would try to sneak out of the room without anyone noticing, ducking the stares and snickers. But someone always noticed. The social stigma can be debilitating and can lead to children feeling like outcasts. Even teachers themselves would participate in the targeting. The teacher's lounge at a school where I did my student teaching often became a den of gossip. They flagged a kid's particular name and warned the teachers in later grades of what they were in for when so-and-so got to their class.

Knowing that my little guy doesn't have to face that kind of cruel scrutiny for his temporary issue is a relief for me. Instead, my son takes online public school for three of his classes, and he's now a grade ahead of his same-age peers in those classes. I know he would never have been afforded that opportunity to shine in a mainstream school if he was forced to shuttle back and forth to special classes.

AS YOU CAN see, all of the answers to the "why are you home-schooling?" question are rooted in the central idea that you can give your children something at home that they can't get at school and significantly increase their quality of life. Whether that means academically individualized lessons, flexible schedules, an emphasis on values, or the ability to creatively coach a child with specific developmental needs without pharmaceutical intervention, more and more families are choosing to bring learning home.

Now that we know some of the reasons why you've chosen to homeschool your family and the big issues you might encounter, let's now look at how we'll approach the methodologies in more detail.

TWO:
Educational Methods and
Approaches 101

Methods and means cannot be separated from the ultimate aim.[1]

- Emma Goldman, political activist

IMAGINE that you've taken the plunge into homeschooling. Your children were doing fine in school, but you had a hunch that they could be doing even better, so you worked up your courage and pulled them out. One of your neighbors living down the street homeschools, and she shared her favorite Charlotte Mason resources with you. Her kids seem quite content and the material looked easy to teach, so you went ahead and bought the Charlotte Mason materials for each of your kids. It was pricey but you decided you weren't going to spare any expense to do it right.

A month in, the kids are complaining. Their discontent has you confused. The family down the street is so bright and happy. Why aren't your own children enjoying the materials, too? Power struggles start popping up daily and now you're starting to doubt your decision to homeschool. Is it because the materials are simple and slow-paced, while your children are eager, fast-paced students? Does the plan you purchased really allow your kids the flexibility to learn what interests them at their own pace? Does it inspire them?

You start to think that there must be something out there that would be a better fit for your kids at home, but how do you find it? You browse the Web and find some other curricula, but you're gun shy about buying now. Your chest feels heavy with doubts. How can you decide what's best for you and your family? You'd never heard of Charlotte Mason before your neighbor mentioned it. A disturbing thought creeps into your head: *What else haven't I heard of?*

The aim of this book is to make sure you start with your best foot forward. Already started? Maybe that scenario sounds familiar, but never fear. It's never too late to make a fresh start down the right path for you and your children. We've established that there is no one right way to teach. But what if you're only familiar with one method? Do you wonder if there are alternative approaches that might work better? What are the odds that the only strategy you know is the best teaching strategy for your child? Many parents who discuss homeschooling would argue that what is lacking in methodology is made up for with love, nurturing, and genuine enthusiasm. Those qualities are definitely cornerstones of a truly successful homeschool, and I would never recommend a method that crowds out that kind of environment. I just think all parents can do better.

Along with the real joys of taking charge of your children's education, parents also face insecurities. Every committed parent hears that inner voice that demands time and time again, "How can I do better?"

The simple answer: Know your options.

Even when you think things are sailing along smoothly and you've got this school thing down, it pays to stay abreast of the basic schools of thought in education and information delivery. Why? Because we know that children aren't static beings. As your children grow and mature physically, they will be changing mentally and emotionally. Will tomorrow's child have the same educational needs as yesterday's child? It isn't likely. To keep pace, we must be constantly tweaking our pedagogy to keep our budding students engaged and challenged. Just when I feel that I've got my kids figured out, they grow and change, and so, too, do their needs both socially and academically.

We also know that siblings differ from each other, so an approach that works for one child may not work for a brother or sister. Once in a while, you'll find that siblings do travel down very similar paths of progression and this makes it easier for homeschooling. For the most part, though, siblings are no more likely to have the same educational needs as a class of non-related students. I often hear parents relate that the differences among their children were evident from moments after birth. Don't let this rattle you. At home you have a much more manageable student-to-teacher ratio and a great chance of succeeding using a multi-format teaching approach.

A thorny problem does remain: How do you master a variety of teaching methods and learn schools of thought that you don't even know are out there? How do you begin to look up something that you can't identify? Over the next few chapters, we'll tackle five popular educational methods, namely the Montessori method, Waldorf education, Trivium, Charlotte Mason education, and unschooling. For each method, we'll consider the following to decide what appeals to you and what doesn't:

- History
- Guiding principles
- Defining characteristics
- What the critics say
- The homeschool spin
- Activities
- Ideal for...

By the time you're done with this book, you'll know enough about each of the five widely discussed educational methods to feel confident in adapting the activities to meet the needs of every child. You may not practice all of the methodologies in whole or part, but the odds are good that you'll glean inspiration from more than one of them. In fact, when I set out to interview homeschooling families for this book, I had a bit of trouble finding families who used just one method over all of the rest. Most homeschooling parents I talked to said that they are "eclectic" homeschoolers—meaning that they pick and choose what works for each of their children from any number of methods, and end up with an educational plan that looks totally different from what anyone else is doing.

I'm a believer that this "cover-all-your-bases," broad-spectrum of understanding works especially well for families with more than one child studying similar content. As you learn about the different methods, you're bound to find something that works particularly well for one child but not for others. Use the material in this book like a multivitamin—helping you fill in potential holes in your academic "diet" for balance.

> Use the material in this book like a multivitamin—helping you fill in potential holes in your academic "diet" for balance.

History: How a Method Came to Be

To understand why and how a method of teaching came to be popularized, you must look at its roots and that's exactly what we'll do. Everyone in history who has pioneered a new school of teaching has done so with a desire to improve the quality of children's education. Often that begins with a few fundamental beliefs about how a child learns, and then those beliefs are elaborated upon until a methodology is formed.

As parents, you must decide what parts of a method will work for your children, and you can do that more easily when you understand the context from which a method grew. Knowing whether it blossomed out of a social setting with very specialized needs, such as the Waldorf method (Chapter 4), or as a college studies framework like the Trivium (Chapter 5), will help you determine which aspect of a method matters most to you. These roots matter because just as each child has certain needs, so, too, did the generations and societies from which individual teaching methods sprung forth.

> As parents, you must decide what parts of a method will work for your children, and you can do that more easily when you understand the context from which a method grew.

One must also weed through all of the surrounding contextual factors in order to get to the heart of the method. Understanding these more peripheral issues will help you distinguish between the practices that are the result of a methodical investigation into the mind and how it responds to differing forms of instruction, and those that are simply the result of academic lore and other lesser scientific means.

An example of a practice that I see as not relating to the scientific foundations of a teaching method, but that has somehow become a central focus to those who teach it, is the use of beeswax crayons in Waldorf schools. Just as an experiment, I did a Google search for "Why beeswax crayons in Waldorf?" I waded through several pages of search results before finding a result that wasn't an ad for the sale of Waldorf style beeswax crayons. When I finally found what looked like an answer to my question, I found a fanciful description of the beautiful art found in Waldorf schools; beeswax crayons were credited for helping create this environment of beauty for the child to experience.

In my opinion, the beauty of the artwork comes through from the use of color, which you can create from a standard box of Crayola crayons. While it's true that beeswax crayons are a more natural product, which

Waldorf prizes, their popularity probably came about because of their availability at the time. Somehow people attached an importance to the crayons that persists to this day, even when their use may never have been more than a matter of sheer convenience. Sadly, I hear parents who still say, "I love the feel of Waldorf schooling, but I can't afford all those pricey art supplies." Being tied to a method without understanding the context of why the method was put in place can unduly limit your options.

This calls to mind the old story about the woman who was upset when her schedule made it difficult to do laundry on Thursdays and who felt great stress over this. When a friend suggested, "Why not do the laundry on Tuesdays when your schedule permits?" the woman responded, "Because Thursday is laundry day!" The friend asked why and the woman said, "That's when my mom did laundry!"

Viewing a methodology from its historical perspective allows you to use the "why" behind the details of a practice to separate out the essential from the peripheral. Regardless of what educational philosophers and curriculum sales people want you to believe, it's possible to practice methods piecemeal—taking parts that work for you, leaving those that don't—and still reap the benefits! Swap out beeswax crayons for Crayolas, and you can still enjoy the benefits of a Waldorf education. Ultimately, knowing the historical nuances can help you make better decisions about a method.

Guiding Principles: The Heart and Soul of a Method

We'll also look at the guiding principles of each of these major methods. What theories or ideas were understood to be *fact* during the development of each approach and how did these "truths" guide the early practitioners of these methods? These are very important to consider.

The idea that childhood is a unique time and that a child is not just a small adult was considered by Maria Montessori to be an undeniable fact and the Montessori method (examined in Chapter 3) was formed with that guiding principle in mind.

Every method has at least one guiding principle; some have many. We'll look at these guiding principles to better understand the next area of study: the defining characteristics.

Defining Characteristics: Tell-tale Signs

Defining characteristics are the little things that clue you in as to what method is being used. For instance, when you have finished this book, you'll hopefully have a pretty good guess that a child studying Latin at an early age is likely to be part of the Trivium movement (Chapter 5) because teaching the "mother languages" is a defining characteristic of that approach. Other things like the widespread use of natural materials in Waldorf education (Chapter 4) and in the Montessori method (Chapter 3) are defining characteristics to a lesser degree. This will be the section where I give you some of the outward evidence of those aforementioned guiding principles.

What the Critics Say (and Why You Should Listen)

Every system has critics; schooling approaches are no exception. Every time experts feel that they have come up with the definitive answer to how to best teach children, of course other experts counter with their own thoughts on what would be a better and more reliable approach. There is a lot to be said for this kind of debate and constant churn. My own belief is that because there is no one right way to educate all children and everyone speaks from his or her own experiences, there is much value to be unearthed in looking at what the naysayers have to say. We'll consider then the prevalent critiques and potential drawbacks of a method with a fair mind.

My husband used to joke that someday we'd write a book called, *Why You Don't Need Self-Help Books.* Ideas championed by so-called experts in one book are later refuted to some degree by other experts in another book. This is true in almost any area and especially so in parenting and education where you often find a wide range of interpretations and positions jockeying for your attention. The field is heavily influenced by the personality and temperament of the experts that dominate—aspects that are hard to quantify but can often influence our perception of a method or practice. Remember that practices can be made compelling just through an advocate's personality and certainty. If experts were to say, "This *may* apply to your child," instead of saying with confidence, "This is absolutely what is best for all children!" how many books would they sell? Not too many I would imagine. Unfortunately, as much as we would like otherwise, that parenting panacea that makes every child-centered gray area dissolve into black and white just doesn't exist, no matter what the experts and pundits claim.

Even experts that tout reams of data should be approached with caution. Data resulting from a study or experiment can be easily manipulated or slanted by an investigator to support a claim about what's best for child learning. There are a number of ways that statistics can be distorted and misused, from overgeneralization of findings to mixing up correlation with causation. I don't intend to give a mini-class on statistics here, but I encourage you to always stay mindful of the context of how information is gathered and presented.[2]

> Listen to what the critics have to say and use it to make balanced choices. Keep the parts that you feel could enrich your child's life and toss out parts that don't resonate with you.

Going through the methods in this book, keep in mind that some practices simply make sense and work, while others seem far-fetched and outdated within today's educational context. Knowing the points of view of the critics for each method helps put their ideas into perspective and helps you draw your own conclusions. Understanding the intentions of the originators—and the criticism they received—goes a long way in helping you make informed choices.

The bottom line: Don't let serious criticism of a method make you throw the baby out with the bath water. Instead, listen to what the critics have to say and use it to make balanced choices. Keep the parts that you feel could enrich your child's life and toss out parts that don't resonate with you.

The Homeschool Spin: From the Classroom to Your Living Room

When you go through the book and consider the various approaches presented, inevitably you will be thinking, *How would this look in a homeschool setting? Can it work in my home?* In this section, I'll give you a few examples of how each approach might look in the homeschool setting. Of course, the creative parent will find many ways to adapt each of these methods to their classroom. Based on my experience with each method, I'll toss out a few ideas to get you started.

Activities: Tips to Try at Home

Here you'll find a list of activities related to the method for several age groups: preschool, elementary, and upper grades. The lists aren't meant to be exhaustive; they are starter suggestions to get your imagination in gear for more activities you could design on your own. The examples provided also give you a more concrete picture of what the method would look like in the homeschool setting. If you like what you see, I encourage you to search for more activities, and I give you my own personal recommendations and favorites for other resources, including books, blogs, and websites.

Ideal for... Families that are a Best Match

Finally, for each method we'll consider what families that particular method would appeal to. Parents have their own personal style and goals that inevitably guide how they choose to homeschool their children. My personal philosophy is that it's best to look for a method of teaching that *complements your natural style rather than one that matches it.*

We all have days that are a bit more harried than the norm. For example, in times of prolonged family crisis, such as an illness or a big move, we might have an extended period of time during which we'll still be teaching our kids, but with less focus. Maybe we'll only cover the essentials, or be unable to spend the usual amounts of time planning each minute of the day. By choosing a method that's different from our own natural style, we ensure that our children get a balanced approach.

Here's an example from my own classroom: I'm typically fact- and detail-oriented, drawn to organized lessons and schedules. If I'm not being mindful, nurturing can take a backseat to memorization and mechanics during the day. To counterbalance this, I conscientiously plan my lessons with one of the more nurturing approaches in mind.

In contrast, I have friends who are consummate nurturers, and when they aren't being attentive and their time isn't planned out, they can lose all academic focus. In catering to their children's whims and fancies, they might end up with a three-hour long tea party that displaces any organized lessons for the day. That's fine once in a while, but it might not form the basis for the educational program you envision for your child. For these families, I would recommend a more academically focused method to supplement their natural teaching style.

So you see, it can help to be mindful of your own tendencies, strengths, and shortcomings as a teacher when choosing a method. Make a choice that fits with your own beliefs and values, but one that doesn't mimic your natural style completely. By making an effort to employ other methods different from your teaching style, you ensure that the whole child is attended to.

HOMESCHOOLING ITSELF ALREADY carries countless stressors from inside and outside the home that are beyond your control. This particular stress—the pressure of being unprepared for the next phase of your child's education—is one that you can mitigate simply by educating yourself. Even the most committed homeschoolers can be so overwhelmed during times of transition that they consider throwing in the towel. Don't. Once you become comfortable pulling from a variety of methods, you'll be able to take a single lesson and teach it in a way that meets the needs of multiple learners all at once.

Now it's time to dive into some of the most popular educational frameworks at play in modern homeschooling.

THREE:
Montessori Method

Our intervention in this marvelous process is indirect; we are here to offer this life, which came into the world by itself, the means necessary for its development, and having done that we must await this development with respect.[1]

- *Maria Montessori, educator*

WHEN I arrived at Audrey's house, her children had not yet returned home from a midday matinee of a flamenco show at the local fine arts theater. As we waited in the kitchen, I noticed fun Montessori activities on a small, child-sized shelf, similar to the ones that I had made for my own boys when they were toddlers. When the kids arrived a few minutes later, we did our quick hellos, and then I followed them upstairs to the schoolroom.

I was immediately wowed by their school space. What looked to be a finished attic intended to be a master bedroom had been converted to a schoolroom with child height shelving all around, endless supplies of wooden Montessori activities on trays, and natural sunlight flooding in from large windows. It was schoolroom perfection. As I would expect in a Montessori environment, everything was in place and kept neat and orderly.

Audrey gathered the four kids, ranging from a 2-year-old to a sixth grader, around on the floor for circle time. They each grabbed a small American flag and sang a patriotic song. A girl who looked to be about 6-years-old said a prayer, and then they all turned and said the Pledge of Allegiance facing a vase filled with the mini flags they had just waved around during their song. Circle time had a distinctly patriotic flare to it.

Next, Audrey demonstrated a game where the children would take turns walking around the group holding a bell. The aim was to walk carefully enough to avoid ringing the bell. The first child to try tripped just a bit and the bell rang a teeny tiny ring. I was expecting her brothers to make some sort of disappointed noise or to lightheartedly tease her about it, but no one did. They all simply put their hands to their mouths and giggled right along with her, and she happily went on her way. In fact, over the hour or so that I was there, there was never a time when there were loud outbursts of, "Way to go!" or "Oh, too bad." The tone remained neutral and non-judgmental throughout.

During story time, Audrey asked the kids what continents they could identify on a map in the book. Her daughter pointed to Africa and identified it as Australia. Instead of correcting her or saying she was wrong, Audrey simply looked to the other children and asked, "Do you guys agree?" Audrey never ever said that a child was wrong. She simply let the correct answer resonate from the others without the sting of a formal correction. My own son once had a speech teacher say that the reason he wasn't performing well in her class was because he didn't like to be told he was wrong. She went on to say that hearing that you're wrong is a part of life that everyone has to deal with. Not in Audrey's house! She is masterful at redirecting attention towards a proper answer without correcting or scolding.

After story time, Audrey announced that it was work time. With little prompting, the kids headed to the shelves, grabbed a tray, and got down to business. The eldest boy worked with pushpins and thin metal bars of various lengths, shapes, and colors, pinning designs to a board. I ventured over and asked him what he was up to. "I'm making a double heart," he said quite matter-of-factly. After making and disassembling several other designs, he ended up with a fairly precise version of the Israeli flag. Audrey immediately set about finding other examples of the flag to show him.

The younger boy put together several small models of things like a virus and a bacterium. At the same low table, his sisters worked side by side on a letter puzzle. One by one, as the children finished a task, they silently put the materials away and got a new work tray. The only sounds that could be heard were of Audrey working with the 2-year-old when needed and the occasional request from the kids for Mom to look at someone's finished work.

During work time, the 2-year-old really knocked my socks off! At one point, she had an accident in her chair. With minimum feedback from Audrey, this tiny little thing set to work cleaning up her own potty accident. Audrey, of course, went over the area with a Clorox wipe—

again, never chastising the child for having the accident in the first place, just making sure everything was properly sanitized. Then, the 2-year-old and Mom washed their hands together. At this, the pint-sized beauty tossed her paper towel in the trash, and declared, "All better!"

Without dwelling on the accident, the little one then headed over to an "object basket." She reached into the container filled with tiny objects and pulled out a little cloth bag. "Dis is a bag," she said. Audrey repeated the word "bag," and then the tiny girl whose words were still unclear, reached into a well-organized box of movable block letters (typical of a Montessori classroom) and spelled out the word b-a-g right there on the table.

Whoa! It was amazing to me, and still there was no outbursts of joyous congratulation, but simply an acknowledgment that the letters did, indeed, spell "bag." On they went to the next thing.

With the extreme organization I witnessed in their learning space, as well as the extensive collection of somewhat pricey wooden Montessori materials, I had to ask Audrey, "Were you ever a formally trained Montessori teacher?" And bluntly, I also had to know how much money had been invested in this very fine school environment. I've visited the homes of many homeschoolers, and I have never set foot in a room so well equipped and stocked with materials.

Audrey told me that she had been formally trained in the Montessori method for children up to 7-years-old, the pre-primary ages. She went on to say that they had only invested a few thousand dollars in the room. A typically furnished Montessori classroom generally costs about $10,000, so she felt they had done quite well with their budget.

As we talked about the money that was invested, she brought over a tray of materials that looked more like our family's Montessori materials.

"See these?" she asked. "They are sound cylinders that I made back when we couldn't afford to buy the nice wooden materials. And look. I couldn't even afford to cover them with solid colored contact paper. I just used what I could to make my own materials."

Admittedly, the sound cylinders stuck out like a sore thumb in this room filled with the perfect wooden materials. They are a charming reminder of how they began and how far they've come.

I should note that Audrey's older children attend a high-tech charter high school and were not present while I was there to observe. It seems that Audrey's hard work in the early years has laid a foundation for her children to move on and find success in a more rigorous-than-average institutional setting. I asked how she felt about Maria Montessori's less implemented ideas about high school. While it was clear that she doesn't do a full Montessori high school program for the older children, Audrey doesn't feel that Montessori's ideas about adolescence are all that far-flung (we'll discuss those ideas shortly) or impossible to implement. In fact, she also fills her children's home time with activities geared for her older kids, such as caring for their small farm animals and raising a big vegetable garden to fully experience the cycles of life.

I left Audrey's house simply dazzled by the calm, uplifting atmosphere. I often hear homeschooling moms talk about how chaotic homeschooling several children can be, but there wasn't a single moment during my visit where it looked like Audrey's children felt that their needs weren't being met, or that any of them were irritable or vying for her attention. And at the same time, there was nothing at all to suggest that this was a show being put on for a guest. They were so comfortable in their routines and it was clear that being mellow and industrious is the norm for them.

History

Maria Montessori was an Italian medical doctor in the late nineteenth and early twentieth century whose studies became deeply focused on understanding how the brain develops and synthesizes information. Her studies were initially centered on understanding and aiding the development of disabled children, but her practices, which came to be known as the "Montessori method" of education, quickly found favor with educators of children with typical development as well.

After news of her work spread across Italy, she was asked to head a preschool in Rome, whereupon she began developing a variety of materials for students to touch and hold that would engage the child in self-led, "sensorial learning." She would observe the children and their interactions with the materials, and then adapt the materials in order to lead the children to delve deeper into concepts of their own accord. Towards the end of her career, Maria Montessori and her son Mario continued their study of the human brain and adapted her methods to the changing needs of elementary-age children.

Montessori schools have become wildly popular and can be found all around the world. Famous names to have been educated in this method are Anne Frank (Holocaust survivor), Jacqueline Kennedy Onassis (former first lady), Julia Child (renowned chef and author), Jeff Bezos (founder and

CEO of Amazon), Gabriel García Márquez (Nobel Prize-winning novelist), and Sergey Brin and Larry Page (co-founders of Google). With names like these to its credit, the Montessori method is easily one of the more popular methods of choice for homeschoolers.

Guiding Principles

The uniqueness of childhood should be respected. Montessori believed that children absorb information from their environment in a completely different manner than adults. Central to the Montessori method is the idea that the child isn't simply an adult in a smaller body, but is a completely unique being that has yet unrecognized potential.

> Guiding Principles:
> * The uniqueness of childhood should be respected.
> * The child is a self-motivator.
> * The hands and brain are interdependent.

The child is a self-motivator. In the Montessori method, there is the basic belief that children, given the proper stimulating environment, are capable of teaching themselves and can be motivated to learn as much as they can on their own. Montessori explains: "The environment itself will teach the child, if every error he makes is manifest to him, without the intervention of a parent or teacher, who should remain a quiet observer of all that happens."[2] A child's potential for investigative learning is only limited by the environment and the teacher's ability to guide him or her toward broader concepts. This thinking differs greatly from other schools of thought that believe that children, left to their own devices, will idly squander away the most formative years of life.

Another cornerstone of the Montessori method is the belief that children's natural curiosity needs to be protected from undue external influences, such as external rewards or punishments. Praise or congratulations, as well as scolding or criticism are rarely given or administered because it's thought that external motivation can be counterproductive to child development. According to Montessori advocates, children already possess their own internal motivation when they enter the world, which should be allowed to develop naturally and not be unduly influenced by others. Teachers, therefore, take a backseat as observers or "living resources," rather than heavily involved administrators.

The hands and brain are interdependent. Much of Montessori education is dependent on specialized materials designed to accentuate learning through hands-on, tactile experience. Montessori believed that our hands are intimately connected to our brain, and that touch was a phenomenally effective mode of information transmission. Children can't learn simply by being told, for instance, that ice is cold; they must feel the sensation for themselves to fully grasp it. Even letters of the alphabet had to be touched to be understood. Writing a letter wasn't sufficient; children must run their hands along the letter and feel its curvature and form.

In addition, Montessori predicted a link between how children handle and experiment with objects and their ability to develop a strong work ethic later on in life. She once stated, "An adult who does not understand that a child needs to use his hands and does not recognize this as the first manifestation of an instinct for work can be an obstacle to the child's development."[3] This is a controversial concept particularly in today's institutional classroom. For many, the quiet absorption of material (e.g., reading and writing) is seen as sufficient for learning; allowing young students to be "physical" in how they learn (e.g., using their hands, playing with objects) would lead to a chaotic classroom. For advocates of the Montessori method, however, tactile, hands-on learning is the heart of child development and education.

Defining Characteristics

Tactile materials are essential. There are many practices that are unique to the Montessori method of teaching, none more so than the use of materials. Montessori developed an unbelievable arsenal of materials for every concept that crossed her scientific mind. Carefully dyed spools of silk were used to guide the students' understanding of subtle differences in color. Blocks that were the same in dimension but of different weights were used to teach differences in heaviness and mass.

Listing all the Montessori-inspired materials here would no doubt test your patience. If you find that this approach interests you, you may want to investigate Montessori materials more in depth. The cost of purchasing these materials can be an eliminating factor for many families, but if your heart rests with the Montessori method, and you're creative and motivated, you can easily make your own budget versions of most of the Montessori materials. I've done a lot of this myself, and plan to compile my ideas in a blog post (or even in a future book) about creating virtually free, D-I-Y Montessori materials at home.

Self-paced learning dominates. In the Montessori method, children work at their own pace. Once in a while, teachers lead sessions on concrete ideas, but it's usually up to the individual child to take those lessons in a direction that he or she chooses. This means that after a lesson, the teacher will not only observe, but also accept the direction that a child takes his or her new knowledge. Often times, a child will mention something in conversation with the teacher, and then the teacher will create an activity around the child's current interest. Of the novice teacher, Montessori said, "The most difficult thing to make clear to the new teacher is that because the child progresses, she must restrain herself and avoid giving directions, even if at first they are expected; all her faith must repose in his [the child's] latent powers."[4]

Defining Characteristics:
- Tactile materials are essential.
- Self-paced learning dominates.
- Mixed-age learning environments are the right backdrop.
- Test-free environments are best.
- Individuality is prized.
- Self-sufficiency is a core lesson.

Mixed-age learning environments are the right backdrop. The Montessori classroom consists of children of different ages, but within an age range: birth to 3-years-old, 3- to 6-years-old, 6- to 12-years-old (sometimes temporarily, 6 to 9-years-old and 9- to 12-years-old), 12- to 15-years-old, and 15- to 18-years-old. In these groupings, younger children can learn from older children, and older children can solidify their understanding of concepts through the mentoring of their younger classmates.

Test-free environments are best. Montessori teachers typically don't administer tests in a traditional sense. Historically, Montessori teachers observe children closely and monitor their progress using a variety of checklists, rating forms, and narrative descriptions, often referred to as "qualitative evaluation." Montessori once said, "My vision of the future is no longer of people taking exams and proceeding from secondary school to University but of passing from one stage of independence to a higher, by means of their own activity and effort of will."[5] For Montessori proponents, personal mastery and accomplishment are valued above arbitrary grades and accolades. Grading scales simply show how well students master valued or prioritized material created by evaluators or test creators. Montessori saw children as individuals that can learn from lessons and absorb details and ideas outside what can be evaluated on tests.

However, with mandated standardized testing and pressures to show more quantitative proof of student performance, some Montessori schools now use alternative testing methods. These include having children make up "assessments" and giving them to other children to take, while the teacher observes both the assessment giver and taker, as well as other, low-pressure forms of assessment.

Individuality is prized. The individual child is the focus in the Montessori school. As such, the nurturing of individuality is the focus more than the development of cooperative and social skills. Social interactions are not as highly prized as they are in others methods. This may be partly a result of the self-paced learning emphasis, but it also seems to be a deeply rooted concept on its own. In Montessori's words, "Child life is not an abstraction; it is the life of individual children. There exists only one real manifestation: the living individual; and toward single individuals, one by one observed, education must direct itself."[6] Montessori didn't view the child as a tiny adult, but as a unique individual undergoing delicate stages of cognitive development. This uniqueness goes beyond any single stage in life. Every aspect of being fully human is embraced, with no assumption about a child's needs based on superficial factors, such as age or gender.

Montessori, herself, was the first woman to graduate with a medical degree from an Italian college, and had spent much of her life breaking through stereotypes that society at the time tried to impose upon her. She appears to simply have taken this respect for individual aptitudes that she spent her life seeking out, and integrated it into her work on child development and education.

Self-sufficiency is a core lesson. Many of the activities that you'll find implemented in a Montessori setting are focused on preparing children to meet all of their own needs. Montessori stated, "Any child who is self-sufficient, who can tie his shoes, dress or undress himself, reflects in his joy and sense of achievement the image of human dignity, which is derived from a sense of independence."[7] Domestic tasks, such as slicing bananas, folding socks, and ringing out sponges, are commonly employed in Montessori schools. In her own classroom, Montessori had children practice buttoning buttons and fastening loops like those found on shoes as part of their regular daily exercises. All tools and utensils are child-sized (e.g., miniature sinks and chairs, smaller forks and pencils) and two-step stools are used to help children access areas that are typically off-limits to children on account of their height. In a Montessori classroom, the learning environment is created with the child's needs in mind to instill self-sufficiency and independence.

What the Critics Say

John Dewey, a renowned American psychologist and educational philosopher, criticized the Montessori method as being restrictive and placing too little emphasis on social interaction. Other critics have argued that the method isn't restrictive enough and doesn't give children the skills to tackle tasks that they didn't choose for themselves. Being that there isn't any formal written work or the traditional "desk work" like what you would find in other educational settings, it's often assumed that a Montessori-educated child may find it difficult to transition to a traditional, institutional classroom.

In addition, critics speculate that children who have never undergone formal assessments may not be able to display their knowledge with standardized testing. With most Montessori schools not exempt from the required state standardized testing, this lack of testing experience among its students has become a growing concern. While preparation for annual standardized testing in other educational settings exposes students to the bubble sheet and other multiple-choice testing formats, can children who have never been given a pencil and paper test intuitively fill out the forms in a way that displays their knowledge and learning? There is, as of yet, no definitive answer to that question. Critics also raise concerns that Montessori students, upon entering college or pre-collegiate institutions, will face testing formats with increased and possibly debilitating anxiety.

Most of the concerns about Montessori education center around the fear that children who spend their formative years in this free-style environment wouldn't be able to find success in mainstream classrooms.

The fact that Montessori is rarely available (and some question whether it was ever meant to be) for children beyond the elementary ages (past sixth grade), lends some credibility to this concern. That said, the list of Montessori alums I gave at the opening of this chapter suggest that some students do, in fact, go on to thrive and succeed in the real world after going through a Montessori-style education.

The Homeschool Spin

The Montessori method is one of the easiest methods to adapt to the home environment for children of lower elementary ages—and even beyond if your child is still thriving with the method.

Create the materials with your children. With a little creativity on the parent's part, the materials can usually be made at home. Your crafty ingenuity can even be its own lesson since building your own materials at home demonstrates the value of improvisation and initiative. Children often enjoy joining in and helping with this, too, which allows them a sense of ownership not only over their own learning, but also over their physical environment.

> The Homeschool Spin:
> * Create the materials with your children.
> * Turn chores around the house into lessons.
> * Learn how to assess self-paced learning.
> * Take advantage of the emphasis on mixed-age activities.

Turn chores around the house into lessons. Also contributing to their sense of ownership over their environment is the focus on domestic skills. When your day is spent in the home, having the skills to participate in home-keeping activities is a major plus.

Learn how to assess self-paced learning. Self-paced learning, as I've said before, is one of the greatest advantages of homeschooling, and this method wholly embraces this concept. As you study Montessori's work in more depth, you'll gain greater insights into how to monitor your children's progress and identify signs of readiness for more challenging activities. The qualitative evaluations make it easy for you to assess your children's progression; however, if you reside in a state that requires you to show more quantitative evidence of progress, you'll need to combine Montessori-style evaluation tools with more traditional methods. I find that if you examine your state's framework for content, you'll easily be able to determine the specific Montessori activities that you can do that cover each of the stated benchmarks.

Addressing state mandated evaluations often eliminates one of the major criticisms of the Montessori method by accustoming children to standard format testing throughout their childhood. While it's true that strict Montessori adherents firmly believe that testing can be damaging to children, I personally believe that this only applies in an environment where the weight of the test results is emphasized, and where children are given the idea that something major hangs on the results.

If you're homeschooling, you can simply take your children in for their testing when the time comes and reassure them that the results of the test matter very little and completely eliminate the undue stress associated with the long, annual testing period that almost all children in institutional schooling experience. This gives your children the testing experience they will need later in life, gives the state the numerical value of mastery that's required, and gives you a feel for the possible gaps in content knowledge that you can address.

Take advantage of the emphasis on mixed-age activities. The nurturing mindset in the Montessori method works well in a variety of homeschooling environments. If you have children who are relatively close in age, this method is ideal because the activities that Montessori outlined in her writings are easily adaptable within an age range.

The Montessori attitude is such that there is no wrong way to use materials (except for maybe throwing them out of a window) so your younger children can always observe and mimic older siblings' work without the fear of failure. Its multi-age classrooms and focus on mentorship, with older children teaching younger ones, translates beautifully at home with sibling relationships.

Activities

Preschool

Note: Many preschool activities will look a lot like chores. At home, be sure to provide your children with a stepladder to easily access counter spaces without adult intervention, or provide child-height workspaces.

- Sort silverware from the dishwasher into the silverware tray.
- Wash and slice fruits and veggies before meals.
- Wring out sponges and wash play dishes in a tub of water or sink.
- Pour dried beans or rice from one container to another.
- Arrange cut paint chips from lightest to darkest.
- Arrange varying objects from lightest to heaviest.
- Move craft pompoms from cup to cup using tweezers.
- Button shirts and lace up shoes.
- Begin learning letter sounds working with a movable alphabet.

Elementary

- Use letters and numbers cut out of sandpaper (the usual tactile medium for Montessori numbers and letters) or other tactilely unique surfaces like felt or foam.
- Give children trays of colored sand or salt, infused with scented oil, and have them use their fingers to write in the sand.
- Provide small objects to move around during math lessons.
- Use a dropper and small cups of colored water to explore how colors combine and become new colors.
- Provide a set of lowercase letters and a group of objects whose names can be sounded out within your children's current spelling level.
- Have children handle their own laundry.

Upper Grades

Montessori rarely spoke of a vision for secondary education until a series of lectures she gave at the University of Amsterdam in January 1920. Her ideas about secondary education reform were based around the concept of *Erdkinder*, meaning "children of the earth." She advanced seemingly radical ideas about pubescent children needing to live apart from their parents in a rural, commune-like setting. In Montessori's vision, groups of adolescents would live off the land, side-by-side with a few adult teachers around.

Montessori's ideals related to secondary education are often perceived as more impractical and less elaborated upon than her in-depth research into elementary education. Unlike her ideas about the learning of younger children, her ideas about the education of older children never really took hold. Throughout Europe, though, there are many secondary schools that claim to be Montessori-inspired, although few of them go the distance that Montessori spoke of in becoming a full-time "farm school." And in the U.S., the Montessori secondary school is a rare bird, indeed.

Without sending your teenager to live on a farm, the best way to maintain a Montessori feel in the upper grades is to maintain the virtually test-free environment and to continue to emphasize student-directed learning. This means continuing to allow older children to follow their own interests and letting them explore those interests to their natural limit. This doesn't mean letting other subjects fall by the wayside, of course. Formal lessons should still be offered so that the learning of new material continues unabated; lessons are merely kept within a timeframe that allows the students to pursue their own interests and projects.

Interests allowed to blossom into passions in one area can certainly lead to learning across a variety of subject areas. Let's say you have a child who's interested in web design. Your job as a living resource means that you encourage your child by supplying him or her with all the books on web design you can find. You then allow your child time to work on his or her own creative projects, and encourage your child to write about the process and to teach the new skills to peers.

As Audrey demonstrates with her children, hard work is an aspect central to Montessori's vision for older students that can be easily adopted at home. Physically demanding work on a farm or a ranch (e.g., chopping wood, bailing hay, and so on) fall under this banner. Audrey mentioned that they chose their property with the children's Montessori education in mind. Of course, if you live in an urban area, similar opportunities may be difficult to find. For those of you without access to manual labor at home, helping your child choose a summer job that's physically demanding or challenging might be a good choice. Summers are a great time for homeschoolers to encourage their older students to stay active with a job that requires working outdoors or physical labor. As a parent, your job is to remain simply a ready resource to guide your teen.

Recommended Resources

My absolute favorite Montessori resource is Brilliant Minds Montessori (brilliantminds-montessori.com), which is an actual brick and mortar school that also sells fairly comprehensive math and reading kits on Amazon. What is unique about their supplies is that their kits come with corresponding teacher scripts and worksheets so that even the non-trained parent can find success with their materials. Brilliant Minds offers reasonably priced math kits for both lower and upper level math that come with brightly colored beads and wooden manipulatives. Priced between $50 and $260, it's well worth the investment and easy for even the most inexperienced teacher or parent to use.

Audrey pointed me to Montessori Outlet (montessorioutlet.com), which featured a smorgasbord of Montessori resources I never imagined. Prices also varied from the affordable to the posh, so there's something for everyone. The drawback to buying from the Outlet is that you simply get the materials without any instructions or guides on what to do with them. So, if you aren't trained in the Montessori method, you'll have to do some extra research on your own, like finding video tutorials on YouTube. I did this myself after I got home from Audrey's house and found that it wasn't too hard to find someone demonstrating how to use a particular set of materials online.

Montessori Print Shop (montessoriprintshop.com) is a website that I've found that offers affordable, printable materials. Many of the resources are free, and there are hundreds more that are available for just a few dollars. My children's daily grammar activities are rooted in materials from the Montessori Print Shop that I purchased, printed, and then laminated for durability. The site even gives you strategies for organizing your materials and provides attractive, printable labels for your storage containers. In terms of longevity, the items we've purchased from this site have been the most used over the longest period of time of any of our

Montessori-specific educational purchases and also happen to be the cheapest.

When making my own materials, I find it helpful to browse the websites of brick and mortar Montessori schools, as well as teacher blogs and YouTube videos. Despite being a somewhat smaller corner of the education world, Montessori advocates seem to have banded together on a variety of online channels and forums. It's easy for any parent with an internet connection to hop online and find teachers and parents sharing various how-to videos. On the Web, you'll find many teachers that demonstrate not only conventional ways of using typical Montessori materials, but also creative ways of turning those materials into, say, complex games. What I'll often do is watch the videos and adapt the ideas using more homemade, low-cost materials. (You get all of the fun, with none of the expense!) Several YouTube channels I use and recommend include: myworksmontessori, AtHomeMontessori, InfoMontessori, unitedmontessori, and montessoritraining.

Ideal for...

Parents that are natural nurturers and materials-focused: The Montessori method works well for families with preschool- to elementary-age students who appear to learn best through hands-on, multisensory methods. The nurturing climate created in Montessori-inspired environments is sure to benefit the whole family.

If you have money to burn on materials, you'll have a bonanza. There are many online stores (like the ones I just mentioned in "Resources") with a wide inventory of materials. If money is an object, and you don't have the time (or inclination) to create the materials on your own from scratch, then Montessori may not be for you.

Families that value process over performance: The Montessori method addresses the whole child and postpones formal academic content of the pencil to paper kind and abstract learning until late elementary (what would be fourth, fifth, and sixth grades). In contrast, your child's traditionally schooled peers would be pushed to dive into writing and abstract concepts immediately upon commencing formal kindergarten education. If your goal is to support the whole child and nurture the learning "process" more that the learning "performance," then Montessori could be for you.

On the flip side, if you value a large amount of data absorption that can be demonstrated in any setting and easily quantified at an early age, read on.

FOUR:
Waldorf Education

Those who judge human beings according to generic characteristics only reach the boundary, beyond which people begin to be beings whose activity is based on free self-determination... Characteristics of race, tribe, ethnic group and gender are subjects for special sciences... But all these sciences cannot penetrate through to the special nature of the individual. Where the realm of freedom of thought and action begin, the determination of individuals according to generic laws ends.[1]

- Rudolf Steiner, educator

I sat at my desk, staring at the computer screen as I eagerly awaited the familiar sound of an incoming Skype call. I was scheduled to meet Rebecca, a Waldorf homeschooling mom in Ontario, Canada for the very first time to observe her family's circle time. We have enjoyed using bits and pieces of Waldorf curriculum in our home, and I was eager to finally meet someone trained in the method and using it for homeschooling.

As the computer rang and I picked up the call, a man's face filled the screen. We introduced ourselves, and then he stepped aside. There on the screen was Rebecca standing with her two beautiful daughters, 9- and 8-years-old, all smiling and cheerful. They were the perfect picture of sweetness and family unity. Their living room looked small and tidy, and fluffy couches were arranged around a circular rug. After a few short greetings and some talk about what they were about to do, they began their circle time.

The first activity of their circle time involved reciting a few long prayers with large, sweeping gestures, presumably to act as a memory aid. Then, to my surprise they began saying the same prayers with the full motions faster and faster. It was like watching a beautiful dance in fast forward. They reached a seemingly impossible speed and when they finished, the girls grabbed onto Rebecca with hugs and giggles that suggested the thrill of accomplishment.

After prayers, they recited a few rhyming verses about standing straight as an arrow and about the seasons. (Everything they did, from prayers and poems, to math and French all had accompanying coordinated movements.) The lessons transitioned gracefully from one to the next, and Rebecca didn't just sit and watch or instruct; she moved right along side her girls, physically participating in their movements. It was breathtaking. With her stance and actions, Rebecca had the demeanor of a mentor or team captain rather than a teacher or administrator. There was a definite line of authority there that was never crossed. At no time did either of the girls try to take circle time in their own direction. Rebecca would state the next step, and the girls seamlessly moved on to the next activity like ducklings following their mother.

In the math portion of circle time, each girl, in turn, was asked to be the Wise Giant. Rebecca explained that an imaginary king needed the Wise Giant's help to solve a problem. Here was a question: "The King has 30 sheep and his five shepherds have each returned with five sheep. He is sure some are missing, but he can't figure out how many. Can you help him, Wise Giant?"

Instead of blurting out an answer, the student who was assigned the role of the Wise Giant did something quite different. The Wise Giant wasn't allowed to speak; the Giant could only stomp the answer loudly on the floor. This was so much fun to watch. One of the girls really needed time to think and Rebecca left the room for a moment and returned, giving her daughter time to think without the pressure of someone staring at her in anticipation.

Soon, the girl's face lit up, and she started to speak.

"No, no, Wise Giant! You cannot talk!" Rebecca interrupted. "You must stomp your answer for the king!"

The girl backed up, and then lunged forward to make five ponderous, heavy steps. It was the right answer. The king was ever so grateful.

The next portion of the math segment was conducted in French. Not only was the segment in French, but it was also a brainteaser. As a math teacher by training, I found this to be the most intriguing math activity I'd ever seen. Here's how it worked: Rebecca would establish a pattern linked with movement, and the girls would have to repeat and extend the pattern. To make things more challenging, the activity was all done in French. The pattern was as follows: 1 (step forward), 2 (step forward), 4 (hop forward), 2 (hop backward), and then 3 (step forward), 4 (step forward), 6 (hop forward), and 4 (hop backward). So, they would hop over every other odd number, and then hop back before continuing. This required the children not only to identify and extend a pattern, but to be familiar enough with linear number lines and numerical relationships to skip count in both directions. And they did it all in their secondary language! It was clear that these girls were really working their brains to pull this off. Different patterns required them to skip around different numbers and become really comfortable navigating the relationships between different values. It was such a great exercise, drawing on linguistic and numerical skills.

After math, it was time for music. I couldn't tell if they were using recorders or the pentatonic flutes that are so popular within Waldorf education, but they pulled their beautiful instruments out of what appeared to be hand-knitted pouches woven from a rainbow of colors. I suspect that the girls made the pouches themselves. During their music lesson, Rebecca played a measure while the girls watched, and then they played the measure back. Afterwards, each was asked to play a song that they knew well. One played the tune to which they had recited their spring poem, and the other a song that I didn't recognize; both performances were beautiful.

When they were done playing, they put away their instruments and left the room, so Rebecca and I could chat. I asked Rebecca about all of the movement and whether or not that was part of the Waldorf activity called "Eurythmy," which I admitted I really didn't know anything about.

She laughed, saying, "No one really seems to have a grasp on Eurythmy. I don't! So, we engage in joyful movement. That is what is important." She went on to tell me how she feels that traditional schooling separates body from mind. In contrast, Waldorf education allows the two to remain in harmony. Rebecca also brings heart into the learning process by having her young students recite prayers from their religion, the Baha'i Faith, and bringing the joyful movement into those sacred rituals as well, bringing mind, body, and heart into their class time.

As with Audrey, I asked about teacher training. Rebecca talked about having taken the foundation courses for Waldorf education, not necessarily as a career move but mostly to use at home. Where they live now, the closest Waldorf school is a five-hour drive away, and so she enjoys taking her teacher training courses online to keep her teaching skills limber and to learn new ways to provide a nurturing education that she feels is best for her children.

School time at Rebecca's home was filled with hugs between activities, snuggles between turns, and a lot of smiles and laughter. Still, within the laid-back style of circle time, the girls were respectful and encouraging to one another. Not once did activities, as exuberant as they were, become unruly. Everyone stayed focused on the assigned tasks and carried out directions with joyful hearts; after all, that's the aim of Waldorf education, and Rebecca's family is a lovely example of joyful learning in action.

History

Rudolph Steiner, a well-respected scientist, published literary scholar, and philosopher in post World War I Germany, was the father of what is now called Waldorf Education or "Steiner Schools." In 1919, Steiner was invited to open a school that would service the children of the employees of the Waldorf-Astoria cigarette factory in Stuttgart, Germany. Upon accepting the offer, he began training the teachers of this new school in his revolutionary techniques and philosophies on education.

Steiner's teachings centered on a concept that he referred to as "anthroposophy," which he described as "a path of knowledge which leads the spiritual in the human being to the spiritual in the universe."[2] Steiner's unique spiritual beliefs influenced his educational ideals and his mission was largely to create a learning environment where the spiritual nature of the child could be unleashed and given the freedom to flourish.

Waldorf schools have become popular around the world, and are often associated with the upper echelon of society and the affluent. Both Waldorf and Steiner are protected names, effectively owned by the Association of Waldorf Schools of North America (AWSNA), which sets guidelines and criteria for schools using this name. As a result, many schools that are influenced by Steiner's methodology but fail to meet the AWSNA's rigid standards—namely the pricey, formal training courses and accreditation, as well as constant monitoring of content without flexibility to stray from the formal curriculum—can only refer to themselves as Waldorf-inspired. Notable graduates from Waldorf or Waldorf-inspired schools are Jennifer Aniston (actress), Sandra Bullock (actress), Kenneth Chenault (CEO of American Express), Shana Blake Hill (internationally recognized opera singer), and Dr. Wolf-Christian Dullo (oceanographer).

Guiding Principles

The early years are experimental. Steiner believed that the early years of childhood required experimental learning. This meant that children should be free to follow their instincts and be allowed to try and fail without an adult intervening too frequently. In fact, Steiner likely wouldn't have seen anything the child did as an actual failure, but rather as learning. Within

> Guiding Principles:
> - The early years are experimental.
> - The child is a social being.
> - Human beings are spiritual in nature.

a richly prepared and inspiring environment, young children should be left to dabble with whatever materials and objects they encounter in their day-to-day activities. Parents will certainly be able to think of a time when they saw their toddler twist a doorknob over and over to see how it controls the latch, or drop items from the highchair, much to their chagrin, to see what happens. In Steiner's view, this type of activity is exactly what youngsters should be involved in, and parents should resist the urge to intervene except for reasons of safety.

The child is a social being. Within the Waldorf method, the child is regarded as a highly social being, and social interactions are considered to be a basic need, on par with nutrition and rest. Steiner has said, "A healthy social life is found only, when in the mirror of each soul the whole community finds its reflection, and when in the whole community the virtue of each one is living."[3]

To encourage socialization, Steiner designed the classroom to give children freedom to interact with each other and learn from one another through planned group activities throughout the day. While individual activities are not forbidden, children are greatly encouraged to attach themselves to a group dynamic. For example, teachers will lead their classes in games that take place in large circles, such as reciting poetry as a group, making up plays, and engaging in group imaginative play. This is drastically different from the Montessori classroom where individual students are all separately engaged in their own activities with little regard for what others are doing. Clearly, Waldorf prizes the community over the individual.

Children's emotional and social needs are also highly regarded because of their impact on how well each individual child integrates into the community and alters the mood of the community of which he or she is a part. When children's emotional or social needs aren't being met, their minds become distracted, closed to the world around them, stunting learning, group socialization, and eventually spiritual development. It can also hinder the group's easy, cheerful interactions, moving the group focus from team pursuits to individual interests.

Waldorf educators monitor and nurture the emotional states of children in non-intrusive ways through love and support. Negative feelings are viewed as disruptive to the learning and social process, causing disharmony in the group. Any individual's negative feelings must be resolved to ensure the integrity of the classroom community. This isn't to suggest that children are discouraged from expressing negative feelings. Rather, it means that every effort is made to let a child's negative emotions play out and find resolution in a healthy and expedient manner so that he or she isn't hampered by them for a prolonged period of time.

Human beings are spiritual in nature. Steiner believed that childhood is a time during which our souls are adjusting from a spiritual life in the womb to the physical life on earth—and that life is in an enduring state of reincarnation. He explained how the spiritual and physical worlds were intertwined: "When you undertake a single step forward in the knowledge of spiritual realities, take at the same time three steps forward in the development of your character toward the good."[4] In fact, many regarded these anthroposophy teachings as a kind of religion.

Believers considered the spiritual realm intellectually comprehensible, a world that one could reach and access through the self-development of virtues and rational investigation. Steiner drew a connection between scientific methods and personal development. Understanding and cultivating one's own spirit could be achieved through thoughtful investigation as easily as one could study and understand any other physical phenomenon.

Steiner focused on training teachers to view and treat their students as spiritual beings. But in practice, the focus seemed to be on nurturing children's "incarnating spirit" rather than lecturing them on matters of the spirit. To nurture the spirit, teachers would tailor their interactions with children according to their individual temperaments. Prayers and celebrations honoring somewhat obscure religious holidays, such as Michalemas, were encouraged. Teachers would also encourage the use of color in artwork and teach specialized painting techniques like "Lazure painting," all thought to be soothing and nurturing to the child's spirit.

Defining Characteristics

Children have different educational needs based on their personality type or temperament. Waldorf teachers classify student personalities as sanguine, melancholic, phlegmatic, or choleric—divisions taken from a theory of psychology known as "humorism." I'll describe the purely academic or psychological aspects of the four humors later in the book in Chapter 10, but for now we'll talk about Steiner's own, somewhat more liberal interpretation of the temperaments.

In Waldorf education, the teacher assesses each child's temperament and treats each student differently according to his or her personality type. Using a child's behavioral characteristics, physical build, and even choices of clothing, Waldorf teachers carefully assess a child's type and then every interaction with that child is dictated by Steiner's advice on what that type of child needs.

Defining Characteristics:
- Children have different educational needs based on their personality type or temperament.
- Imaginative play is prized.
- Literacy development is delayed.
- Group progression and bonding are central.
- Art accentuates all subjects.
- Main lesson blocks enhance learning.

To give you an idea of how finely tailored every interaction is in a Waldorf environment, you need only look at Roy Wilkinson's book, *The Temperaments in Education*.[5] The use of physical appearance was often used to gauge how to interact with a child. For example, Wilkinson describes the "choleric child" as one with a bulky body type who digs his or her heels into the ground when walking; who likes spicy foods and wears clothing that is unique from that of his or her peers. Wilkinson does describe more social aspects of each type, but only after giving an in-depth description of physical appearance.[6] For Steiner, visual cues were important because teachers often see children before they get a chance to interact with them.

Wilkinson goes on to describe detail about what the choleric child needs and typically will do in the classroom: "The teacher should make sure each story has passages that will appeal to each temperament. Cholerics like boisterous action..." Even discipline has its own prescription. "The choleric must get the red flag removed from before his eyes before he can be reasonable. Remind the child of the misdeed later, and discuss it with him/her."

Steiner even thought out defined guidelines for teachers on how to interact with the parents. I once had a neighbor who had attended a Waldorf school and had, himself, gone through a portion of Waldorf teacher training. He was very excited when he found out that I was an educator, and showed up on my doorstep the next day with a book—barely a book, it was so tattered and well-loved—that was a manual from his brief time undergoing Steiner training. I paged through and found a chart detailing the temperaments with statements consistent with those in the Wilkinson book, but it went even further and had ways to assess the parents of students and how to address issues with them in the proper manner. There were special recommendations for every combination, such as "the phlegmatic parent of the sanguine child." All these years later, I don't recall what each prescribed interaction was, but it was clear that every one had been thought out and calculated for maximum impact.

Imaginative play is prized. Imaginative play is taken to the next level in Waldorf education, and you need look no further than the use of dolls, gnomes, or other play figures for evidence of this. Waldorf dolls in their purest form have plain clothes and faceless heads. It is thought that by not giving the dolls faces, children would be encouraged to use their imagination to fill in the blanks. By leaving a doll without a face, just a sphere with hair, the child's imagination fills in the gaps according to the circumstance in play. Dolls with faces stuck in frozen expressions are considered limiting in their imaginative scope.

Imaginative play is thought to promote learning and development in all subject areas, not just art. Rebecca's use of creative storylines and physical movement during a math lesson exemplifies imaginative play in action across disciplines. Imaginative play is also considered to be healing and therapeutic. Children who are struggling with an internal conflict can, through this type of play, act out a range of scenarios, envision their outcomes, and make choices about life without having to face any real world consequences. Emotional trauma can be healed through play scenarios where that trauma is avenged, soothed, or healed in the imaginative world. According to Steiner, the therapeutic energy cultivated in the imagination can cross over into the real and physical world of the child.

Literacy development is delayed. Followers of the Waldorf method feel strongly that "joyful movement" is essential to childhood, and that reading and writing, being largely sedentary activities, should be postponed until around the ages of seven or eight. Yes, this means no formal training in reading. A child may have a book, enjoy looking at the pictures or retelling what they can remember of the story, but a teacher won't sit down with the student to teach him or her any phonetics until much, much later. In addition, children are taught to write before being taught to read. Writing lessons often include games of movement, such as posture games meant to teach children about straight lines. At a Waldorf school, walking with a beanbag on your head is considered training for handwriting. This stands in stark contrast to mainstream education where children are largely taught to identify letters, sounds, and words either before writing them, and where reading skills are generally taught alongside writing skills.

Group progression and bonding are central. Because Steiner emphasized the emotional bond between students and their teacher and classmates, children educated at Waldorf schools keep their teacher and stay with their cohort for either the duration of a three or seven-year learning cycle, or through their length of stay at a particular school. This group progression is central to the Waldorf method and evidences the importance placed upon the group dynamic. It's thought that children can't progress naturally if they are separated from a cohort and have to repeat the bonding process each year with new classmates. Social bonding, according to Waldorf proponents, must be reinforced and cemented before children can focus on learning. Social interactions are regarded as a part of child development and education.

Art accentuates all subjects. Subjects studied by students are complemented or even introduced through artful expression. In language arts, before learning to write letters, children are taught to copy abstract forms, which the teacher slowly replaces with letters, sometimes without ever actually telling the students that they are writing letters. In a process called "form drawing," young students learn writing by first drawing abstract pictures. In this way, they feel none of the stress associated with perfecting handwriting in rote drills.

Science is often taught through artistic expression as well. In early grades, children will draw things they see on a nature walk or observe on a "nature table," a space set aside for the display of found, natural objects and/or magical scenes inspired by nature, like gnomes sitting around a pile of acorns and fall leaves. In later grades, students may perform experiments and draw detailed accounts of each step.

In fact, students often make their own textbooks on the content they study. Looking at homemade textbooks, or "good books" popular at Waldorf schools, I get the feeling that I'm looking directly into Darwin's field journals or Da Vinci's sketchbooks. Pages are filled with drawings and diagrams and marked with copious notes around the margins.

A central part of Waldorf education is that students are encouraged to express themselves through art regardless of the subject. Special art supplies, often beeswax crayons, high quality watercolors, chalk, sculpting beeswax, and other materials, are given to students. For Waldorf educators, effective learning requires a classroom and school environment that is beautiful and inspirational. Art is central to creating that setting.

Main lesson blocks enhance learning. For a great part of the day, Waldorf students are engaged in some form of self-expression or exploration through crafts or group projects. But for an extended period of time, often for two hours at a time, students are given a lesson. These periods of focused teaching center around one single topic for a set number of weeks, and then move on to an entirely different topic for the next cycle or block. A typical school year may include a few language arts blocks, a few math blocks, a couple of science blocks, and sometimes a couple of art blocks, each lasting anywhere from three to six weeks at a time.

Examples of these blocks include "measurements blocks" for math, during which children measure and weigh all sorts of things, perhaps cooking in the kitchen to follow dry ingredient measurements, making tables in their "good books" comparing metric and standard units of measurements, making estimates, and so on. For language arts, there may be blocks devoted to fables, where students study Aesop's fables and listen to stories, and later work in groups to illustrate them and plan elaborate plays.

Long periods of time spent in intense concentration on a particular topic was once unique to the Waldorf experience, but has since been adopted by many public school systems. Steiner may have been on to something with the lesson blocks concept. Research done at non-Steiner schools that have tried block scheduling found that over time about 80 percent of teachers lectured less and engaged students in more active learning formats.[7] As a result, students were less passive in the classroom, and the number of students on the honor roll increased. While teachers covered slightly less content with block scheduling, the content covered was more thorough.

Many educational advocates now believe that longer, focused lessons provide students a chance to delve deeper into their work. Topics are less rushed and can be explored in more detail; learning isn't cut off as students are shuffled constantly to their next class when the bell rings.

What the Critics Say

The most controversial aspect of Waldorf education is Steiner's teaching on spiritual matters. He believed that there are three 7-year stages (referred to as "mystical numbers") in which the child's soul gradually reincarnates from the spiritual world to the physical. Through the three stages, the "physical," "etheric," and "astral" bodies of an individual are brought into what he calls their proper relationship to foster the incarnation of the "I" that has been "evolving" between death and rebirth.[8] For most people, this belief system can feel like fringe thinking, and any teaching that has its roots in such mystical ideas can feel like a potential threat to personal and/or religious beliefs. That said, many people around the world strongly identify with these concepts and either adopt them religiously, or find a way to integrate them into their own existing religious beliefs.

A group called People for Legal and Non-Sectarian Schools (PLANS), comprised of former Waldorf students, parents, and teachers, was formed to counter these teachings. PLANS warns that the Waldorf method—more specifically the concept of anthroposophy at the core of Waldorf education—is actually an esoteric, occult religion unto itself. More specifically, they complain that the governing board that dictates what is and isn't Waldorf is too rigid and tied to arcane, medieval dogma, and that the emphasis on social interactions and non-intervention of adults creates an environment ripe for bullying.[9]

Much has been said about the esoteric religious undertones in Waldorf education, and many religious families steer clear of it for that reason. I asked Rebecca about this, and she maintained that while Waldorf education does have spiritual undertones, she feels that there is nothing within the Waldorf curriculum that conflicts with her own religious beliefs. It's important here to draw a clear distinction between what's part of the curriculum and what beliefs inspired the curriculum's creator.

I will pause here and say that I spoke to families from many religions, including mainstream Christians, Latter Day Saints (Mormons), Baha'is, and Jews, and I found that members of all those faiths share different opinions about Waldorf education. Some are comfortable with Waldorf teaching; others aren't. When I looked for a Waldorf family in my local community, which is predominantly LDS, I was frequently told that I wouldn't find any Waldorfians because the beliefs conflict with their religion. In desperation to find someone to interview, I contacted the writer of our favorite Waldorf math book and explained my situation.

"What part of Utah do you live in?" the author asked. "I'm LDS and live in Utah just over the mountain range from you, and we have a thriving community of LDS families who use Waldorf here!"

When we spoke, I also asked how their community balanced the seemingly fringe beliefs of anthroposophy with their own LDS beliefs, and she assured me that, in her view, the two can work in perfect harmony. Her opinion was that those who think otherwise either don't understand what their own church teaches, or don't understand what Steiner taught. Needless to say, a fair share of controversy around this aspect of Waldorf education abounds.

I've personally used Waldorf-inspired math for all of my kids at different times because of its gentle, story-driven approach to mathematics. While my study of Steiner's beliefs have led me to the conclusion that his spiritual ideas don't harmonize with my own, I've found that none of his anthroposophy beliefs are evidenced in the curriculum that we've used. After vetting the content, I don't hesitate one bit to use the materials that I've deemed the best for meeting my children's needs at that particular time.

To me, the larger controversial issue by far that trumps even the uneasiness caused by Steiner's mystical belief system is the postponing of literacy development. In a world that is increasingly focused on early literacy intervention, Waldorf seems to be advocating the unthinkable by delaying actual reading and writing until sometimes as late as age 9. Of course, Waldorfians claim that form drawing and posture games are actually forming a foundation for letter recognition and composition. Still, many of my personal acquaintances who have chosen to send their children to Waldorf schools because of their nurturing environment will admit in closed quarters to teaching their children to read at home. Many of them simply don't trust the decision to postpone literacy training.

Waldorf schools aren't the only places you'll find people delaying the introduction of literacy skills. Countries like Finland, which does very well on international tests on reading, don't start reading lessons at school until students are 7-years-old when cognitive development is more advanced.[10] In the U.S., perhaps the most well-known proponents of delayed literacy are Dr. Raymond and Dorothy Moore. They have written many books directed at homeschoolers and ran, while they were alive, the still operational Moore Academy, which provides distance learning to homeschoolers over the internet. In their 1975 book, *Better Late than Early*, the Moores justified delayed literacy instruction by writing that children don't reach psychological readiness for formal learning until around ages 8 to 10.

The Moores also argued that most successful homeschoolers delay literacy instruction—an assertion that, as far as I can tell, doesn't really have any factual support. I've been in the homes of countless homeschoolers, and in my own experience, none of the families I met chose to delay literacy instruction intentionally. Sure, there are parents who wait for their children to initiate reading on their own before perusing regular reading instruction, but the norm among homeschoolers appears to be engaging in literacy training at either the public school typical age or before.

Parents who find that a child is struggling with reading and writing, perhaps even to a degree that it's interfering with harmonious family interactions or social development, may find comfort and reassurance within the Waldorf framework. When I mentioned this upside to methods that promote delaying literacy instruction to a friend and professional educator, she remarked, "Sure, having books to back that up is nice if you assume that negative interactions or late literacy instruction are the only two options. There is a way to teach young children to read without stressing anybody out." I think many would agree with her. Still, for many parents and educators who find themselves at their wits' end when it comes to teaching a child to read and write, the Waldorf approach may ease their nerves.

The Homeschool Spin

Like Montessori, Waldorf is quite easily implemented in the home. Unlike Montessori, there isn't a special emphasis on special materials other than encouraging the abundance of art supplies. No specific materials are otherwise required (unless, of course, you find beeswax crayons a must-have!).

Provide D-I-Y learning opportunities. Self-led experimentation and manipulation of the environment is easily accomplished with a little planning. There are a variety of resources on the Web (see the "Recommended Resources" section in this chapter for a few recommendations) to help parents incorporate the arts into other academic subjects.

The Homeschool Spin:
- Provide D-I-Y opportunities.
- Encourage imaginative play.
- Emphasize community and social harmony.

Encourage imaginative play. More than any other educational method, Waldorf encourages imaginative play, which can be ideal for young students because it comes so naturally. Artistically-minded children will enjoy participating in the creation of their own textbooks, props, and manipulatives, which Waldorf encourages. For the creative and/or visual student, the possibilities are endless in the Waldorf-inspired setting. More than with any other method, the innocence of childhood seems to be preserved if not prolonged, and imaginative play takes precedence.

Emphasize community and social harmony. Teaching concepts of community and respect for each person's basic rights is a common practice among homeschoolers already, so Waldorf-inspired teaching should be a natural fit for families that value social harmony. Those families who homeschool only one child may have to reach outside of the home and make a concerted effort to plug into the local community, while homeschoolers with multiple children may find the family unit to be the perfect community for teaching these values.

Activities

Preschool

Dyed-in-the-wool Waldorfians don't recommend any formal activities for the preschool set, and even go so far as to ridicule any formal lessons for the youngest of children. The main focus is to surround children with a beautiful, natural environment and to provide resources for play. A lot of play. Those who feel merely Steiner-inspired will admit to encouraging youngsters to work on handicraft activities, like finger-knitting and loosely guided art activities before the school years, but maintain that no formal literacy or numerical skills should be taught at this early stage.

Elementary school

- Create and hang up letter cards similar to those alphabet cards that run above the white board in a standard elementary schoolroom.
- Copy doodled forms from a chalkboard to paper; zigzags, loops, and abstract shapes all prepare the creative mind for formal writing.
- Memorize playful poems and rhymes that connect with the season, time of day, or nature.
- Make simple, faceless gnome toys or dolls to act out math problems.
- Try kitting and wet on wet water coloring.
- Add movement to poetry and songs to connect the mind and body.
- Pass bean bags around a circle in rhythm with skip counting during math.
- Make up imaginative story problems and illustrate them.
- Write a group story, passing a page around and each person adding a sentence at a time.

Upper Grades

- Encourage students to make their own textbooks filled with sketches, observations, and text.
- Take nature walks and encourage copious note taking and drawing.

- Select medium-scale building projects, such as building dog houses or play structures for charity.

- Stage elaborate plays, and encourage students to write, choreograph, and make costumes.

- Read books and allow ample amounts of time for critique and discussion.

- Take artistic endeavors to the next level with advanced knitting, wet felting, needle felting, and painting projects.

Recommended Resources

Great illustrated books on form drawing abound. There is *Form Drawing for Beginners* offered by Christopherous Homeschool Resources (christopherushomeschool.org), as well as generic books on form drawing broken down by age level available through Waldorf Books (waldorfbooks.com). If you're interested in exploring "Vimala handwriting" (believed by some Waldorfians to be a spiritual aid, as opposed to simply handwriting), read *Soul Development Through Handwriting: The Waldorf Approach to the Vimala Alphabet* by Jennifer Crebbin. For more reading on the Waldorf approach to literacy and links to books on form drawing, visit Waldorf Curriculum (waldorfcurriculum.com).

A Little Garden Flower (waldorfjourney.typepad.com) offers great resources specific to the Waldorf homeschooler. We've used their math book and I can attest that the material is charming and engaging, while being thorough and easy-to-use. It's not, however, a stand-alone complete curriculum, and it assumes a previous understanding of Waldorf basics.

Another fabulous resource for those with young children is Over in the Meadow (overinthemeadow.wordpress.com), which outlines an entirely free curriculum for children from birth to grade two. It also has links to tons of free online books on topics from handwork to cooking and running a home, from very old math textbooks to books on helping children start a business. It's an invaluable resource for those interested in Waldorf education but who aren't quite ready to make a huge financial investment. However, without grounding in the basics of the Waldorf method, the site's tools might be difficult to implement with meaning.

As with the Montessori method (Chapter 3), there are extensive blogs and how-to videos online that are free to access, including Waldorf Without Walls (waldorfwithoutwalls.com) and a blog called Ancient

Hearth (ancienthearth2.blogspot.com). Just like Montessori fans, Waldorf proponents represent a vibrant subculture of educators that has thrived and developed into a tight-knit community. *A word of warning:* Many of the Waldorf bloggers and vloggers out there are hardcore believers in the anthroposophical aspect and it tends to enter into every area of their discussion. If the spiritual aspect rubs you the wrong way, take what you like and leave the rest.

Ideal for...

Child-centered households that value self-expression: Waldorf works well in homes that prefer child-centered approaches to learning (similar to Montessori) and value self-expression above strict adherence to textbook-style learning. This may be a good approach for families with children who are discouraged by early efforts to read and need a little more freedom and less structure during their regular day. But if you have a child who's naturally inclined to read and absorb information more systematically, then you might want to look elsewhere.

Families comfortable with the spiritual dimensions: While some people with strict religious beliefs may feel initially put off by the spiritual underpinnings, I feel strongly that you can implement a Waldorf-style learning environment with all of the nurturing practices—minus the reincarnation bells and whistles. I encourage anyone who feels initially drawn to the beautiful and gentle approach of Waldorf-inspired education, but may be put off by the fringe ideas that notoriously infiltrated much of Steiner's writing, to examine why you're attracted to the elements that appeal to you. Implement the Waldorf ideas you value most, and simply leave out the rest.

Families wanting to balance rigid teaching styles with more creative and emotion-focused learning: Those with a preference for fact-based, academic-focused learning will likely appreciate other methods presented later in the book a bit more than Waldorf. However, if your natural style of teaching is somewhat more rigid and systematic, and you're looking to balance that out and provide creative outlets for your children, then Waldorf education is a beautiful choice to add softer, imaginative, and emotion-centered elements to your planned school time.

For example, you may choose to follow a more rigid curriculum schedule, but accent subjects with Waldorf-inspired projects and activities.

Montessori Method vs. Waldorf Education

Parents who have toured various schools in search of the perfect fit for their children often ask, "What are the differences between the Montessori and Waldorf methods? The classes look just about the same, and the kinds of families who choose these two schools appear quite similar... " I've also read comments on homeschool forums where countless times parents insist there isn't much difference between Montessori and Waldorf.

At a glance, the actual practice of each method may appear quite similar. Both are child-centered and have a slightly less structured instructional approach within a highly controlled and prepared environment. Their hands-on and test-free classrooms do tend to serve a similar portion of the population—families who gravitate toward more earthy, free style, and artistic approaches to teaching. Both methods serve the preschool- to early elementary-age child, with a few Waldorf schools running the entire K-12 spectrum. Upon closer look, however, these methods are quite different. The real differences lie in the ideals that drive them. Understanding these key differences will affect how you blend either or both methods into your homeschooling plans.

Montessori – Self-sufficiency and intellectual development: Montessori focuses on the individual child over the group, most likely as a result of Maria Montessori's location on the globe and the time in which she lived. Montessori mainly worked with the underserved, impoverished Italian children who received little education. Montessori opened her first school in 1907, a period of time in Italy where poverty was rampant and industrialization and harsh working conditions plagued many families. It was undoubtedly an environment where an imagination was almost a key to survival for a lot of children whose parents were mostly factory workers. Working long hours, parents had little time to teach the practical skills of self-sufficiency that their children sorely needed in order to endure the long stretches of time that they were left to fend for themselves. In short, the environment was imagination-rich and instruction-poor. As a result, Montessori focused on practical skills and intellectual development that utilizes the teacher as a resource rather than as an instructor.

Waldorf – Imagination and socialization: Rudolph Steiner, on the other hand, lived in a different time and place. World War I had just ended and in Germany, a sober ability to get by and take care of one's self and family was a skill mastered by mostly everyone who had survived the war and now faced a recovering, fragile economy. The postwar landscape was severely lacking in imagination and heavy in basic survival. The most that the average child had to look forward to was an adult life working in an un-stimulating position in a factory. Steiner's approach with his Waldorf schools was driven by a need to change and usher in a generation that wasn't overwhelmed or demoralized by the conditions of industrialization. Later after World War II, he sought to create a society of free thinkers where atrocities like those that had just been committed during the wars would never be repeated.

In their time, both sought a balance... Both Montessori and Waldorf approaches to education appear to have stemmed from an effort to balance out the harsh, one-sided existence of the children of each given time and place. If children lacked imaginative play and hope, Rudolph Steiner was going to give it to them and encourage free thinking. If what they lacked was the simplest of self-governing skills, Maria Montessori was there to advocate an approach to fill the need. Today, an individual's experience within either of these systems depends largely on the interpretations of the teacher/parent and what aspects of the method are prioritized. Both are highly nurturing, child-centered methods that come from unique and sophisticated theories on the basic needs of the whole child.

Use elements from both. In the home setting, there's really no need to explicitly choose one method over the other. Montessori is undoubtedly more academic, while Waldorf clearly has a more artistic tilt. Still, being child-led, the same child's education within either of these systems might look very much the same. Artistic children will self-initiate artistic pursuits in whichever child-centered environment they may be in; the academic children will follow their more intellectual pursuits.

In our home, we use elements from each of these styles with great success. Montessori grammar has really been a game changer in our home, and it's something that my preschooler can work on right alongside his fourth grade sister. It's clear and no-frills, and it gets the job done. I also find Montessori teachings to be indispensable for the preschool years. Having a 4-year-old with practical life skills is a lifesaver when older students need more quiet time in the school area, and a little one is in need of a place to focus his attention without being disruptive. For example, my little guy folds towels and cuts up food for the next meal while his older siblings continue with their school work.

We've turned to Waldorf math with its whimsical characters and tales for group learning. The young ones can appreciate the little gnomes in the land of Numeria, while also gaining gentle exposure to the math concepts; the older learner gets a pressure-free lesson. Also, I never would have thought to challenge my children's artistic skills had it not been for my time looking into Waldorf schools. The crafting skills advocated by Waldorf practices go far beyond what most people would ever expect a child could learn. Waldorf embraces craftsmanship to a degree that it has inspired me to give my children every opportunity to pursue advanced crafts. Last year, my daughter crocheted her own holiday gifts for friends and has completed several quilts at the ripe old age of nine. All of the children can hand sew and knit, and their wet on wet painting is spectacular.

As you can see, parents can certainly blend both approaches to meet the needs of individual members of their family. Take a look at the lives of your children and their personalities and temperaments (more on this in Chapter 10) and choose the method that most balances your children's inner and outer needs for development, self-expression, and self-mastery. We'll go over how to blend everything together and implement different educational methods and teaching styles in Chapter 11.

FIVE:
Trivium

...the sole true end of education is simply this: to teach men how to learn for themselves; and whatever instruction fails to do this is effort spent in vain.[1]

-Dorothy Leigh Sayers, writer and Christian humanist

VISITING Emily's home, I was honestly expecting a little chaos. Not because there is anything at all chaotic about Emily herself, but because she has four boys at home. One mom and four boys all day long at home? It sounded like recipe for a noisy, rowdy, boisterous schooling experience. But as we approached the front door, I didn't hear a thing. There was no sound or commotion coming from the inside. At one point, my kids, who were along for the visit, asked if I was sure I was at the right address because it seemed as if no one was home. I double-checked the street numbers thinking maybe they were right, and we'd gone to the wrong house. But this was, indeed, the place.

When Emily opened the door and welcomed us in, two boys stood quietly behind her. Leading us inside the house, she warned me with a smile that there was a naked 4-year-old somewhere around the corner. Yet, I never saw anyone streaking by, and only met him when he was properly dressed. Now, I'm most certain that if my own boys found themselves naked at the moment the doorbell rang, there would be no keeping them from flashing our guest. Curiosity would get the best of them, and they'd just need to see who was at the door before they could concentrate on dressing themselves. This was my first clue that Emily's little fellows were gentlemen.

Her 6- and 8-year-old boys led my kids down to the toy room to play with their 2-year-old brother. Then, I followed Emily to observe "school time." Soon the two boys returned and classes began for Emily's sons. Standing in the middle of the room, she gave them the choice of what to do first. The eldest chose to work on handwriting; he got out his materials and settled down on the living room floor, sitting by the coffee table to get to work without much discussion. The younger of the two chose to work on some poetry memorization before moving on to a reading lesson with mom and then choosing a storybook to read aloud to her. He was quite the impressive reader at the age of six!

When the eldest finished his handwriting activities, he moved quietly on to math. He got out a math book and some transparency sheets. He carefully paper clipped the transparencies to the page and wrote the answers in marker on the clear plastic sheet to leave for Emily to check at her convenience. Such a great idea! Both boys knew right where everything was, and where they were in each book. They could seamlessly move from one subject to the next without Emily needing to interrupt what she was doing to give them a page number or to help them find their things.

Emily's consistent organizational scheme has spared her from the fairly common time-waster of answering questions about where a missing book, pencil, or marker might be, what page to work from, or even how to address a problem. There was none of this. If the eldest son ever did encounter a math problem he didn't understand, he must have marked it for later because he never once interrupted the other child's reading time to get Emily's attention. It was clear that their family had embraced the Trivium ideal of teaching children how to learn on their own.

Even when interruptions took place, the boys showed remarkable restraint and discipline. When the phone rang in the middle of school time, the eldest boy rose to get the phone and answered it with impeccable manners. I was reminded of my days at a "finishing school" in Tennessee, where the long-lost etiquette skills of properly addressing a letter, holding a teacup, and answering the phone were taught to students. The call was for Emily; she took it, getting up to find an address for the caller. It was not a super short call, but the boys just sat silently where they were, finishing work without her, and then simply waiting patiently when they were done. To me, their ability to sit silently and wait without becoming distracted was nothing short of miraculous! Their ability to be self-sufficient learners was evidenced by this ability to stay focused and maintain order in Emily's absence. When she returned, they picked up right where they left off without any prolonged discussion about who the caller had been or what the call was about.

As impressive as her school-age boys were at self-initiating work and waiting patiently, what was just as exciting to watch was her 4-year-old son who wandered frequently into the living room where class was taking place. He was generally quiet and undisruptive as he went about his business. I watched as he made his way behind the kitchen bar, where I couldn't see him from my seat. As he wandered around, I heard him make a comment about how one of the other boys didn't do his job of putting away the silverware. He sounded almost exasperated.

Then I heard him rustling around. I couldn't resist, so I snuck up to peer over the counter to see what he was up to. Lo and behold, the little tyke was emptying the dishwasher! No one had told him to do it, but apparently it's one of his chores, and so perhaps routine just dictated that he put the dishes away. You better believe I immediately added, "How in the world did you get him to do that on his own?" to my list of follow up questions for Emily later.

Emily's home is characterized by relative order and a sense that family members know exactly what their roles are in the well-oiled machine of the home. With self-directed preschoolers doing the dishes, and older children working at their own pace without falling into daydreams or disruptive behavior, the day clicked along briskly. Such pleasant contentment must be the result of careful planning and routine, as well as a heavy dose of nurturing and love.

History

The Trivium approach to learning, sometimes referred to as the "classical style" of education, seems almost to be as old as time itself. Its absolute origins are unclear, though it was a common way to organize studies as far back as the oldest medieval universities and centers of education. In these medieval liberal arts institutions, the trivium was considered the lower group of basic studies comprised of grammar, logic, and rhetoric. This was a common course of study intended to prepare pupils for the later quadrivium, the higher group of studies that included music, arithmetic, geometry, and astronomy.

In comparing the trivium and the quadrivium, it helps to think of the trivium as the standard bachelor level course of study in these esoteric institutions, while the quadrivium was more on par with doctoral courses. While these subjects were once considered highly evolved levels of thought, they inspired what is now considered primary pre-collegiate education. Many of our public school curricula, in their focus on core subjects, are more or less loosely patterned after this system.

Today, what is most distinctive about the Trivium approach isn't the content, but the method and sequence of how information is presented to students. Trivium advocates consider us to be fundamentally thinking beings, whose capacity to absorb information is divided into three defined stages. They believe that our brains are suited to absorbing information in a particular sequence through these stages. In education, this translates to teaching students to master information in successive levels: Mastery of basic material prepares students for more advanced material at the subsequent level.

Learning is focused on two areas: to obtain general knowledge and to learn *how to learn*. Learning as a skill is considered largely lost or ignored in our modern educational systems. Modern adherents to the Trivium approach assert that current teaching trends only teach a child to learn on a task by task basis, requiring a trained adult to tell them where to go next for the subsequent piece of information. Under Trivium, children theoretically develop the skill of learning—they learn how to learn—that allows them to pursue knowledge on their own without the need of a guide telling them what questions to ask.

Trivium is a popular movement among homeschoolers and the one you're most likely to associate with those whiz kids who win the Scripps National Spelling Bee every year. The easiest way to give you a list of famous adherents to the Trivium method is to say that it's the formal education style of the Ancient Greeks, Romans, and early Puritans—so just consider what great thinkers fall into those categories. It's not hard to imagine why you'd choose this teaching method when people the likes of Aristotle and Socrates were schooled in this system!

This is a good time to note that in the university setting the Trivium is rarely studied by pre-professional teachers under the name, "Trivium." During all of my time as a teacher in training, I never heard the terms "Trivium" or "classical education" uttered. In fact, it wasn't until long after I began homeschooling and studying trends in home education on my own that I made the connection between Paideia schools and the Trivium method. When I sat down to research, fact check, and elaborate on these concepts, it struck me that Paideia was undeniably an outgrowth of Trivium.

Where did Paideia originate? In the mid-eighties, an American by the name of Mortimer Adler proposed a method of school reform as the answer to what he termed the "antidemocratic" schooling system that the U.S. had adopted over time. Schools around the world eventually adopted his plan as their foundation for education and many changed their names to include the term "Paideia."

You won't find followers of the Paideia Proposal who profess outright that it's the Trivium method in disguise, but upon investigation you'll often find the same breakdown of age groups and a similar organizational structure to the content. What Adler seems to have done is combine the structure and sequence of the classical education system with what were hot topics in the world of education at the time, ideas such as, "all children are capable and worthy of being educated" and "true education is not limited to the classroom and institutions of higher learning, but will be lifelong pursuits that create impeccable citizenship."

These popular and unoffending catchphrases, combined with the academically accelerated methods of the Trivium were an easy sell to the tired and lackluster institutions of the 1980s. Until the advent of Paideia schools, the now hackneyed phrase, "All children are capable of and worthy of being taught" had been tossed around in the halls of higher education institutions, but in reality failed to impact the lower elementary grade levels.

I can't say that the reforms brightened the institutional education scene for younger children to any great extent except in the case of special education. Before Adler made the Paideia system popular, children with severe mental and physical handicaps were relegated to "schools" that were often no more than glorified daycare centers. The thought that these children either couldn't or shouldn't be educated had led to a system-wide attitude that children with special needs were nothing but burdens on the taxpayer. With the arrival of the Paideia Proposal, students who had previously been shuttled to second-rate institutions were now being reintroduced to mainstream classrooms and being given the opportunity to study alongside their same-age peers and receive the same basic education.

Guiding Principles

Grammar, logic, and rhetoric are the three basic stages of learning. Under the Trivium method, learning is divided into three basic stages: grammar, logic, and rhetoric. A child at the early grammar stage, before the age of 10, is expected to memorize seemingly unrelated tidbits of information. Sometimes called the "parroting" stage, it's evidenced by children's natural enjoyment of repeating verses over and over or awkwardly spewing facts that they think might interest their audience.

From ages 10 to 13, children are considered to be in the later grammar stage where they begin to understand more abstract ideas and their knowledge base is broadened to encompass the less concrete ideas necessary for higher levels of thinking. All concrete, basic building blocks of knowledge are considered essential materials at this stage.

From ages 13 to 15, children move to the logic stage, sometimes called the "dialect" stage. They can now begin to reason for themselves and ask more questions. At this stage, students are trained to analyze information and to reason in a logical and methodical way to determine whether a statement or assertion has value or truth. Children are expected to understand metaphorical writing, mathematical symbols, and other abstractions, and daily exercises in the abstract are increased.

> **Guiding Principles:**
> Grammar, logic, and rhetoric are the three basic stages of learning. A child learns facts, then how those facts fit together, and finally how to convey those facts and practice what's been learned.

Finally, from ages 15 to 18, in the "rhetoric" stage, young people are expected to express their own thoughts and articulate information from their studies in a clear and thoughtful manner. When they reach this stage, they are expected to engage in intellectual conversations about sophisticated topics, giving their personal take on the subject at hand, and to support their position with cited evidence. In the rhetoric stage, the fine art of debate is honed both through speaking engagements and writing. When you hear students who've been reared in the Trivium approach speak at this stage, it becomes quite clear that they exude confidence in their own knowledge and communicate at a level of intellectual discourse akin to sport. The jocular and cerebral banter that can be witnessed when two Trivium heads get together evokes an episode of *Frasier*, an old TV sitcom where the two brainy siblings exchange witty comments and dueling conversational barbs.

In a nutshell, Trivium emphasizes this learning sequence: A child learns facts, then how those facts fit together, and finally how to convey those facts and practice what's been learned.

Defining Characteristics

Content delivery is specific: whole to part. "Spiraled content," sometimes called the "inverse spiral," is a way of visualizing the sequence of how material is presented. Typically, Trivium education moves chronologically at each stage, starting at some ancient point in history and progressing to modern times. Over time, content gets re-examined at a finer and finer level. This broad to specific, or "whole to part," approach is represented by an inverted spiral that gets tighter each time it passes a given point. The dynamic of "whole to part" and "part to whole" is discussed in more detail in Chapter 8.

> **Defining Characteristics:**
> - Content delivery is specific: whole to part.
> - Great literature is studied over textbooks.
> - Mother tongue fluency and linguistics are the foundations of literacy.
> - Christian foundations are emphasized.

Trivium demands a very dynamic, disciplined way of presenting content. While content delivery occurs in stages—grammar, logic, then rhetoric—that go from simple to complex depending on the student's age group, the *content within a given stage* is taught from whole to part, where broad concepts are introduced first, followed by increasingly fine-grained detail.

Here's how the spiraled content works: During the elementary years, in the grammar stage, students may study ancient times; they do art projects, memorize lists of rulers and ruling families for various areas, and read basic versions of epic tales to gain familiarity with the time.

In middle school, when they reach the logic stage and come across this same period of history again, students read passages from the original texts and complex pieces of literature that they merely touched on in elementary school. The lists of rulers that they memorized before will have more meaning as they study how each came to power; students then begin to understand the nuances of the various political struggles and victories.

Finally in the rhetoric years, students revisit the full texts and draw parallels to current affairs and news reports. They analyze historical contexts and make their own assumptions as to how things might have gone differently; they choose what are, in their estimation, pivotal points, and use their reasoning to speak with authority in discussions about current social, economic, and political themes and issues.

Great literature is studied over textbooks. Developing a broad, usable vocabulary is essential in the grammar stage and sets the foundation for all other learning and advancement at the later stages. In Trivium, literacy skills are of utmost importance because once children learn how to read, they can learn how to do anything else by simply reading about it on their own.

History and ancient cultures are studied primarily through literature. Only books that are anointed the "greats" or "classics" are used. Through classical texts, children come to feel connected to characters whose shoes they can step into through the words on the page; thus, Trivium students develop a deeper feeling of connection and understanding to the time and culture. For a Trivium advocate, textbooks are ineffective as learning tools; they break down information into non-sequential paragraphs and present only the most sterilized of facts, which don't allow children to connect to the content in a way that directly studying the literature of the time can.

The exception to the textbook rule is in mathematics. Math is the only subject thought not to be readily accessible through literature; therefore, textbooks and drills are essential. Arithmetic and geometry were traditionally only studied once the scholar reached the level of the quadrivium, for which the trivium is the basic framework. However, as the Trivium method evolved into a formal method for the education of younger and younger students, a broader range of mathematical concepts were introduced to the spiraling framework to support the formation of logic skills and to make room for the more complex math topics of which pre-collegiate students are now expected to gain mastery. While reading and literacy hone students' abilities to independently learn and expand knowledge on their own, mathematics sharpens logical thinking skills that are needed in the logic and rhetoric stages of learning.

Mother tongue fluency and linguistics are the foundations of literacy. It's quite common for Trivium students to study Greek and Latin—the languages known to be the roots of many modern languages. A basic understanding of these root languages is thought to help students decode definitions of words by breaking them down into their component parts even if those words are outside of their own spoken language. This is how those Scripps National Spelling Bee kids are able to use the answers to the question, "Can you tell me the language of origin?" to spell unfamiliar words.

Some followers of the Trivium method take this language learning to the next level, using it to gain access to original works, particularly religious texts, that have either not been previously translated, or for which the translations have varying degrees of accuracy. By becoming fluent in these mother tongues, individuals can gain an understanding of biblical meanings on their own, apart from relying on previous scholarly interpretations.

Christian foundations are emphasized. While it's true that many of those who are devout followers of the Trivium method are also devout Christians and visa versa, I'm not convinced that the Trivium method is, in itself, a Christian-based method of training, regardless of what the blogs and books say. For me, it's a "chicken or egg" scenario. Study of the mother languages, for example, provides a skill that enables one to delve deeper into biblical texts. For intense biblical study, this can be an absolute draw for Christian families who want to take their faith studies to the next level. Still, if you dig into history, you'll find that the method actually originated in polytheistic cultures that predate Christianity. The idea that the Trivium method and Christianity go hand in hand is merely the result of modern-day expediency (i.e., it made Bible study easier).

The Bible is thought to be the single most quoted book in all major works of English literature (and I suspect the same could be said for literature of other languages as well). The Old Testament itself is a foundational text for other major monotheistic religions, such as Islam and Judaism. It's no wonder that academic scholars, regardless of religion, would have at least a similar level of interest in studying the mother languages and building upon this time-honored tradition of educating great thinkers.

Still, the stereotype seems to hold true; classical or Trivium-inspired education in the homeschooling context is often associated with a strong Christian focus. While it remains surprisingly uncommon to meet a family without strong Christian convictions engaged in Trivium education, I would venture to say that the exception disproves the assumed Christian foundational connection.

What the Critics Say

It's too focused on intellectual development. The most common criticism of the Trivium method is that it only serves the intellectual development of the child and neglects the emotional and spiritual needs. This is, of course, an interesting complaint considering the established Christian-bent of Trivium followers. I presume this thought comes from an understanding that knowledge of textual information regarding religion is quite different from that nurturing of an individual's spiritual development. This is often a point made by atheists who can quote scripture from every major religion.

This "all brains, no heart" criticism of Trivium seems to come most often from those who practice a less ritual bound form of their religion and view the human spirit to be less a thing nurtured wholly by systematic study and more a thing nurtured by expression.

There is a lack of social and emotional development among learners. Another common criticism is that children who "graduate" from the Trivium method may be less successful in social situations as a result of a purely academic focus. The Trivium framework offers very little about the social or emotional needs of the child, but I think that this is a criticism best reserved for use on a case-by-case basis. Parents can choose to adopt the Trivium method as an educational framework and still provide a nurturing environment that attends to the non-intellectual needs of their children. Only when the Trivium is used as an absolute guide for teaching can it become a limiting factor in their children's social development.

But let's face it—there are children taught under every system who aren't naturally inclined to be socially successful by society's standards, anyway. Those individuals would remain who they are regardless of how they are schooled. It's up to the parents to decide whether their children who feel less comfortable in the social sphere and community setting would thrive in Trivium's more academic setting. For this reason, the Trivium method may appear to have a disproportionate amount of nonsocial types flocking to its use.

In Chapters 9-10, we'll go over child learning styles and personality types and discuss in detail how you can use your children's natural gifts and temperaments to select and adapt a teaching method.

The Homeschool Spin

It's all about reading and self-study. Trivium's emphasis on reading makes it a comfortable fit for the home. Larger families can easily integrate this method at home by having older students read to younger students and then discuss the content in a methodical way. The emphasis on using "great literature" and clas-

> The Homeschool Spin:
> • It's all about reading and self-study.
> • Go in-depth and promote deep readings and study.

sics makes it highly affordable; you can opt out of purchasing a pre-formulated curriculum and hit the library instead.

Go in-depth and promote deep readings and study. There is no mention of art or creative expression in the formal Trivium framework, a stark contrast to other methods such as Waldorf education (Chapter 4). However, Trivium does promote deep reading of literature, which can lend itself nicely to art projects with a little adaptation and ingenuity. Many of the boxed curricula that lay claim to the Trivium style include art projects of all kinds. Be mindful with the younger students, though. Don't overlook creative activities altogether if you opt for Trivium's cerebral, knowledge-centered approach.

Activities

Preschool

- Memorize letters and sounds, progressing to digraphs (multi-letter combinations that make a single sound such as −tch and -sh).
- Count objects using one-to-one correspondence by touching or moving each object once as it is counted or sliding it across a mat.
- Memorize sight words and basic arithmetic facts.
- Memorize rhymes, poems, adages, and other useful information.
- Learn the days of the week and the months of the year; making up songs can be helpful for this.

Elementary (Grammar Stage)

- Memorize lists of items related to current studies (successions of rulers, animals that belong to the same phylum, dates of major battles, etc.).
- Read the "kid" versions of great pieces of literature so that when the original is read in later stages of learning, young learners feel familiar with the stories despite the advanced language.
- Begin formal Latin or Greek studies.
- Memorize longer passages of poetry or sections of important documents, such as "The Gettysburg Address" and the "Magna Carta."
- Work on fact fluency for all arithmetic facts, including addition, subtraction, multiplication, and division for numbers zero to 12.

Middle Grades (Logic Stage)

- Read selected passages from great works of literature.
- Learn the context surrounding lists memorized in the previous stage.
- Study the relationships among events and people in history.
- Make connections between natural phenomena, refining the broad knowledge of environmental factors down to more specific details.

Upper Grades (Rhetoric Stage)

- Study argument styles and write argumentative papers on current content areas.
- Read literature classics that relate to current areas of study.
- Encourage students to participate in debate teams, mock trials, and local youth government committees.

Recommended Resources

Susan Wise Bauer's 1999 book *The Well Trained Mind* (welltrainedmind.com) is considered the sacred text of classical education for homeschoolers and is ripe with extensive resource lists. Anything I list here will just be duplicating her already brilliant work. Check your local library for the book.

The Classical Scholar (classicalscholar.com) offers countless articles, links to free resources, as well as assessment tools and frameworks all geared towards busy parents.

Trivium Academy (triviumacademy.blogspot.com) is a long running blog with all sorts of Trivium-related content, as well as endearing personal stories of struggles and difficulties. The writer has had many upheavals in her personal life, and it can be reassuring to see someone who has gone through a divorce, a re-marriage, and all the drama that comes along with that still be able to keep it together to homeschool her kids in a formal manner.

Trivium Pursuits (triviumpursuit.com) is another site rich in resources and articles. Here you'll find free, printable downloads of seminars, a blog, and a bookstore with resources geared toward Trivium education.

Ideal for...

Families that prefer individualistic, academic study to an emphasis on socialization: This method is an obvious fit for children who are uncomfortable in settings where socialization is prized. That said, it's important not to let academic learning become an excuse for never encouraging students to develop meaningful, interpersonal relationships.

For parents who are natural nurturers, this method makes a nice complement and helps bring students back to an academic focus. For inexperienced parent teachers, or for those who seek more direction in how to teach, the marching, clear-cut sequence of presenting content ("spiraled content") can be reassuring.

Children that thrive on individual expression and rigorous thought: Even if your child is highly emotional and needs a more gentle approach that allows for greater blocks of time for individual expression, don't count the Trivium out altogether. While some families find that

Trivium may not suit their needs during the early years, they often see its value in educating children in the upper grades. In fact, the last stage of the Trivium method focuses greatly on expressing individuality and original thinking. Debate seems to be a natural fit for children who always desire to exert their own force upon the world. With the Trivium approach, informed argument is a central focus for older students.

Still, for younger, more sensitive children, or for nurture-focused parents for that matter, the Trivium can feel a bit overwhelming and stifling.

SIX:
Charlotte Mason Education

But give the child work that Nature intended for him, and the
quantity he can get through with ease is practically unlimited.
Whoever saw a child tired of seeing, of examining in his own
way, unfamiliar things? This is the sort of mental nourishment
for which he has an unbounded appetite, because it is that food
of the mind on which, for the present, he is meant to grow.[1]

- *Charlotte Mason, educator*

STEPPING into Janel's house, I felt like I was coming home.
Sure, she's got nine kids, and I've only got three, but the tangible energy
was the same. There wasn't a quiet moment during my visit; no, quite the
opposite.

A young girl sat at a sewing machine, happy to show off her quilted
purse project. Off in one corner, some boys playacted sword fighting with
sticks. Scattered around were musical instruments, an ant farm, and a
tadpole habitat. Laughter and occasional interruptions abounded—though
not the rude sort, but the kind that say, "I'm comfortable enough here to
interject my own thoughts, and I know they will be valued." This was a
home that was lived in and loved in. What a breath of fresh air.

I knew from our first e-mail exchange that I was going to love Janel.
Her honesty about their family's challenges in finding the right schooling
fit for her family was so touching that I got a little weepy reading it.

"I don't really feel that we chose Homeschooling, as much as it was
chosen for us," she wrote in one of our e-mail exchanges. "I started to
think about it from the time my oldest was in first grade, but kept
ignoring that feeling because he was such a difficult child that I needed
my time away from him. As time went by, and we were going to the public
school about four or five times a month to pick up my son yet again, to

take him home after his latest blow up, we started to really worry about him and his future. We did a lot of praying, thinking, and asking around. At this point, there really only was one answer: homeschooling."

Janel homeschooled her family off and on because they simply couldn't find a method that worked for them. When they discovered Charlotte Mason education, their kids, one by one, chose to come back home.

As Janel called seven of her children in for history time, a 7-year-old spun around to where I was sitting behind the couch and said with an impish grin, "Our history is awesome! And sometimes we get to do two!"

What a fantastic attitude towards school work! As they all rolled in and piled on couches or sprawled across the living room floor, Janel began to read a narrative-style story about the Renaissance artist, Giotto. The younger kids colored in coloring books that precisely matched the time period about which Janel was reading; the older kids just sat and listened. The oldest two didn't seem quite as engaged in the story, but they were polite and didn't disrupt in any way. When Janel stumbled over the pronunciation of an unusual Italian name, those two jumped right up to offer her a consensus on how they would pronounce the name, showing that they were, in fact, paying a great deal of attention.

There were giggles when Janel got to a section about a young Giotto painting a fly on the nose of a man in a painting by his mentor. Later, the oldest boy teased his mom with what appeared to be an inside joke, remarking, "Mom, you should read your favorite story. You know? Your faaaaavorite story?" All of the kids snickered and laughed, elbowing each other and exchanging knowing glances.

Janel laughed it off, adding, "Yes, that is a funny one, but I think we'll stick with this one today."

I have no idea what funny story they were referring to, but this little exchange highlights what I enjoyed most about Janel's family, which was the way they all related to one another. While there was no indication that Janel wasn't in control, it was clear that the children felt safe treating her as one of their own. There was a trust that you only get when there is no fear, just mutual admiration.

After finishing, Janel asked for verbal narrations from the kids, a hallmark activity in Charlotte Mason education. As soon as the first child began to narrate, hands shot up around the room from kids who wanted to contribute their favorite details to the retelling of the story.

Next, she gave them each their own independent reading assignments. The eldest son, it turns out, had read ahead the day before so that he wouldn't have as much to read today. It was a surprise to me, having read about the difficulties he had faced in public school. Clearly he's a self-motivated young man, choosing to work ahead when he enjoys his work.

Before I left, Janel showed me salt dough castle models that the kids had made when they learned about all of the essential parts of castle architecture. This opened the floodgates for the kids to begin showing off their favorite things. The eldest son told me about when they had made their own paint, just like Giotto, from egg whites and colored chalk. "It smelled so bad," he said.

At this, one of the daughters exclaimed, "Mom! We should show her your painting of the sunset!"

Janel smiled an embarrassed smile. "Oh, that's out in the garage somewhere. She needs to go."

As I headed back to my van, the little girl snuck out to meet me in the driveway. In her hands was a canvas, one of her mom's beautiful paintings. It was one of the most charming displays of pride I've ever seen from a child.

It's clear that Janel's family has finally found their fit. The children are lively and engaging, plunging right into the day's lessons without any prodding. They seem quite self-motivated and have a slew of self-initiated projects. And best of all, any negativity that they were experiencing at institutional schools seems to have dissolved into love and easy learning at home.

History

Charlotte Mason, who lived in the late nineteenth and early twentieth centuries, was a brilliant British educator whose ideas not only revolutionized schools around England, but trained parents by the thousands. Upon the passing of her father at a young age, Mason attended the Home and Colonial Society for the Training of Teachers and earned top ranks among her peers.[2] During her years teaching in institutional settings, she started developing her own ideas about how to perfect the liberal arts education in England. After some time, she was invited to give a series of lectures on her personal philosophies on education. It was during the course of her lectures that she became convinced that the best way to help children was to first educate parents. She believed that many parents lacked even the most basic understanding of what children need to thrive and of how to properly train them.

Later, Mason gave a series of lectures that would eventually be published under the title "Home Education" and started the Parents' Educational Union. The Union quickly evolved into a training institute for governesses and later into a national school for teacher training. That teacher training institute would eventually supply teachers to schools that were popping up all around the country using Mason's works as their guiding principles.

The County Secretary for Education, Mr. Household (as he was known among the inner circle of Mason followers), became immediately interested in Mason's work and tirelessly spread the interest. He eventually began supplying schools with books on her methods.[3] Many books and even a periodical were born out of Mason's own words and writings, giving her great influence over parents, home childcare providers, and educators alike.

To truly understand how revolutionary Charlotte Mason education was for its time, we must look at the educational system that was in place in England. Children then were taught in a very rote manner: The main subjects taught were the three R's (reading, writing, and arithmetic)—no more, no less—and drills, recitation, and memorization were standard. Students were required to sit with perfect posture on hard chairs while performing flawless mental calculations and were frequently punished physically if their work didn't measure up to the stifling standards. In fact, it wasn't uncommon for teens to be caned or "given the strap."

Mason's radical new spin on education was described by Sir Michael Sadler as "a shaft of light across the land."[4] If you can imagine how dreary an existence and life most children led, it's easy to see why Mason's methods were so warmly welcomed. Mason took the Latin word for education, *educare*, meaning "to feed and nourish," and developed around it a new concept of proper education—one that nourished the soul.

Adding to the somber landscape of learning was the debate over the education of girls. This was a time when feminist education was being hashed out at institutes of higher learning, as well as in churches and political forums. The debate centered on what constituted proper education for young girls and women. Was the perfect woman one who had accomplished many frilly undertakings and was a "trophy" of sorts to a husband? Or, was the ideal woman one who had been soundly educated? Mason's philosophies on liberal education included a broad-based approach for all children, male or female, noble or common, wealthy or poor—upending debates over political correctness or stereotypes.

Mason also breathed new life into a struggling scouting movement.[5] Interestingly, some of Mason's works were compiled and became a sort of proto-handbook for this early form of boy scouts. During Mason's time, children engaged in learning in the classroom, sitting passively at desks and doing indoor tasks. Her ideas about the importance of nature and "learning by doing" resulted in a sudden boom of boys being encouraged by their governesses to go outdoors to climb trees and tie knots.

Guiding Principles

The child is a fully formed individual. Mason firmly believed that the child isn't born a blank slate to be written upon, but comes into the world as a fully formed personality that needs to be valued and respected. When we try to burden children with mounds of facts and lessons, we deny the essence of their formed personalities. Mason advocated that teachers supervise but not drill students in their lessons.

Guiding Principles:
- The child is a fully formed individual.
- Education requires the right environment, an emphasis on the right kind of discipline, and real-life experience.
- Knowledge is assimilated when it is reproduced.

Education requires the right environment, an emphasis on the right kind of discipline, and real-life experience. Mason often stated that education is "an atmosphere, a discipline, a life."[6] This "atmosphere" is the environment from which the child pulls information. For instance, nature study is valued in Charlotte Mason education, but you can't fully experience nature or learn about it in the truest sense while sitting indoors. The immersion of the child in an atmosphere rich in possibilities enhances learning and cultivates curiosity.

Mason also believed that children needed to be trained in good habits if they were to grow up to be self-guided thinkers. Discipline was regarded as a centerpiece of education and Mason believed that good training led to good habits. She wrote, "This subject of training in becoming habits is so well understood... that I need only add that such habits are not fully formed so long as supervision is necessary."[7] Bear in mind that Mason was referring to English society that purported to have child "training" down to a fine science. Perhaps, if writing today, Mason would feel compelled to expand on her ideas. To Mason, properly trained and disciplined children did what was right out of good character, whether or not they were being watched or threatened with punishment. To build good character, one needed good habits—and that required training. Good training was the foundation of a good life because it was seen as having numerous applications across all areas of life. For instance, the formation of good hygiene promoted health; good study habits promoted intellectual growth; upstanding moral character promoted spiritual success, and so on.

Today, there is strong scientific basis for these beliefs about training and character development. Physiologists have long reported how our brain structures respond to habitual lines of thought and action, offering scientific support to Mason's theories on the importance of establishing good habits early on in life. A study led by Ann Graybiel of MIT's McGovern Institute shows that "important neural activity patterns in a specific region of the brain change when habits are formed, change again when habits are broken, but quickly re-emerge when something rekindles an extinguished habit—routines that originally took great effort to earn."[8] The study illuminates how early habit formation determines behavior, and how truly malleable our brains are. With good training and habits, we can reshape our neural connections and change our behavior.

This reminds me of my own experience playing the flute. I haven't played the flute on a daily basis for over 10 years, but when I do pick up the instrument, there are complicated songs that I can play without a second thought. If I try to read sheet music, the notes turn into a jumbled mess. It's as if my fingers just know what to do on their own. Scientists will tell you that this phenomenon all comes down to muscle memory or motor memory, which is refined and developed through practice and discipline. The songs I could play on the flute today were pieces I had spent hours practicing years ago. Practice drilled the notes into my fingers. Now, imagine if we were able to ingrain character and work ethic into our children through the power of habit and practice. Mason believed that we could!

Finally, real life was where Mason believed that true learning took place. For this reason, she believed that home life was more important than school. Learning was less a thing for the classroom and more a thing for the great wide world. Her heartfelt belief in this made her schools obviously different. Formal instruction was limited to mornings; afternoons were reserved for real-life teaching experiences, such as nature walks, self-guided science experiments, and art projects. This also impacted reading and literature choices to a great extent. Children were encouraged to read stories and narratives that allowed them to mentally associate with the daily lives of other children in other places and times.

Knowledge is assimilated when it is reproduced. Mason believed that children couldn't really learn something until they could recreate it on their own terms in a variety of situations. "As knowledge is not assimilated until it is reproduced," she wrote, "children should 'tell back' after a single reading or hearing: or should write on some part of what they have read."[9] This differs greatly from the monotonous recitations prevalent at the time. Mason's belief manifested itself in the practice called "narration," which we'll explore more fully in the next section.

Defining Characteristics

Living books: Not all reading is created equal. Mason taught that children would connect most with written content that bonded them to a particular character and made them feel like a part of that time and place. You can't get this intimate connection from a textbook, so of course, literature became a common substitute, often referred to as "living books." To Mason, living books draw in students to the content through deep connections to characters that are forged through deep, immersive reading. These connections to characters evoke the same bonds that students might have with close friends.

Defining Characteristics:
- Living books: Not all reading is created equal.
- Narration over Q&A is emphasized.
- Formal testing is downplayed.
- Rather than dwelling on passages or re-reading content during lessons, students quickly move on.
- Nature walks and field journals are prized.

"Let him, on the contrary, linger pleasantly over the history of a single man, a short period," Mason said, "until he thinks the thoughts of that man, is at home in the ways of that period. Though he is reading and thinking of the lifetime of a single man, he is really getting intimately acquainted with the history of a whole nation for a whole age."[10] This beautiful statement about living books captures the power of literature and reading.

Not all books were regarded as living books. Textbooks were out, but also were commonplace children's books. Mason's distaste for children's books came from a view that most of them talked down to or belittled children's intelligence. Perhaps Dr. Seuss books would have been out had Mason lived today. Mason believed that the child needed to connect personally with a character of great charisma rather than characters that mindlessly spoke in rhymes or performed silly acts. She advised parents against giving children books of whimsical content or that lacked hidden morals to teach and inspire children.

Today, Charlotte Mason advocates encourage both parents and educators to carefully examine what books should be made available and to consider what actual educational value they have. This stands in marked contrast to current thinking that any reading is good no matter the source or the content. I dare say that the likes of Captain Underpants would alarm Mason's sensibilities.

Narration over Q&A is emphasized. Mason once wrote, "Direct questions on the subject-matter of what a child has read are always a mistake. Let him narrate what he has read, or some part of it. He enjoys this sort of consecutive reproduction, but abominates every question in the nature of a riddle."[11]

Reading this, I think instantly of how often my own children have retold a dream or a story with such unbelievable detail and excitement the moment their father walks through the door. The desire to recapture the drama of a moment seems a natural part of childhood. The practice of encouraging these reflections is central to Charlotte Mason education, as Mason herself observed how the enthusiasm for learning can be dampened when children are quizzed rather than allowed to discuss material on their own terms.

Formal testing is downplayed. In a Mason-inspired environment, testing is shunted in favor of "narration." For example, to assess reading comprehension, teachers ask children to re-tell or narrate the story in their own words. Sometimes children are asked to do so in writing; younger children's verbal accounts are often recorded as a record of assessment for the school board. As children recount the story in narration, they are never interrupted or questioned, but are encouraged to be as thorough as possible.

Narration takes a bit of time to master, especially in our fast-paced world, and requires gentle patience considering the meandering way many children can speak. But Mason-advocates consider narration fundamental to preserving the dignity of the child and a catalyst to developing a child's innate curiosity and natural desire to learn.

Rather than dwelling on passages or re-reading content during lessons, students quickly move on. The interest and value of a piece of literature is in the newness or novelty of its content. When a child reads a selection, be it a paragraph, a chapter, or an entire book, but can't narrate it with any success, the teacher must be prepared to just move on. Rereading a passage to pick up on details that were initially missed is viewed as the quickest way to squash a child's natural attention span.

According to Mason, insisting that a child re-read material to absorb it can be potentially damaging to the child's sense of achievement. Children are thought to have amazing powers of attention and focus—as long as the content before them is novel. If a teacher questions a reading and points out that they could have done better, then their sense of achievement becomes skewed, potentially stunting learning. Children undergoing Charlotte Mason education won't be tediously rereading their work or being corrected for their mistakes. Teachers keep students moving along without lingering on what's been missed.

Nature walks and field journals are prized. Mason's emphasis on "learning by doing" is most evident in the regular practice of nature study. Nature study in the Mason method was two-fold: 1) by communion with natural surroundings, and 2) by documentation in a field journal or notebook.

Mason recommended regular interaction with natural surroundings for students: being outdoors and getting direct exposure to nature. To Mason followers, understanding the greater world started with first understanding the immediate surroundings. Education is the science of relations—not of whole and part as you'll see emphasized in the Trivium method, for example (see Chapter 5)—but of self to surroundings.

Mason is quoted as saying that "it is an evil that children get their knowledge of natural history, like all their knowledge, at second hand."[12] To Mason, children naturally strive to understand that which is important to them; firsthand, sensory experience was considered the shortest path to feeling that earnestness of what's important. Nature study through direct, personal discovery was central because it was the means by which students come to understand their place in the world. Nature studies also helped students build upon existing knowledge; learners could understand the "small parts" and then later grasp how those parts fit into the "big picture."

During nature walks, a teacher doesn't interrupt too often with formal lessons, but simply calls attention to things of interest and makes short descriptive comments. Inclement weather was no excuse to stay indoors, either; examples of natural phenomenon—lightning, thunder, rain, snow, cloud formations and other climate conditions—are on display only during bad weather. So, Charlotte Mason students are bundled up appropriately and marched on outside to appreciate the day that is at hand.

The second part of nature study is the documentation of nature. The terminology here differs among practitioners. Some people document in what they call a "nature notebook," others in a "field journal." Either way, students are required to take a small and manageable notebook along on all nature walks and studies. During these walks, students and the teacher (yes, the teacher has one as well!) sketch objects and organisms of interest and jot down accompanying notes, such as sensory descriptions that can't be drawn.

Other forms of nature documentation include poetry and essays. Mason also encouraged the use of calendars, sometimes inside of the notebook or journal, on which to document "firsts" and "lasts" of natural events, such as the sightings of the first ducklings, the first colored leaves of autumn, the last spring rains, and so on.

Children are encouraged to commit reasonably long periods of time focused on their documentation. In this way, nature documentation and record keeping are seen to aid in the mastery of various subjects and help children improve their writing mechanics on a regular basis. Yet even with the importance placed on notebooks and documentation, these writings and drawings are usually kept as personal records and never graded or formally evaluated.

What the Critics Say

After much research, I've found almost no outright criticisms of either Charlotte Mason or her methods. The only concern that I can highlight is the same as with other non-testing methods. Children who are reared in Charlotte Mason education and then, for whatever reason, must proceed in a more formalized institutional setting, may find testing difficult. The same is true of all homeschooled students who reside in states with stringent standardized testing requirements, or who plan to go to college and will need decent ACT or SAT scores.

The Homeschool Spin

Because early education during Charlotte Mason's time took place in the home, usually with a governess, much of her writing is directed explicitly to mothers and nannies, making it an ideal complement for home education.

> The Homeschool Spin: Home and hearth is where learning starts... The home is not diminished as a place where the child merely eats and sleeps, but is lauded as a place for learning, too.

Home and hearth is where learning starts. Every activity is one that can be done in or around the home. With "life" as one of the three prongs of education, the home is not diminished as a place where the child merely eats and sleeps, but is lauded as a place for learning, too. In the U.S., Charlotte Mason is rarely mentioned in any depth with regards to institutional education the way it is in other countries, such as England and Japan, but is the focus of many general homeschooling approaches. In many ways, it's the easiest educational framework to adapt for the homeschooling context. Charlotte Mason education is viewed as a natural fit for homeschooling. In fact, many boxed homeschool curricula and parenting guides are built around Charlotte Mason education. Of all of the approaches that are touched upon in this book, the Charlotte Mason approach is the most clearly intended for use within the home and is quite minimally covered in teacher pre-professional training in the university setting.

Activities

Preschool

- Make available high quality picture books for children and call their attention to details in the pictures.
- Include children in family discussions and chores.
- Assist in the early formation of hygiene habits.
- Correct bad behavior and eliminate bad habits, however minor or seemingly age-appropriate. Good training requires good habits to be instilled from an early age. This can feel initially time-consuming, but will free your time once good habits are formed.
- Get outside and observe; call attention to small, frequently overlooked elements in nature.

Elementary

- After a reading, have the children tell you about the passage and write down their own words, or have them write a conversational narration of their reading.
- Supply nature journals and take time each day to wander outside, observe, and do nature sketches.
- Write and read poetry inspired by the natural world.
- Provide logical, story-based math problems.
- Gradually increase household responsibilities and assign housework that can be completed by the children.

Upper Grades

- Expand reading selections and have informal book reports replace verbal narration.
- Encourage children to engage in self-initiated investigations and projects.

- Let children take on the majority of chores. By this age, children should be able to complete any and all of the household tasks that the parents can do and stand in for mom or dad when need be. This doesn't mean that a single child should be responsible for the running of an entire house, merely that children are trained in every aspect of running a house, from laundry to lawn care.

Recommended Resources

Charlotte Mason education is such a widely embraced form of homeschooling that there are ample resources and support groups available online. If you're looking to try the approach on for a while with no major financial investment, Ambleside Online (amblesideonline.org) is your best first stop. While use of the site does require a basic understanding of Mason's teachings (which you now have from reading this chapter!), everything you need to give the approach a test run is there. The outline and booklists are free, but it does require you to purchase various books from the list. Many of the books Ambleside uses can be purchased for next to nothing as Kindle editions.

Similarly, Simply Charlotte Mason (simplycharlottemason.com) offers free book lists, but with more curricula to purchase than to use for free. That said, the resources available for purchase are clear and comprehensive. I was able to flip through some of them at Janel's house and came home to purchase some of my own for things like handwriting and copy work. The site also hosts a blog with thorough and practical posts about designing your school day, choosing curriculum, and planning out each year of study. I can't say enough good things about this site. If you're ready to spend a small amount of money and commit to the Charlotte Mason way, this is the best site to help you choose what to buy and how to fit it all in.

The Tanglewood School (tanglewoodeducation.com) boasts a classical educational focus with a Charlotte Mason education delivery style. They offer free book lists and year-by-year outlines and sell very affordable PDF format parent planning books. Tanglewood also offers a step-by-step "create your own curriculum" section with forms and questionnaires designed to help you make your own personalized plans specific to your family's needs.

In addition to these affordable, D-I-Y approaches to Charlotte Mason education, there are companies that offer a "wonder box" approach (discussed in Chapter 11) with everything the company has decided you'll need in one single parcel of mail. These are fabulous if you feel overwhelmed with choosing and sifting through materials at other sites, and just want to know that everything you might want is already someplace on your schoolroom bookshelf.

That convenience does come with a high price tag. Living Books Curriculum (livingbookscurriculum.com) offers wonder boxes for grades K-8 at a cost ranging from $300 to $600 depending on the grade. You also have the option of buying individual books, but all for a generally higher price than you would expect to pay at a bookstore.

There are also tons of great blogs and websites that offer free printables, discussions, and topical guides to various elements of Charlotte Mason education. Mason lovers have a blog carnival (blogcarnival.com/bc/cprof_2378.html) featuring links to topic-specific Charlotte Mason blog posts. The Handbook of Nature Study blog (handbookofnaturestudy.blogspot.com) offers beautiful notebook pages for nature study that can be downloaded and printed, as well as loads of posts on seasonal ideas for nature study. The woman who runs that site also runs Harmony Art Mom (harmonyartmom.blogspot.com), which also offers beautiful, free printables relating to art and music study.

Practical Pages (practicalpages.wordpress.com) features an entire page of free, printable resources. Plus, this mom, a certified teacher, also has a very thorough section dedicated to the ins and outs of proper handwriting instruction, from mechanics to styles and methods, and one major section with oodles of art study guides. Don't just look at the tab for "free pages;" gems and free goodies are also featured in every section of this site.

Ideal for...

Most families that want a gentle, academic approach to home education: Most families will find that they can implement Charlotte Mason education methods with ease. This nurturing, yet academically focused approach is a clear fit for many homeschoolers.

Those who may be uncomfortable with this approach are those who want a clearly focused, step-by-step approach with a lot of instruction and assessment (e.g., Trivium discussed in Chapter 5). Those who live in states that require periodic testing may feel the need to practice testing skills, though some concern has been raised as to whether or not the testing practice in itself undoes the intended good of the method.

Charlotte Mason education can serve as a guide regardless of other educational approaches you use, and any type of lesson can be executed with Mason's core principles in mind.

SEVEN:
unschooling

I hold that the aim of life is to find happiness, which means to
find interest. Education should be a preparation for life.[1]

-S.E. Neill, educator

SARAH'S home looked like a chic boutique crossed with an art
gallery. Eye-catching and beautiful, the bright rooms were covered in
whimsical art of all kinds: the kids' artwork, quilted crafts, glass and metal
creations, even a plant growing out of a cool pair of rain boots. Sarah's
three girls also embodied this bold, whimsical spirit, marching to the beat
of their own drum; they exuded confidence, as well sweetness and
kindness. The oldest daughter was dressed in a cute and trendsetting
outfit and sported a hat that was something like a toy teacup and saucer
balanced upon her head with some hairpins. The middle daughter had a
killer horror movie scream, which had landed her the best screaming roles
in all the local theaters. The youngest, still shy and sensitive, wore a
sequins-laden outfit that made her look as if she should be perched atop
an elephant. They each glided through the house like ethereal spirits on a
mission. It felt as though a kind of magic pervaded Sarah's home.

With her eldest daughter, Sarah had practiced "attachment
parenting," a parenting style characterized by sensitive and emotionally
available parenting. From that experience, Sarah began to feel that there
would never come a day in her daughter's childhood where Sarah would
want to send her daughter away. "I would miss her too much," she
explained. "I felt like I was meant to be with her during her young years."
Sarah then started looking into becoming either a Montessori or Waldorf
trained teacher herself, in an effort to remain a part of her daughter's life
once the school years arrived.

As Sarah did her research, she stumbled upon a technique called TCS (Taking Children Seriously). "The concepts of TCS changed my life. Completely. All of a sudden, everything was open to discussion and thought... I knew I was home. S. [her eldest] was less than 6-months old at the time. So, I am proud and grateful to say that 'unschooling' and the TCS concept of common preferences have been our touchstone for pretty much the last thirteen years."

"Unschooling" sounds like the antithesis of schooling, a method intrinsically at odds with any educational system, so I asked Sarah to explain.

"My definition of unschooling?" Sarah considered my question thoughtfully. "Well, in my ideal world, unschooling is living a full, interesting, happy life in the absence of school. As if school didn't exist," she explained. "To me, it's not eclectic, child-led, or un-parenting; it's a true experience: individual, unique, and hopefully, very fulfilling. It's like having a guide helping you to find resources that will lead to your most inspirational life."

Sarah and her husband don't impose many rules on their girls—even when it comes down to chores, sleep times, or food preferences. For Sarah, the lack of obligatory rules and enforcement is about prioritizing ideals rather than fitting into a conventional system. "Some people have an easier time letting go of educational ideals than they have letting go of arbitrary rules," she points out. "I have always wanted to honor my children's circadian rhythms and food choices. So we don't have bedtimes, monitor the TV, or make arbitrary food rules."

The differences between Sarah's style and my own were humorously highlighted when my 4-year-old became upset at me while Sarah was over at my house. My son had asked to eat an avocado five minutes before I would be serving dinner, and I said no. When my 4-year-old pouted and left the room, Sarah turned to me and asked, "Why can't he have the avocado? I'd love it if my kid asked for an avocado!"

I knew this must have looked nuts to her, coming from a no-food-rules home, and I admire her no-nonsense approach. With a sheepish grin, I responded, "Well, because if he eats the avocado, he won't be hungry for dinner!" She laughed at me, reminding me of the healthy fats in avocados and that it wouldn't do my son any harm to let him have his way (in fact, it would be a nutritious indiscretion!). But I just couldn't budge. Family meals are a cherished constant in our home, and I wasn't willing to let go of it for an avocado. Later, Sarah and I would share a laugh about how our two belief systems came head-to-head over something as innocuous as an avocado.

In addition to no food or bedtime rules, Sarah has steered clear of using a curriculum unless her kids have specifically asked for it. "Around fifth grade age, S. decided that she would like to academically match her schooled peers in math," explained Sarah. When I asked Sarah why S. suddenly decided she needed to have more concrete math instruction, she said she didn't really know. No one was unkind to her or pressured her to buckle down on math. She thinks that maybe she just wanted a math book like everyone else.

"So, knowing her intense love of story, art, and color, we drew on the most beautiful math materials I could think of. We used Waldorf stories, rainbows, glass counters, beautiful books, and lovely games. I wanted it to be gentle and to her liking...a game. I wanted her to love math as I do. Even this backfired a bit and ended in tears, and math 'curriculum' was shelved for a bit.

"This year, she is at grade level [seventh grade] due to her begging for math. We chose Teaching Textbooks since she loves autonomy and the computer. This year, she still doesn't love it but she likes it. It is a goal of hers; I support her and got her the tools I thought would support her. Even though I don't tell her to, she does math every day and got to skip half the curriculum."

Through that self-motivated spirit, the girls have found success this year as they have transitioned to more traditional schooling through an online high-tech school. Sarah admits to trying to talk them out of it, arguing, "We won't be unschoolers at all!" But the girls really wanted to give it a try, and Sarah helped them enroll. Enrolling means that this year, for the first time ever, the girls have had to take daily classes. How does that work in a house where the mom never tells the kids what to do?

I couldn't help but interrogate the eldest, S. "So, let's say that it's getting late and you haven't done your classes yet. Does your mom let you just not do them and get kicked out of the program?" I asked. "Does she remind you to do it? What happens when you don't do what you have to do?"

S. shrugged at my slew of questions. "Well, she'd say, 'Do it now or do it tomorrow.'"

Sarah laughed at S.'s response. "Yeah. That's about right. Now or tomorrow, it will get done."

Sarah's middle daughter, E., also transitioned to a more formal school-at-home program through the high-tech high school and has enjoyed great success even without any prompting from Sarah. In fact, next year E. and her sister will have the chance to submit a business proposal to their online school to be evaluated for the chance to get some startup cash to start their own businesses. What amazing opportunities these girls have found for themselves!

This begs several questions: Are these amazing kids able to thrive and develop so beautifully without any rules or formal lessons because they are innately self-motivated individuals? Or, have the philosophies of TCS and unschooling helped them develop their own inner compass? I can't definitively say, but whatever the mainspring for their success, it's clear that Sarah's daughters are brilliant and happy and have a bright future ahead of them.

History

In 1977, John Holt, an American educator and author, began circulating his revolutionary thoughts on education in a bi-monthly newsletter called *Growing Without Schooling*, or GWS. The years of Holt's life leading up to the newsletter were a frenzy of national media attention on his controversial books, *How Children Fail*, and its follow-up, *How Children Learn*. During his time as a fifth grade teacher, Holt recognized a stark contrast between the timid, seemingly beaten down fifth graders he taught all day and the bold, assertive toddlers of his sister's friends. After much observation of his students, Holt determined that schools were more of a problem to students than a benefit. A quick glance at the kind of venues that featured Holt's ideas prior to the release of GWS demonstrate how widely people were interested in what he was saying, whether they agreed or disagreed. He wrote op-eds for *USA Today*, had articles publishes in the *Christian Science Monitor*, and was a visiting lecturer at both Harvard University and UC-Berkeley.

The second issue of GWS contained the first known use of the term "unschooling," which at that time simply meant not sending your kids to school. There was no such thing as "homeschooling" as there is today, and this was an attempt to shorten the long explanation of, "Our kids don't go to school because we teach them at home," to a simple, "We unschool."

By the mid-eighties, the term "homeschooling" had caught on, and soon the word "unschooling" would come to represent a unique subset of families who opted out of not only institutional schools but also formal schooling methods altogether. Today, John Holt is often referred to as the "Father of Unschooling."

Still, the idea he popularized has its origins even further back in history. In 1921, a revolutionary thinker and teacher named S.E. Neill started the Summerhill School, which now resides in Suffolk, England. This was the first, and still the most famous, democratic or "free school." Neill's aim was to "free" children from the oppression of forced knowledge and enable them to pursue only the knowledge that they felt they needed to further their own individual, creative endeavors.

In the 1960 book, *Summerhill: A Radical Approach to Childhood*, Neill wrote, "I ask what earthly good can come out of discussions about French or ancient history or what not when these subjects don't matter a jot compared to the larger question of life's fulfillment—of man's inner happiness." He went on to say, "I am not decrying learning. But learning should come after play. And learning should not be deliberately seasoned with play to make it palatable. Learning is important—but not to everyone."[2] The result of Neill's ideas was a school that offered classes democratically chosen by students, and emphasized creativity, play, and bliss. Summerhill still operates today and maintains a student body of close to 100 students, ages 5 to 18. Many of the students live at Summerhill full-time. To date, democratic schools have spread as far and wide as Israel, Japan, and New Zealand.

It would seem that in the 1920s, Neill cut school out of the institution, and then in the 1970s, Holt took the institution out of schooling. These two momentous events together appear to have culminated with today's unschooling movement characterized by a lack of connection between formal education and meaningful living.

Today's unschoolers are a broad spectrum of families, ranging from the radical believers who shun all things academic, to those with a softer concept of child-led learning. Every unschooler seems to have a different definition of unschooling, but the definition I've liked most and feel most broadly applies to the bulk of unschoolers is this: Unschooling is about allowing children as much freedom to learn in the world as their parents can comfortably bear. This focus and respect for the child is an idea we've seen in other methods, such as in Montessori (Chapter 3) and Waldorf (Chapters 4).

While no wellspring of hard data specific to the impact of unschooling exists yet, there is increasing academic attention to the importance of informal learning. Institutions like the University of Pittsburgh Center for Learning in Out-of-School Environments

(UPCLOSE) are cropping up throughout academia. Centers like UPCLOSE launch projects that monitor parents and children on field trips, such as outings to botanical gardens and museums. Researchers make careful observations of child-parent interactions and quantify specific actions and lines of questioning with the hope of gathering enough information to draw conclusions on learning in an "everyday context." It's only a matter of time before substantial evidence is gathered on the benefits and drawbacks of informal, delight-driven learning as opposed to traditional frameworks for education.

In a report titled "An Analysis of Research and Literature on Creativity in Education," Anna Craft found "that highly creative pupils have self-perceptions, values and motivations that differ from those of other pupils."[3] In addition, it was found that "teachers tended to devalue independence of judgment and also the involvement of emotion, which are two factors associated in personality studies of creativity with high creative potential. ...teachers [also] put a very low value on creativity traits within the school environment and that their perceptions of creativity were centered around its intellectual aspects and problem-solving processes." Similar research also indicates that highly creative and intuitive children might be stifled by formal education, and suggests that a looser form of child-directed learning might be a better environment for cultivating creativity.

In her paper, Craft goes on to cite other studies that conclude that nurturing creativity in the formative years is a must. Young people won't be able to thrive in today's ever-changing world if they can't think outside-the-box, or if they are accustomed to being passive receptacles for information and never encouraged to explore and discover things on their own. Nurturing creativity in the classroom can guide students later in life, providing them the instincts to respond to challenges, crises, and change. It can also give students an entrepreneurial mindset, such as the courage to try new things and to venture out in unexpected directions.

While the studies cited by Craft never completely detach from the central idea of classroom-based, directed-learning, they nonetheless demonstrate that there are advantages to setting children free from force-fed learning. Give children the freedom to make choices and to use their creativity to navigate the great wide world—and they may very well get the best education of their lives. Independent thinking, unshackled from conventions is a very special skillset that is being inadvertently squelched by a system that steamrolls discipline and demands a uniform educational standard.

Guiding Principles

Life and learning are inseparable. At the heart of the unschooling movement is the idea that children learn what they need to learn when they need to learn it, and they certainly don't need a teacher telling them that they need to learn it. Children in unschooling families learn from life experiences or seek out knowledge and investigate when they're curious about something. But it's certainly not considered education; it's just life.

> Guiding Principles:
> - Life and learning are inseparable.
> - Learning doesn't have to be coerced and should happen in a natural context.
> - Happiness is the purpose of life.

Learning doesn't have to be coerced and should happen in a natural context. Children learn best when learning happens in real world settings. Consider a lesson on money and budgeting: Rather than sit through a math class to learn about money, an unschooler might start a business or look at their allowance and see what they can buy. Unschoolers believe that if you take the concept of money and give children actual situations in which to use and manage their money, they would learn much more than if they were just given lessons. To an unschooler, children learn better when the learning comes naturally and isn't imposed by a teacher.

Happiness is the purpose of life. The idea that learning without joy is useless goes all the way back to Summerhill and is still a strong theme in the unschooling community today. The children, not the adults, set the pace of their own learning. If learning biology doesn't make a child happy, then the child doesn't learn biology just then. Maybe someday the child asks about it because there is something he or she wants to understand that requires knowledge of biology. If that day comes, then the child will exert the effort to learn biology. Until then, force-fed learning isn't worthwhile.

What you'll never find an unschooling parent say is, "Everyone needs to know about biology. So sit and listen!" Children who find no joy in particular lessons won't absorb the information and may even develop a distaste for learning and curiosity for curiosity's sake. What a child enjoys and wants to learn dictates the lesson plan for the day, week, and year.

Defining Characteristics

Classes are not required. The American author Samuel Langhorne Clemens, more famously known as Mark Twain, would probably have been one of the biggest supporters of unschooling. He once remarked, "Education consists mainly in what we have unlearned." He is also generally thought to have said, "Never let your schooling interfere with your education" and "Soap and education are not as sudden as a massacre, but they are more deadly in the long run."[4]

> Defining Characteristics:
> * Classes are not required.
> * There are fewer no's and rules.
> * Children are encouraged to have intense and diverse interests.

These ideas are echoed in unschooling in its most basic and obvious characteristic: the lack of required, formal classes. This doesn't mean that children never experience gymnastics or art classes, or study math or biology; it means that sanctioned school activities are never foisted on children against their will. There are no "required" classes in unschooling, and unschoolers steer clear of replicating institutional style schooling in any form.

There are fewer no's and rules. One of the hallmarks of unschooling is that parents make an effort not to tell their kids "no" unless they absolutely have to. For some, this just means thinking before answering a child's question and taking a moment to evaluate whether or not something really deserves that reactionary "no." For others, it means not telling your kids "no" if they want to eat candy canes for dinner every night. You'll find a whole spectrum of personal limits and interpretations on this particular point, but certainly most modern unschoolers in general limit how often they say "no" to their children. Interestingly, all of the unschoolers I know personally don't have rules about bedtime, television consumption, or diet and meals.

But the thinking on this topic of rules and no's appears to be evolving. John Holt's newsletter *Growing Without School* often featured articles that contained statements like this by an unnamed mother: "...we justify it by the fact that we are their parents and, we think, of all the people on earth, are the wisest when it comes to their upbringing. We monitor their socialization just as we do their TV and sugar consumption..." This stance demonstrates how open to interpretation the rule on "no's" is for many families.

Even with these startling "exceptions" published in his GWS newsletter, John Holt remained the authority until his death and is still regarded as the "Father of Unschooling."

Children are encouraged to have intense and diverse interests. Unschooled kids have abundant amounts of time to spend on whatever their heart desires. Maybe it's a stereotype, but unschooling families always seem artistically motivated and highly creative, so it's no surprise that the kids in these families often have interests in creative activities, such as dance, drama, fashion, art, and other expressive and imaginative activities.

While this may sound similar to the Waldorf method (Chapter 4) with its emphasis on self-expression, the mode of expression among unschoolers seems to be more genuinely unique to the individual. Waldorf students are encouraged to explore creative outlets within preselected modes or formats—specific ways of painting or the use of dolls, for example. With unschoolers, no set limits or parameters are given; children are allowed to express themselves any way they wish. When life is about following your bliss, you're going to want to express that bliss! It's not uncommon to find unschoolers with packed schedules of creative classes and activities. Children pen their own scripts, make movies, write books, or make their own clothes. The time to fully develop an interest is a luxury afforded to unschoolers above all others.

What the Critics Say

Of all of the educational philosophies discussed in this book, unschooling is easily the most controversial. There is no lack of families and educators who describe unschooling as a form of neglect, who call it dangerous and even describe it as a political statement (e.g., a rejection of the values of a formal education) that risks the future of the children involved.

TV show *Good Morning America* ran a segment on "radical unschooling" in which their panel of so-called parenting experts were vocal about their concerns.[5] Ann Pleshette Murphy, parenting expert and regular *Good Morning America* contributor, had this to say: "This to me is putting way too much power in the hands of the kids, something that we know kids can often find anxiety-producing, and it's also sending a message that they're the center of the universe, which I do not think is healthy for children." Dr. Reef Karim, a psychiatrist on the panel, agreed: "The whole concept of cooperating with your kid is kind of cool in theory," he said, "and if a child was a little adult I think it would be great, but he's a child."

That segment inflamed the unschooling community and general public alike, getting the show enough mail and calls to run a follow-up piece. *Good Morning America* revisited the family of unschoolers from the first segment and gave them a chance to respond to both the criticism from experts and the massive public response. The family maintained that there are many paths from point A to point B, and that many unschooled individuals are all grown up and in college, holding jobs, and raising healthy, happy families. They reminded viewers that it's only the media that makes unschooling seem new, that it's actually been around a long time and it's not as much an experiment as a choice.

Many of the prominent voices of the unschooling movement blame the controversy surrounding their practices on society's entrenched biases about school culture and education. They argue that if individuals were not so attached to wielding absolute control over their children, or so brainwashed by their own conventional upbringing, then they would see that unschooling is, in fact, what's best for all children.

Sandra Dodd, an influential figure in the unschooling movement, refers to "traditional, culturally-indoctrinated parents" frequently in her blog (sandradodd.com) as one of the problems with education today. Unfortunately, there are few moderate voices in the clamor that surrounds the concept of unschooling; name-calling from both sides is the norm. It's rare to discuss unschooling and get a neutral, middle-of-the-road response from either advocates or critics.

Do the arguments by critics on either side have any merit? It's impossible to judge the philosophy underlying unschooling against other frameworks. From the outset, we must acknowledge that unschooling families appear to have different goals for their children. If my goal is to go to the car wash and your goal is to go to the grocery store, your criticism of my road map is moot. So, if the goals of unschoolers are for their children to be consistently joyful or curious, while the goals of others are that their children get into the right college, it's natural to expect that unschooling will be vastly different from other methods of education.

In her blog, Sandra Dodd enumerated the differences between what unschoolers want for their kids and what the rest of the world seems to want:[6]

> Each little experience, every idea, is helping your child build his internal model of the universe. He will not have the government-recommended blueprint for the internal model of the universe, which can look surprisingly like a school, and a political science class, a small flat map of the huge spherical world, a job with increasing vacations leading to retirement, and not a lot more.

With my different set of goals about what education should be, I read that and think, *Gee, I'd love for each of my kids to be able to get a job with increasing vacation days and a retirement plan.* Clearly, Sandra and others who share her views are looking for something else in education.

The Homeschool Spin

Provide a focus on the practical and quotidian. Unschooling, being characterized by a lack of school, makes this educational "framework" all about everyday life, which generally happens in the home. If you value child-led parenting, homeschooling just makes so much more sense than sending your children to a democratic or "free school."

> The Homeschool Spin:
> • Provide a focus on the practical and quotidian.
> • Use unschooling to (un)structure your child's free time or vacation days.

In fact, I was looking at the admissions page for a democratic school where there are no required classes, where kids just do what they want all day in the halls of a giant mansion on beautiful wooded acreage—and was floored by price tag: $7,000 per student per year in tuition fees! It sounds to me like a brilliant business model if you can talk parents into paying that kind of money in exchange for merely being around as a resource for their kids all day.

As a parent, if that level of freedom is what you want for your child, then why not do it with them at home for free? Why miss out on watching them become the joyful people you want them to be? Unschooling is tailor-made for the home.

Use unschooling to (un)structure your child's free time or vacation days. Many of the families that I interviewed during my research described themselves as "summer unschoolers" or "afternoon unschoolers"—implying that while they let their children take the lead for the better part of the day, they also make sure that the basics are covered in a testable way should their kids ever need it. For example, the mornings may look very much like public school at home (or be filled with practices and activities previously discussed in other methods), but after lunch, the children are set free. With the blessing from their parents, the children are allowed to make whatever choices they want concerning their free time with little to no adult input or pressure to be "productive" in any traditional sense.

While afternoon unschoolers may say "no" less often like their purist counterparts, they're also likely to put in place some predetermined limits. Sure, purist unschoolers might accuse these parents of being less trusting of their children and taking what's convenient, but I would argue that their fundamentalist stance is the same rigid attitude toward education that the movement, at its heart, has always set out to change.

Remember, this is your homeschooling adventure and you can take what you like from wherever you find it. If you want to be an afternoon or part-time unschooler, go for it!

Activities

For unschoolers, activities may be unpredictable and vast. Every happy, child-chosen activity is an unschooling activity, from shopping at the mall or farmer's market, to playing video games or making up a play with the neighborhood kids. I would say the burden in providing activities for unschoolers lies in parents staying out of the way and not interfering with their children's self-driven interests. This can be hard for parents who want only the best for their children and believe in taking decisive steps and actions. The parents' role is to be a ready resource for their children.

With unschooling spanning all age brackets, parents of older children often find it more of a challenge to get their children to all of the places they want to be. I have a friend who's an unschooler who once wanted to join our group of moms for weekly social time while our children played together. But with her kids and their widely varied plans, my friend just didn't have the time to join our social group, busy as she was getting her kids to all of their activities. She exclaimed, "This unschooling thing is really cramping *my* social life!" Far from being lazy parenting, unschooling often requires a great deal of sacrifice from parents.

Recommended Resources

There are many blogs devoted to providing information on unschooling from parents that either fully unschool, dabble in unschooling, or aspire to it. These include Sandra Dodd's website (sandradodd.com), which I would consider to be quite radical and uncompromising. Sandra is an unapologetic, leading voice in the current unschooling movement and her site has everything from unschooling blog posts and audio recordings of her speaking engagements, to schedules of her upcoming speaking engagements. With its wealth of information, her site should be your first stop.

Unschooling Ruminations (unschoolingblog.com) is a straightforward, zero fluff blog dealing almost exclusively with unschooling topics. Cassi responds gracefully to questions about why many unschooling bloggers seem so very anti-schooling instead of embracing everyone's right to decide for themselves. She also writes about common unschooling fears like, "If we don't set down rules, what if they just watch television all day?" This site is a great stop for those who are leaning towards a more democratic home but may have some nagging reservations.

A blog ring called Christian Unschoolers (christianunschooling.com) offers links to a collection of blogs by Christians who identify as unschoolers, claiming to "disciple instead of discipline." This group seems to be a very unique subset of unschoolers; most prominent voices for the unschooling movement seem to be from those who don't identify with any particular religion—one of the core values of unschooling being independence. So, if you have strong religious beliefs, even if you're not Christian, you may find your online tribe among this list.

Ideal for...

Families that are looking for something radically different:
Unschooling is certainly for the brave and the bold—the educational
rebel. It takes courage to trust its process and to stand up to outside
pressure to become more involved and hands-on in your children's
education. Unschooling is suited for families that rank test-based
achievement below fundamental curiosity and practical life skills. Creative
and free-thinking families will appreciate the nurturing, free-spirited
approach, while families who want to see where their children stand up
against benchmarks and same-age peers in academic areas will probably
lean less toward unschooling.

Families that value personal bliss and self-directed learning:
That said, if you're drawn to the idea of "following your bliss" as an
important educational goal for your children, but aren't quite ready to let
go of standard lesson-based learning altogether, the spirit behind
unschooling can still come through. So-called "afternoon unschoolers"
practice a more forgiving form of unschooling where formal, scheduled
class time exists but is minimized, and children are allowed to pursue
personal projects and interests with gusto, without stifling supervision.
Don't unconditionally discount unschooling; feel free to take the
principles that most appeal to you and integrate them into your own
practices.

———

NOW THAT WE'VE finished covering the five educational
frameworks and philosophies that can be adapted in the home in
Chapters 3-7—Montessori method, Waldorf education, Trivium,
Charlotte Mason education, and unschooling—we'll now shift our
attention in the book to several broad-based theories on learning. In
Chapters 8-10, we'll cover concepts related to "whole and part"
instruction, multiple intelligences, learning styles, and child
temperament—and how you can harness them at home.

As we discussed in the Introduction, think of the educational
methods as home architectural styles: they give style, structure, and form
to your home education plan. Now, it's time to make that home yours.

The learning theories and educational concepts discussed over the next few chapters provide you those personal, tailored touches that truly meet the needs and preferences of your family. These details determine how you'll structure and customize your school time at home in the way you want.

Let's get started.

EIGHT:
Whole and Part
Instructional Techniques

Whether you're looking at a picture of the earth from space or the tiniest speck of life under a microscope, your task is to capture your children's interest and use that to move them closer to a full understanding of their world.

IMAGINE that you've decided to give a lesson on photosynthesis, the process by which plants and trees turn sunlight into energy. How would you go about introducing this topic? Would you start with the broad concepts first, such as the elements of water and sunlight, and how root and leaf systems function through cellular respiration? Or, would you start with the details first, discussing the chemical compounds of water and ATP, and how they interact?

If you have strong opinions about one strategy over the other, consider yourself part of one of the most popular debates among educators: "whole and part" instruction. On one side, you have those who support "whole to part," and on the other side, educators who vouch for "part to whole" education.

The debate is especially relevant for homeschoolers. Usually, every educator you ask will have an opinion on which works best for different subjects and why, and generally many different educational methods and philosophies employ some aspect of whole-part instruction (most explicitly in Trivium discussed in Chapter 5). In this chapter, we'll go over the ins and outs of each camp and show you the fundamental differences between the two, so you can decide what works best for you.

Whole to Part vs. Part to Whole Approaches

Big picture first... The whole to part instructional method looks like this: The teacher first shows the child the big picture, how a thing relates to the greater world, or a single broad ranging topic. Once the student has an understanding of the larger issue, the teacher then breaks it down into more specific areas and each is studied accordingly. An oversimplified example of this would be teaching a child about microscopes and how to operate one and look at a few slides (whole), before covering concepts such as magnification and light reflection (part). The idea is that a child who has an appreciation for the big picture will have a greater desire to understand the component parts.

Whole to part is better suited to some subjects than others. For instance, in language arts, it's typical to encourage a child to read passages from books (whole) before the concepts of grammar and sentence structure (part) are introduced.

A look at the parts... The part to whole approach, in contrast, examines a greater variety of more focused points before tying them all together to convey the big picture or grand concept. For advocates, the idea is that students need to understand the finer details before they can develop a full appreciation for the broader subject or topic. An area where you often see this teaching technique is in cell biology or other science topics. For example, typically the functions of an individual cell are introduced first (part) before different cell types and their different jobs in an organism (whole) are discussed.

A Look at the Reading Wars

Perhaps nowhere has the whole and part debate been more heated than in literacy development. Not long ago, phonics, a kind of standard, part to whole approach to reading literacy, was challenged by the whole language instructional method. Jon Reyhner, a researcher at Northern Arizona University, described how debates about whole and part instruction, which had been traditionally confined within the walls of universities, spilled out into the greater world and turned into battles fought in newspapers, state legislatures, and even in Congress.[1] Central to the debate was this: Do children have greater reading success when they are taught how to break down words into phonetic components and sound words out, or do they learn better when they memorize a great deal of words and expand their vocabularies?

"Phonics proponents led by Rudolph Flesch in his 1955 book *Why Johnny Can't Read* attacked the whole word approach because it did not get students into reading children's stories that did not have carefully controlled vocabularies," writes Reyhner.[2] In contrast, whole language supporters argued that children would be able to access more advanced texts when they could recognize more words at a glance and didn't having to stop and sound words out. These whole language advocates also pointed out that many English words don't neatly follow the rules of phonics anyway.

Both camps have the statistics and studies that support their respective approaches—which is why the debate is a yet unsettled issue. Yes, it's true that about half of the words in the English language can't be decoded with traditional phonics and therefore must be memorized. But that's a lot of words to memorize and the odds are good that you'll never be able to teach them all. With a few phonics rules, however, children will be able to read the other half of English words regardless of whether they have been taught those specific words. To me, that approach sounds more doable.

For the rest of this book, I do my best to stick to an unbiased view of methodologies, but on literacy instruction I'm overwhelmingly in favor of phonics and I have strong opinions about what works well for reading instruction. Quite plainly, I root strongly for the phonics camp; in fact, I think that the educational experiment of whole language to the exclusion of phonics has cost us dearly.

During my years in the classroom as a university student and a teacher, I saw several upper elementary and middle school students who weren't good readers embarrassed when asked to read in front of others. They struggled to read unfamiliar words because they lacked the basic understanding of how to sound out words. In contrast, I've never seen a child with a solid foundation in phonics struggle to read. Also, far too many children who were schooled under whole to part language techniques return to the basics of phonics much too late in their educational path. For that fifth grader who has to return to the seemingly infantile phonics books after becoming accustomed to reading with whole language approaches, the experience can be emotionally and socially devastating. Sometimes, this backtracking can send kids straight into full-on academic rebellion.

My recommended approach for parents: Once you teach your child to decode language basics through phonics, you certainly can begin to teach them to recognize non-phonetic words and start building their vocabulary bank through exposure and reading practice. For me, though, phonics is still the most efficient way to teach new readers and set them down a path of self-driven literacy.

Today, the debate over which approach—phonics or whole language—best serves the child continues to rage on, even causing proponents on each side to flip flop on actual definitions of whole language and phonetics. The debate has also paved the way for the rise of the latest reading instruction trend called "balanced literacy instruction." To its supporters, there isn't one single way to teach all students how to read; both the phonics camp and the whole language camp are regarded as too extreme. They claim that when you choose one approach to the exclusion of the other, some children will be shortchanged. Balanced literacy instruction aims to blend the two approaches so that that all learners get the benefits of each.

I appreciate this balanced method within an institutional setting because it concedes to my most ardent belief that every child learns differently. When you choose to homeschool, you'll have the benefit of being able to observe how your children learn best and to adapt your literacy instruction using any combination of the two approaches to suit their needs.

What Technique Should Parents Choose and for Which Subjects?

The idea of part to whole versus whole to part is in no way confined to the area of language development. In other subject areas, there's no hard evidence that either approach doesn't work well for different children.

Take what we've learned in sports: In the field of sports science, numerous studies and articles have dissected two approaches for teaching bodily movements, such as lay-ups and free throws in basketball. Do you teach the whole movement and then look at what parts need work, or do you teach each movement in the lay-up and then put them together? Brian Mackenzie, coach and tutor/assessor with UK Athletics, the United Kingdom's National Governing body for Track and Field Athletics, reports on his sports teaching site that "when a skill is complex or there is considered an element of danger for the athlete, then it is more appropriate to break down the complex movement into its constituent parts."[3] He goes on to report that "studies have shown that simple skills (and perhaps simple is relative to each individual) benefit from the whole method, skills of intermediate difficulty benefit from the part method, closed skills are often taught with part instruction, [and] difficult skills are best dealt with by oscillating between part and whole."

Since findings in this area and many others aren't definitive, I recommend parents try both approaches and observe their children to decide which approach is best for different subjects. One seemingly fail-proof combination that is popping up with great popularity is the "whole to part to whole" approach. In this variation, the big picture is briefly and superficially introduced to give perspective to the entire process, then the component parts are studied in depth, and finally the big picture is reassessed with greater detail. If not too much emphasis is placed on the mastery of the whole during the introductory phase (unless your students insist), this method works quite well for the majority of children.

One of the best ways to assess what whole and part variation works for your children is to deliver a few lessons with this "whole to part to whole" approach. Then, observe them: What points in the lesson are they slowing down? Are they slowing the pace of the lesson as they learn the parts or as they learn the whole? Is the slowdown due to difficulty with understanding the concept or with a desire for more information?

A slowdown in the initial whole phase, followed by mastery in the final whole phase, may indicate that you have a part to whole learner on your hands. If this is your hunch, try the next lesson with a part to whole approach, and watch to see if that initial discomfort with the content is mitigated. Does the learner feel more at ease and show more dexterity when you examine component parts more in-depth before looking at how they all fit together? If, on the other hand, your student slows down a great deal in the central phase where you examine the component parts, then in your next lesson, try a heavy-handed whole to part style and see if the more focused look at the whole allows your student to feel more at ease with the details.

As a homeschooler, you should keep experimenting.

Integrating Whole and Part Instruction at Home

Keep in mind that a student needing part to whole instruction in one subject may still benefit from whole to part in other subjects. My disclaimer and preferences aside on the value of part to whole in reading instruction (i.e. phonics), I don't see any issues with customizing different approaches for different subjects. No uniform, across-the-board way works for every family. You may find that science topics or history are better presented part to whole, or that it makes more sense to teach social studies using whole to part.

My own homeschooling experience over the years has revealed just how different my children are when it comes to learning, so I tend to look less at the subject matter when deciding what whole and part approach to use, and more at the child.

> book less at the subject matter when deciding what whole and part approach to use, and more at the child.

Hannah Jane really responds to part to whole teaching; she pours over details for long stretches of time, and then later has her own epiphanies about how things all fit together. She doesn't ever seem to want to be taught the whole. She wants the parts, and then she wants to inform everyone of the whole that she's come up with on her own. Whenever I start with the big picture, she's fidgety and eager for me to get on with things and fill her in on the details.

On the other hand, her younger brother, Hunter, likes me to introduce the big picture first and linger on it in lessons. For example, he enjoys hearing about the ecosystem as a whole, but gets annoyed by discussions of all the little niches within. He loves to belt out songs, but is impatient in choir when asked to work on specific parts to improve his rhythm. As a result, he has repeatedly dropped out of choir, contented himself with sitting by while his siblings participate, and insists that he likes singing alone, his way, where he can always sing the whole song and never have to stop half way through to work on the parts. He likes to read entire books rather than those terse, sometimes senseless readers. Everything about him is whole-oriented. Only after he has worn out a topic does he finally hone in on the details.

These differences among my children can make for a tricky group lesson in our home, so here's how I handle subjects like science that we study as a family: First, I start with a quick and dirty overview segment and lay out the big picture in a very rough way. I give my part-oriented daughter some independent reading and encourage her to take notes on the details that she loves so dearly; meanwhile, my younger, whole-oriented learner and I sit down and look at some pictures and talk about the big concepts. He's not a proficient enough reader yet to be handed a textbook, so this discussion-with-pictures approach works quite nicely.

After that brief period, all of my kids are asked to make a "KWL" chart, which stands for "Know, Want to know, and Learned." We fold a paper into thirds and they fill in what they know and what they want to know. This helps them exercise patience when I'm using an approach that isn't focusing on their favorite part. They know that if they've written something down in the "want to know" section, I'll be sure that we cover it later. My daughter's "want to know" lists are always very specific; my son's lists are much broader, relating to the interconnectedness of the things we discussed in our picture time. When we're all done with a lesson or a unit, I pull out their charts and make sure that they now know everything they wanted to know when we began.

One scenario that teachers and parents often face is having a student who gets bogged down because of heightened interest rather than difficulty. These precocious children suddenly become fixated with a concept or topic, becoming so engaged that they find it nearly impossible to move on in their studies until they have worn it out. This is fantastic, but if it becomes a regular issue that disrupts other lessons and causes students to neglect other work, it may be time to change strategies.

Dealing with this situation requires a more complex examination of the broader needs of your children beyond how they best take in information. Now that you know what sparks their interest, you'll need to adjust the pacing of lessons to manage how their interests develop and peak. If your students always get hung up on the smaller parts (details are where the most intensely curious kids usually get hung up), then you may want to consider teaching with a heavy dose of the big picture up front, and gradually move through the details in measured doses. This ensures that the big picture material gets the right amount of attention before the children immerse themselves in the details.

As a teacher, I once had a student with Asperger's Syndrome in the special education room where I worked who had an intense love of rocks and dinosaurs. When I first got the job, the other teachers encouraged me to make every single lesson for him relate to either rocks or dinosaurs as a guaranteed way to get his attention. The characteristically Asperger's trait of intense focus would kick into overdrive when I related a math lesson to rocks. Later, the boy would become agitated when asked to move on to language arts or even recess. I quickly learned that if I nurtured him properly throughout the day, he would reasonably attend to any lesson I put before him. So, I saved the rocks-related lessons for times when he needed a distraction from a difficult social situation or classroom problem, or when I wanted him to focus on more difficult, intense subjects.

In the years since I had that experience, I've used what I've learned with my own children at home. My most sensitive child, who always feels picked on and who is a serious daydreamer and dawdler, has an intense love for dinosaurs. He has two different dinosaur encyclopedias and he enjoys cross-referencing things between the two sets of books. He'll look at the teeth of an Allosaurus in one book and determine whether it was likely to have been a carnivore, omnivore, or herbivore. He'll then flip open the other book and check the teeth in a picture to see if his assertions are consistent with his findings from the first book. He can do this for a half an hour, the longest anything ever holds his flighty attention.

So, when he's feeling out of sorts and particularly sensitive, I'll give him something related to our current topic to look for and cross-reference among his encyclopedias. If we're in the middle of a lesson on the flora of a certain climate zone, and he becomes upset at something, I quickly diffuse the situation by asking him to do a little research. I might ask, "Can you find any pictures of trees in your books that might be related to a sugar maple?" This gets him in his zone, still mostly on topic, and soon he can emotionally move on with his day.

A caveat: If I were to structure every lesson around his dinosaur obsession, his knowledge base would soon be out of balance. For this reason, I save the cross-referencing strategy for emotional emergencies.

WHATEVER METHODOLOGY AND   educational   framework you adopt at home, whether Trivium, the Montessori method, or a combination of both or others, whole and part instruction (and its variations) provide a wonderful content delivery strategy for homeschooling families.

If you're leaning towards the Montessori method (Chapter 3), you'll notice that the lessons are very much structured part to whole. For example, in grammar lessons, you generally discuss every part of speech before looking at complete sentences. If you have a part to whole thinker, you're all set. If, however, your child needs to see the big picture first, don't hesitate to offer that big picture; look at a complete sentence and point out how all of the words have a different function and work together to produce a complete thought. There's no need to forego using the Montessori method just because you have a whole to part thinker on your hands. If the Montessori method is your vision for your family, you can adapt the framework while still adhering to its principles.

Waldorf education (Chapter 4) doesn't seem to be characteristically one or the other, so the ball is in your court. You can use art to accentuate the parts or the whole in whatever order you need, and you can allow your children time to discuss whatever element strikes their fancy.

Trivium (Chapter 5) has a natural whole to part set-up. Over the years, the same topics are studied in finer and finer detail each time you revisit them. But this doesn't mean you can't let your detail-oriented learners dig into the finer points from the get-go. In our home, we use the Trivium approach for our history studies, and what I've found is that my details-focused learner can always find more details to examine on succeeding rounds. For many subjects, there's always a level deeper, so don't stress over keeping things broad just because that's the layout of your chosen curriculum. Experiment and adapt accordingly.

Being very literature-focused and narration-based, Charlotte Mason education (Chapter 6) makes it easy to adapt to your children's natural inclinations. For example, when they hear or read a story, they'll get the big picture and choose to hone in on details (or not) on their own during narration. If you have a big picture child, don't neglect to ask for details once in a while. While you aren't supposed to question children too intensely during narration, do make it clear that you'd like them to include some interesting details in their re-telling. Get a sense that your whole-oriented children are, at a minimum, acquiring acute observation and listening skills and do notice the details.

Finally, don't worry if the topic of integrating whole and part instruction with other formal educational frameworks feels a bit overwhelming at this time. We'll discuss how to put everything together in Chapter 11.

NINE:
Different Kids, Different Smarts and Learning Styles

I never teach my pupils; I only attempt to provide the conditions in which they can learn.

- Albert Einstein, scientist

OUR goal as educators is to make sure that we give our students what they need in order to become informed thinkers. We can't do this if we simply hand them information in a way that they can't process or use. We must look at all children individually and determine how they think and how they hear what we say to them, before we can even teach them how to learn. Let's take a look at some of the most popular ideas about how to address children's learning needs.

Howard Gardner, an American developmental psychologist, shocked the educational establishment in the early 1980s when he coined the term "multiple intelligences." Before then, schools regarded intelligence as strictly singular: A child either excelled in school subjects and was regarded as smart, or didn't and was deemed average—or worse, learning-disabled. Testing was (and still largely is) based upon reading, writing, and mental calculation. In schools, intelligence was a measure of literacy and mathematical aptitudes, and nothing more; every other aptitude was regarded as extraneous to success or intelligence.

Artistic and nature-loving children were dreamers. Athletic students were mostly "dumb jocks," unless they were also whiz kids in the classroom. Talkers were disruptive rebels that needed to be reformed. Life after K-12 education held two paths: either a path to college, thought to be only for those who tested well, leading to a future in white-collar, corporate America, or a path to a blue-collar factory job, for those who

st well or earn high marks in school. There wasn't yet the focus
nking outside the box or a respect for artisans and the
reneurial-minded making a living in the arts, athletics, the outdoors,
rough some other unconventional way.

Beyond Math and Verbal: Smart in Different Ways

Howard Gardner broadly defined intelligence as an ability to solve
problems or create products that are valued in at least one culture.
Gardner's theories rocked the educational establishment by daring to
consider that other aptitudes and intelligences mattered. His ideas about
multiple intelligences started with his deep concern over the ramifications
of measuring intellect by the traditional means, such as the Intelligent
Quotient (IQ) Test or other testing means practiced by schools. Schools
used these tests to place students in classes, give out awards, and
determine whether students would be held back a year or advanced.

To Gardner, the tests were flawed. Children who didn't test well in
traditional "school subjects," he observed, were treated as less intelligent
than children with more measurable and valued skills—usually those
associated with specific types of verbal or math-based intelligences.
Gardner believed that the children who didn't excel in those subjects
might, in fact, have a high level of intelligence—just in different areas.

The bias toward certain intelligence types wasn't only perpetuated in
testing, but throughout the educational system, from curriculum
emphasis, to how teachers treated students in the classroom. In most
schools, non-verbal and non-math subjects and skills were often devalued,
relegated to afterschool activities that hadn't yet become the all-
important resume boosters and child development necessities they are
regarded as today.

Art, when studied at all, was often treated like an afterthought rather
than a subject for study, like art history and theory, where students read
about art and art trends and memorized facts and dates associated with
great artists. Little class time was actually devoted to encouraging students
to create their own artwork, or to explore art galleries or museums. Time
outdoors was minimized, and recess was often moved indoors to
gymnasiums; it was thought that exercise was the most important aspect
of free time.

Tiger mothers hadn't yet entered the scene and there were more latchkey kids than there were those loaded with afterschool schedules. Young people who enjoyed extracurricular activities, such as sports, dance, or music, but eventually reached a plateau, were expected to "give up" and shift their attentions and energies toward academic subjects. For example, students who weren't "going pro" with these activities were expected to defer them and "get more serious" with their more important studies. I wonder how many dinner table lectures were delivered where Danielle was berated for not putting in the same amount of effort into algebra that she devoted to field hockey practice, or where Tommy was criticized for spending too many weekends drawing cartoon sketches rather than working on his English composition reports.

> Entrenched biases have created an educational system and curriculum that nurtures and rewards only some students—those who excel and test well at particular subjects.

While math, reading, and other academic subjects are undoubtedly important, the problem, according to Gardner, was that the education system valued these subject areas to the exclusion of others. Over time, these entrenched biases have created an educational system and curriculum that nurtures and rewards only some students—those who excel and test well at particular subjects.

What about other students with different gifts and interests? How can teachers and parents use students' innate aptitudes to spark their learning success in other subjects? Can Danielle get excited about algebra through her interest in sports? Can Tommy write his reports by harnessing his interest in the visual arts?

According to Howard Gardner, they can.

Lesson Tips for the Eight Intelligence Types

Gardner divided human intelligence into eight types:

1. Bodily-kinesthetic

2. Interpersonal

3. Intrapersonal

4. Verbal-linguistic

5. Logical-mathematical

6. Musical

7. Visual-spatial

8. Naturalistic

In this section, we'll go through each of Gardner's intelligence types. You're bound to see shades of each one in your children, some to a greater degree than others. For each type, I provide lesson tips to incorporate into your homeschooling so that you can better teach to your children's aptitudes.

Bodily-kinesthetic

An individual who has bodily-kinesthetic intelligence easily masters tasks that involve movement and muscle activity. Don't make the mistake of only including those children who are natural athletes in this category; this type of intelligence also applies to children who simply learn best when moving things around or moving themselves around while learning. Any time children in this category use their body, it's almost as if the information gets stored in their muscles, as well as in their brains. For these children, the mind and body are intimately linked.

Tips for the "Body-Smart"

There are many ways to help your bodily-kinesthetic child at home. Being physically present in a lesson makes learning more meaningful for all types of learners. For body-smart children especially, the simple act of being up and walking around while learning new information, rather than sitting still at a desk or table, may help them retain information better.

In its simplest form, this may mean acting out concepts rather than relying on quiet, book learning. For example, when I taught the states of matter (solids, liquids, and gases) in my home, I had my children get up and act out the behavior of particles in a particular state. For solids, they had a group hug to show that the particles are packed close together; for liquids, they held hands and swayed to demonstrate how liquid particles can move within a confined space; and for gases, they ran wild around the room to show how gas particles spread out and fly off. This up-and-at-'em sort of approach sticks in the mind of my bodily-kinesthetic learner, Hunter, in a much more meaningful way than it would have if I'd simply lectured, "Particles in solid matter are close together..."

Unconventional ways of teaching that harness the pent-up energies of students can turn otherwise sedentary lessons into more active, engaging ones that kids can get excited about. As a public school teacher, I recall the dread I felt when I had to teach a grammar class. My training and interests had been in math, and I dreaded the idea of diagraming sentences. *How am I ever going to make this fun for the students?* I wondered. I suppose I was also secretly thinking, *How will I have any fun teaching grammar?* I hated the assignment, but I eventually found ways to have the students up and out of their seats while learning basic grammar rules. I brought in a Nerf basketball set and arranged the students in teams; students who knew the proper grammar rule were invited to take a shot. I also arranged sentence diagramming races where two students would race from a line at the back of the classroom to the chalkboard and try to diagram a sentence correctly before their competitor. The dull act of diagramming sentences on paper quietly at one's desk was transformed into thrilling games. When kids enjoy learning, the learning sticks.

Here are some other specific suggestions to try at home:

- Try Waldorf-inspired "joyful movement" when memorizing or reading long passages and poetry (see Chapter 4).

- Turn every concept into a game of Charades. "Act out" science concepts that have relationships between parts.

- Take field trips. If you're studying art, take a trip to the art museum. If you've been discussing biology or ecology, take your children to the natural history museum, or better yet, try a nature preserve or go for a hike.

- Take science lessons off the page and into the lab (a kitchen counter lab or garage lab, that is) by doing hands-on projects, rather than simply having your children read textbooks and parrot back what they've learned. Do experiments and build models and dioramas.

Interpersonal

The child with interpersonal intelligence is characterized by an ability to easily make friends, empathize with others, and form strong relationships. These individuals often make excellent leaders or facilitators as they have a knack for commanding an audience and an ability to empathize with others. Social talents can be of grievous concern in the traditional classroom setting, however, if not properly channeled, especially when energies are often put towards private conversations and note passing during class.

Children who excel at interpersonal skills are often said to have high emotional intelligence, or EQ. They understand group dynamics and work well in teams and with others, enjoying the liveliness of conversation, discussion, and debate.

Tips for "Socialites"

At home, make sure that interpersonally intelligent children have ample opportunity to socialize and interact with others, whether that be with siblings, homeschool co-ops, or even just with you. Help children who fall into this category learn a range of subjects by allowing them to explain ideas and concepts to others. The narration technique in Charlotte Mason education (see Chapter 6) is ideal for these students. Re-telling a story or teaching or tutoring others on concepts they just learned goes a long way to promoting academic success for these interpersonally-gifted children. Role-playing or play acting are also great tools for interpersonal learners.

Here are some other specific suggestions to try at home:

- Use phrases like, "Let's work together on this," and "help me understand this."
- Encourage meaningful group work by letting your socially-smart students teach others. If group work isn't possible, have them teach or narrate back to their favorite stuffed animal or even to their pets. I've gone so far as to have Hannah Jane give our family dog, Stillwater, a Latin quiz, just to make sure she had understood the material.

- Turn the biographies of famous artists, writers, or scientists into plays and theatrical productions.

- Join co-ops, study groups, and clubs for homeschoolers (e.g., chess club, poetry writing groups, science fair teams, or other hobby groups) in your area. If you can't find the right groups, use Yahoo Groups or Meetup to locate other homeschoolers and start your own club.

Intrapersonal

Intrapersonally gifted children tend to be thoughtful and introspective. More than other kids, they're in touch with their emotions and can easily access their own ideas on a wide range of topics. Often perceived as shy, these students can fall between the cracks if they aren't provided with an environment in which they feel they can safely express their own feelings and struggles. Children with this kind of intelligence are independent, often thriving when left to work alone on a task, and when they're given the freedom to pursue tasks in an individualized way. Often these children enjoy more analytical subjects and have a great capacity to understand complex and abstract ideas.

Tips for "Solitaire Players"

The home environment is a natural fit for children with intrapersonal gifts as long as they are blessed with parents who can skillfully channel their interests in a productive manner. Sometimes it can be hard for a gung-ho parent or teacher to reel back and allow children with these aptitudes the space to learn. It's easy to say, "We're supposed to be focusing on this and this today!" and be constantly directing and hovering to make sure their children stay on task.

The Montessori method's emphasis on child-directed learning and its natural respect for children's independent and natural psychological development provides a wonderful approach for those with intrapersonal aptitudes (see Chapter 3). For children who tend to be self-reliant and autonomous in their learning style, the Montessori idea of observing and guiding children through their educational development nurtures rather than stifles these intrapersonal learners.

Trivium, with its focus on teaching children how to independently pursue knowledge, can also be a comfortable fit for intrapersonal kids if they are generally content to turn their attention to specified themes. Once parents see that their children have acquired the ability to pursue new content on their own, they can feel comfortable giving their kids the space they crave during school hours. Parents with children who fall in this category should adapt their teaching styles and learn how to be comfortable monitoring success in more un-intrusive ways.

Here are some other specific suggestions to try at home:

- Encourage journal-keeping, such as art journals, diaries, and other types of learning journals, which give intrapersonal learners a more personal outlet for self-expression.

- Turn intrapersonal learners into budding critics and have them write critiques and reviews of curricula and lessons, as well as books, films, and food. These critiques can help students connect with content and others outside of group discussions.

- Provide a lot of books to read and a lot of blank paper for reflecting.

- Allow for uninterrupted blocks of time dedicated to study.

- Support personal, self-chosen and self-guided projects.

Verbal-linguistic

These gifted individuals excel in anything that has to do with words and languages, whether written or spoken. Reading and writing come more easily to verbal-linguistic children and they usually have excellent reading comprehension and advanced vocabularies. These learners like to take notes, write stories, and (for outgoing personalities) talk, talk, talk. Memorization and copy work, as well as discussion-based group work and debates are ideal teaching tools for these children.

Tips for "Word Whizzes"

At home, take the opportunity to make all of your subjects a little more language-oriented. Charlotte Mason's emphasis on narration (see

Chapter 6), as well as the Trivium's stress on expressing independent thought and honing rhetoric skills among older students (see Chapter 5), enhances learning for these children. If your verbal-linguistic learners are talkative and thrive in front of an audience, design recitation or even performance-based activities, like the reading aloud of passages in books or poetry.

Here are some other specific suggestions to try at home:

- Allow verbal learners to come up with real-life scenarios for math problems and relate them to you like stories.

- Encourage children to keep lab notebooks, which can be a dream for kids who prefer writing detailed and extensive notes as they learn.

- Encourage creative writing and journal-keeping to harness the expressive talents of your imaginative learners.

- Have the talkers in your home prepare speeches and presentations of what they've learned and turn one evening a month into "Show and Tell" hour for the family.

- Start a family newsletter and let your natural authors pen the articles (your visual-spatial learners can design and arrange the layout). Send your newsletter to extended family on a regular basis and invite your readers to send "Letters to the Editor" to engage your children.

- Suggest starting a blog where your children can write about their school work, post original stories and poems, and just display their dazzling command of words and verbal expression. Wordpress, Blogger, and Tumblr are a few popular blog platforms to explore. (*Caution:* Customize online privacy and security settings and use password protection to protect your younger students.)

- Encourage your more verbally inclined kids to start or join debate teams and public speaking clubs (check Yahoo Groups, Google Groups, or Meetup for local groups in your area).

Logical-mathematical

Students who display strong logical-mathematical intelligence are generally those who have been traditionally viewed as intelligent. These students are the ones who—forgive me for saying so—have long made the lives of kids with other intelligences more difficult! They're not just math whizzes, but also have a wide range of skills: They can easily grasp abstract concepts, show an aptitude for number theory, and can follow logical arguments with dexterity. They make the complex seem simple and often leave their peers scratching their heads.

Tips for "Logic Lovers"

Logical-mathematical children benefit from having the freedom to pick apart lessons. These children often prefer to spend more time on a subject—not because they can't grasp it, but because they often want to explore topics in more depth. Glossing over a topic in what seems to be an age-appropriate way is often unsatisfying for these students. Hannah Jane, my eldest, is one of these students, and I find that she's often inclined to delve deeper into every topic we cover. Under her barrage of questions, I'm lucky if I have all of the answers on hand. A Google search is a saving grace for homeschoolers with logical-mathematically intelligent children; you can't always anticipate what direction these learners will go with each lesson, so be prepared to do extra research on the side to answer all of their questions.

Also, be content to allow these students more time than you've allotted for a particular lesson if that's what they need. Try to cultivate their investigative and curious natures by providing materials and activities that they can try on their own. To this end, the Waldorf-inspired idea of lesson blocks—blocks of time devoted to a particular topic or subject—works well (see Chapter 4). These analytical children thrive when they can focus intensely for longer periods and thoroughly master topics before moving on. The Trivium's focus on systematic curriculum development that builds on topics can also be a natural fit for logic-minded students (see Chapter 5).

Logical-mathematical learners don't just have organized brains; they also want everything to be organized in their own way. Allow them time each day to implement their own organizational system. Even if their system seems a bit chaotic to you at the outset, there may be a "method to the madness" that they alone perceive. As long as things aren't repeatedly getting lost or misplaced, take a deep breath and let your structure-lovers organize and re-organize as they see fit.

Here are some other specific suggestions to try at home:

- Start lessons with a puzzle or riddle that relates to the content, or can only be solved using the content of the lesson. This gets the attention of logical thinkers and helps them focus on the lesson as a means to satisfy their natural, problem-solving urges.

- Turn lessons in literature or other subjects into critical reading sessions where students identify logical fallacies (e.g., red herrings, shaky assumptions) or appeals to emotion in stories, speeches, and other narrative accounts.

- Encourage games of strategy, such as chess, or hobbies, like computer programming, that encourage analytical and abstract thinking.

- Engage in small-scale engineering activities, like building model airplanes or taking apart clocks, radios, and other mechanical objects, especially if your inventive young students like investigation through tactile activities.

- Provide ample organizational tools, such as folders and dividers, and encourage students to use their own color-coded systems.

Musical

Children with musical aptitudes are those who have a keen understanding of musical components, such as sounds, tones, melodies, and rhythms. There are also many among us who are just naturally inclined to use music to express themselves. I have a dear friend who's musically intelligent, and she once exclaimed, "Wouldn't you just die if you couldn't share your music with someone?" Well, I do play a few instruments, but the idea of dying if I couldn't play for others to express myself was one I couldn't relate to at all. My friend represents one type of musically intelligent child: someone for whom everything is a song or a piece of music.

But the aptitude for music goes beyond just having perfect pitch, or being able to play musical instruments, sing, or compose music. Musical learners also have strong auditory skills and better absorb material delivered verbally through lecture or discussion, rather than through passive reading. The musically inclined can also show high marks in math. Musicians often find topics like fractions easy to grasp. Musical harmonies or chords, in a way, are like fractions. Musicians learn that different pitches played at certain intervals sound nice together (3rds, 5ths, and 8ths), while pitches played at other intervals (2nds, 4ths, and 7ths) sound harsh or dissonant. Rhythm and time are also based on fractions. Music has rhythms that always add up to a whole: A measure is typically a whole note, half that is a half note, a quarter of that is a quarter note, and so on in the standard common ("C") time.

Whether music study directly enhances student performance is difficult to say, but studies have increasingly suggested that the association between music and academic success is worth noting. In fact, students taking courses in music performance and music appreciation scored higher on the SAT than students with no arts participation: Music performance students scored 53 points higher on the verbal portion and 39 points higher on the math portion; music appreciation students scored 61 points higher on the verbal and 42 points higher on the math.[1] Another study found that music majors enjoy a higher rate of acceptance to medical school than any other major.[2]

Tips for "Musical Magnates"

Music can be a great way to introduce concepts that need to be memorized. Many students simply recall things better if they're set to songs or catchy tunes; younger students may respond better in an environment filled with music and sounds, rather than a dead-silent classroom. As your child matures, however, knowing how to incorporate music into lessons can be a challenge, and many homeschoolers must learn how to be creative for their music lovers.

Turn lessons into songs and use well-known songs or music pieces as inspiration for lessons on everything from grammar to cultural studies. I'll never forget watching MTV's Kurt Loder correct Jewel's use of the word "casualty" in a televised interview. I took that little gem to the eighth grade grammar class I was teaching, and they had a field day with it, bringing in more cases of bad song grammar when they came across them.

If you're not musically inclined yourself, you may want to ask a musician friend for a basic course in music reading and music composition to help set you on your way to finding creative ways to integrate music into your homeschool routines. In Waldorf education in particular, it's common to use "transition songs" to move students from one activity to another (Chapter 4). Singing is considered a gentle way to change the pace, rather than simply telling a student, "Okay, it's time to move on now." Waldorf homeschooling moms report this works wonders when used regularly, especially for typically stressful moments like getting younger children to leave the playground without a fit. Mothers simply come alongside their playing child and sing the transition song, and hopefully after some practice with this routine, the child simply joins in and follows along behind Mom as they head back to the family van. If you're interested in adding songs to your daily routine, you'll find a lot to work with within the Waldorf framework.

Here are some other specific suggestions to try at home:

- Teach grammar by having students take lyrics from their favorite songs and diagramming those sentences into their grammatical parts (choose songs that are grammatically correct, of course). Alternatively, have students identify poor grammar and incorrect vocabulary usage in song lyrics.

- Encourage children inclined to write to compose their own lyrics, or to set their writings, such as poetry, to song.

- Break down pieces of music into component parts; for example, notes, bars, and staff lines, can be used to teach fractions and proportional math problems.

- Listen to original music inspired by a period text or character from history or fiction to teach lessons in literature or social studies.

- Ask children to identify motifs, choruses, and refrains in songs, or particular instruments in songs or instrumental music. Close listening teaches observational and analytical skills.

- Use period music to introduce historical topics and/or to contrast historical periods. For instance, listen to Baroque music (e.g., pieces by Bach) and discuss how it differs from later Classical music (e.g., works by Mozart).

- Listen to different music from around the world and different regions to teach world history or cultural studies (e.g., djembe or drum music from Africa, or samba pieces from Latin America).

- Identify rhythmic patterns and motifs in other subjects, such as math or science. For example, point out daily, monthly, and annual rhythms in the world around them.

Visual-spatial

Children with visual-spatial abilities are those with an aptitude for visualization and ability to navigate and see objects in their mind's eye. They notice fine visual details and can solve spatial problems involving maps, directions, and forms. Children who demonstrate this type of intelligence are apt to learn and comprehend ideas better when they can *see* an actual depiction of a concept, either in schematics or drawings.

These children are often quite artistic and creative across a variety of subjects. Visual-spatial learners can be serious doodlers and may show an inclination towards drawing from an early age. With its emphasis on artistic creation, "form drawing," beautiful colors, and fine details, Waldorf is a good framework for these types of learners (Chapter 4).

Visual-spatial intelligence isn't limited to the arts, though. These learners also exhibit an interest and aptitude for subjects as varied as architecture, model building, and geometry—any topics that involve visual forms that these learners can manipulate and investigate through drawing, models, and design. Kids with this inclination learn best with diagrams, illustrations, and physical models. For this reason, the Montessori method is also often a good fit with its arsenal of hands-on, movable materials (Chapter 3).

A good rule of thumb on whether Waldorf education or the Montessori method is more appropriate is to decide if your visual-spatial learner is more creative or analytical. The analytical spatial learner will appreciate the clean lines and no-nonsense approach of the Montessori method's materials, while the creative spatial learner will most likely appreciate the free-spirited and expressive nature of the Waldorf environment.

Tips for "Visionaries"

At home, parents can help their visual-spatial learners in many ways. Use rich, descriptive words in lectures or stories that help visual learners create their own mental models and images. Allow for artistic expression in all subjects, providing unfettered access to paper and a variety of writing implements for making visual representations of content. Scrapbooking and journaling provide a nice accent to class work.

Dioramas and model building are also fantastic for visual learners, allowing them to move parts of a story or manipulate relationships to see how certain arrangements or layouts work. More concrete method math programs work well, too, as the manipulatives and physical tools can be arranged to make concrete pictures out of abstract mathematical concepts.

In particular, graphic organizers are lifesavers for parents with visual learners. Graphic organizers, with their worksheets of visual maps for students to fill in, provide a visual record of knowledge that students can collect and show off. Some visual maps are typical flow charts or Venn diagrams, while others are more creatively organized and detailed. Some can even be downright adorable.

My daughter uses two specific graphic organizers when she writes reports: First, she outlines the entire paper as a giant hamburger, with her opening and closing thesis statements as the top and bottom buns, and her topic sentences for each of the three content paragraphs as the lettuce, tomato, and meat patty. Then, for each content paragraph, she uses another type of organizer that's shaped like a giant ice cream cone. Each topic sentence from the hamburger organizer goes in their respective ice cream cones. Atop each cone are the related sentences as the scoops of ice cream. Once her hamburger and ice cream organizers are filled in, she's ready to go to the computer and begin typing. Everything she needs to have a well-organized paper is taken from her organizers, cutely laid out in her burger and ice cream cones.

Our favorite resource for free graphic organizers is Houghton Mifflin Harcourt's Education Place (eduplace.com/graphicorganizer). I print a ton of them and keep them in a pocket storage hanger on the wall in the schoolroom and the kids use them for everything from brainstorming and analogy building, to paper writing.

Here are some other specific suggestions to try at home:

- Encourage budding scientists to keep lab notebooks, which can be filled with sketches of experiments, ideas, and diagrams.

- Motivate aspiring designers to create their own "lapbooks," elaborate books (often created with folded file folders) filled with pictures and smaller mini-books, which encourages students to be creative, while letting them organize academic content in a personalized way.

- Design a large-scale agricultural field and play with different crop arrangements and watering schemes to better understand why fields are laid out the way they are.

- Build simple machines, automata, and toys to teach the relationship among the different, smaller parts.

- Incorporate video-based lectures into your own, such as those found on Khan Academy (khanacademy.org), WatchKnowLearn (watchknowlearn.org), Teacher Tube (teachertube.com), Brain Pop (brainpop.com), and the RSA Animate lecture series (comment.rsablogs.org.uk/videos/) started by the United Kingdom Royal Society for the encouragement of Arts, Manufactures and Commerce.

- Get inspired and challenge your spatial learners to make their own visual lectures using screencast video tools such as Screenr (screenr.com) and GoView (goview.com).

- Build reports in Microsoft PowerPoint or Visio (visio.microsoft.com), or an equivalent visual mapping program, such as Gliffy (gliffy.com), that allows them to create a concrete visual representation of their thinking.

Naturalistic

Children who are considered naturalistically intelligent are those who have a seemingly innate ability to care for plants and animals and are sensitive to the natural environment. Those with green thumbs, whose gardens flourish while the rest of us have puny harvests, are naturalistic, as well as those who can skillfully tame and train wild or unruly animals with apparent ease (think of those people who are identified as "horse whisperers" or "dog whisperers").

While it's doubtful that young children will have grown a garden or tamed a wild horse, you can still identify more subtle clues that point toward them becoming great outdoorsmen. Watch for signs, such as spending ample time outdoors, demonstrating an intense curiosity about the flora and fauna, examining trees, focused bird watching, and catching creepy crawlies for examination and later releasing them or taking them home to be a part of their growing menagerie (imagine frogs or spiders collected in a terrarium, or ant farms). Among the different intelligences discussed, naturalistic is one of the more difficult ones to quantify and measure, but is no less worthy of consideration.

Tips for "Naturalists"

In the homeschool setting, children who are inclined towards the natural will benefit from having natural objects and nature-based stories as a regular part of their school work. Utilize the nature study ideas advocated under Charlotte Mason education (Chapter 6); its emphasis on outdoor learning lends a suitable framework for children with the naturalist aptitude. Science is, of course, the easiest subject to integrate with nature topics, and the possibilities are simply endless, from biology to astronomy.

Naturalists are avid collectors and they often like to categorize objects in their own creative taxonomies. Anxiety about damage to a precious butterfly collection or the loss of a neat river rock can be insurmountable distractions. So, if your naturalist has siblings, reserve the collection for the naturalist only. If you have multiple naturalists at home, be sure they keep separate collections. I can't overstate the attachment naturalists feel to their collections. To these finicky collectors, an item lost can't be easily replaced.

Here are some other specific suggestions to try at home to keep your naturalist content:

- Encourage the keeping of field journals and spend a considerable amount of time exploring the outdoors.
- Sort leaves according to species.
- Make graphs using pine cones, or measure angles formed by leaf veins or tree branches.

- Read books with natural themes, such as books about historical figures in botany and the biological sciences.

- Study history through the eyes of naturalists of the time and teach natural learners about the great discoveries of the natural world through these historical figures (e.g., read about the great anthropologists and archaeologists who unearthed artifacts and documented the cultural traditions of ancient cultures).

- Allow your nature lover to amass extensive collections of natural items (e.g., butterfly collections and ant farms) and find ways to integrate their collections into other areas of study.

- Start a small-scale garden in window planters or in the backyard, and incorporate your small garden into biology lessons. If space is an issue, look up community gardens in your area and sign up for your own plot for growing everything from flowers to herbs.

- Visit botanical gardens, museums, or zoos to provide the natural stimulus that these learners crave. City dwellers can also take longer educational field trips to national parks and recreational sites (better yet, turn family vacations into learning trips).

- Provide proper organizational tools for collections, such as small hardware cabinets, to keep their objects safe and organized.

Using Innate Aptitudes to Teach

To Howard Gardner, the key to making education more meaningful and effective for students was for teachers and parents to identify the areas where each child excelled and where each needed extra help. Gardner believed that any child who had a high level of ability in one or more of those eight areas of intelligence could be more easily taught other subjects as long as the teachers were mindful of the child's natural aptitudes and nurtured them for other studies.

For example, consider a child who's musically inclined and happens to be having difficulty mastering grammar concepts. Using the concept of multiple intelligences, a teacher might find ways to incorporate music into lessons on grammar; perhaps songs about grammar rules might be used. In the same way, a spatially gifted child might be aided by the use of base-ten blocks and other manipulatives when engaging in math problems.

It's important to note that most people have aptitudes in more than one of the eight intelligences. It's rare that you have a person excel only in a single area. We're all multidimensional and varied in our interests and skills. As you read through the descriptions in this chapter, you were probably reminded of people you know that match each one, and you might also have noticed that many can straddle more than one category. In one way or another, we're all a combination of the eight intelligences.

I consider myself to be a combination of logic-math and musical intelligence (however rough-edged my natural music inclinations may be). My three kids, Hannah Jane, Hunter, and Haven, all have their strengths, too. Since all of my kids seem to have a bit of musical intelligence, we use music for just about everything. We memorize poems and prayers by making songs out of them and by singing them in the mornings during circle time. We watch old *School House Rock* episodes on YouTube when we step into a new grammar concept. Every time I go to the teacher supply store, I keep my eyes open for CDs that present concepts using music. For example, at the moment my three kids are all learning the states and capitols through song with a CD of music that I discovered. We recently made a deal: When they could all fill in a blank map with the correct labels, we would go out for ice cream. Music has made this mundane task of memorization accessible for my kids, regardless of their age.

My middle guy, Hunter, is a serious bodily kinesthetic learner. His body is built for action, so any time I can add an element of movement to a lesson, I will. For example, we sit in a circle, crisscross-applesauce (what teachers used to call sitting "Indian style"), with our knees touching. We pass beanbags around the circle rhythmically as we skip count aloud. This activity appeals to everyone's musical sense, and gives Hunter a chance to move while we work. We also make up games where we shoot baskets or race to stand on certain spots to answer questions. All of this helps Hunter get through the day.

Still, each morning, my children are all asked to do a bit of traditional desk work, usually consisting of them working on a mom-made sheet with about six varying math problems, a few nouns to make plural, a sentence to diagram, and one bit of copy work from the board. Hunter is always moody during this time and the last to finish. But I think it's important that he also learn to be comfortable with spending some time each day working outside his optimal comfort zone.

My daughter, Hannah Jane, is one of those lucky kids who's smart in multiple areas and finds it easy to learn with just about every instructional method except rote memorization. When facing a mess of lines on a page, she can easily set up equations and calculate the angles of each intersection based upon a given angle measure, but she can't tell you what four times four is without skip counting (because of her distaste for memorization). She's a thinker, a nature lover, an avid reader, and quite the flute and piano player. She dabbles in everything and is quick to engage strangers in discussions about the Donner party or the latest atrocities against Muslim minorities living in China. Because she's so multifaceted, I don't have to spend too much time catering to her needs, because she'll easily adapt to whatever activity I've designed to meet the more specific needs of her brothers, or she'll simply go off and create her own lessons and tell me what she's learned when she's done.

Haven, my youngest, just at the kindergarten age, is clearly an interpersonal guy. He stops frequently during every lesson to update me on his progress, to get a high five, or to seek out a compliment. We'll indulge him in a lot of discussion. To give him a chance to show off his knowledge and talk, Hannah Jane often lets him feel as if he's teaching her something new. He's a talker and a charmer and will happily learn whatever he needs to if he knows that he'll get to tell someone about it later. For particularly daunting lessons, I've motivated him to participate simply by promising to let him call his grandma when he's done and tell her what he's learned. Setting up share time as a reward for tasks accomplished works wonders for my interpersonal child. The only challenge is having enough people in our inner circle that he doesn't wear them all out!

So many of our group lessons are designed to appeal to multiple intelligences. Take our science lessons: During one lesson, I'll have them up and about, acting out the states of matter, which helps Hunter feel more engaged. I'll also videotape the lesson and e-mail it to Grandma, so that Haven will have something to talk about over the phone later. We'll debate the merits of work before play, and then let the kids use dolls to act out what would happen in different scenarios. We may then make up a little song about the importance of getting work done first, which appeals to all of them.

Debunking Criticism of Multiple Intelligences

While Howard Gardner's theory may at first seem harmless and delightful, there are those who fear the practical consequences of embracing multiple intelligences. These concerns center on the idea that it could be used in defense of lowered efforts in teaching. If a teacher or parent were to look at Lucy, who isn't a very strong reader, and say, "Well, she's smart in other ways," and therefore never work intensely on improving her reading skills, then Gardner's ideas have enabled another child to fall through the cracks.

But consider another scenario: If that same teacher or parent looks at Lucy and says, "Lucy is clearly very bodily-kinesthetic smart, so there must be some way to address her reading difficulties in a way that appeals to her unique intelligence," then Gardner's ideas will have helped Lucy's instructors cater to her unique needs.

The criticism from some seems more rooted in a fear of the misuse of the theory than a problem with the theory itself. A discerning practitioner can use Gardner's ideas to cater to the individual needs of the child, while a careless one could manipulate its intentions and use the theory as an explanation for why their teaching methods have failed.

Other critics of Gardner's theory also ask: Is this anything more than putting a fancy title like "multiple intelligences" on the age-old practice of appealing to a child's interest to teach a variety of subjects? Gardner supporters would say, yes, that it is a fundamental difference in the way we measure and value intelligence. Intelligence is, by the new definition, more multifaceted than we previously understood.

I've even heard a few people rant about how unscientific Gardner's theories are, and how it remains unsubstantiated by evidence. To these critics, I'd point to the criteria by which something may or may not qualify as an intelligence. Gardner didn't simply pick random, feel-good areas and call them intelligences. The criteria for what constitutes an intelligence included the potential for loss by brain damage, the existence of savants with the specific exceptional capacity, evolutionary plausibility, and susceptibility to encoding in a symbol system, among other things. In fact, the criteria used shows that the theory is more than a fanciful idea devoid of critical thought.[3]

Each Child is a "Blend"

As you begin to understand your child's natural abilities and see beyond conventional definitions of intelligence, you can see how varied each of your children's strengths are. For example, an interpersonal learner may also excel at linguistics, using language as a means by which to connect to other individuals, and may grow up to be a journalist or diplomat. Or, your logical-mathematical child may also be a visual-spatial learner, showing an aptitude for visual analytical skills and problem solving that could be refined into a career as an engineer. The combinations are endless and can be measured on a sliding scale.

The best way I can describe how we all have different types of intelligences is to imagine a music studio filled with different recording equipment. On the control panel are rows of knobs and sliders that are all set at different levels to achieve the perfect blend of sound. A child is much like the final track. One child may have his bodily kinesthetic knob turned way up, his linguistic knob set somewhere in the middle, and his interpersonal knob turned way down. Another child can be a totally different "blend" of smarts.

Regardless of the combinations, each child is a person with unique capacities destined for greatness in some way. By ridding ourselves of those rigid notions that only math and language oriented students can succeed, we can create new learning environments for our children where every child can experience success and find his or her niche in the world. Embracing our children's unique "blend" of intelligences is one of the most nurturing things we can do as homeschoolers.

> We can create new learning environments for our children where every child can experience success and find his or her niche in the world. Embracing our children's unique "blend" of intelligences is one of the most nurturing things we can do as homeschoolers.

Learning Styles: Absorbing Information in Three Different Ways

The simple differences in how we absorb information shouldn't be glossed over. If your children simply can't retain much of what they read but can recall every detail from a lecture, it would be a mistake to have only textbook-based school days. It's the same scenario for children who like to work with their hands and are stuck listening passively to lectures all day. Understanding your children's learning styles—how they learn best—and working with those preferences as you teach will enhance their chance of success.

There are three universally accepted types of learners:

- Visual learners learn best by seeing.
- Auditory learners learn best by hearing.
- Tactile learners learn best by doing.

Most students can tell you what works for them, but some may need some coaxing and experimentation from you to draw out what their learning styles are. Let's take an example from biology: cell division. How would each type of learner best absorb information about cell division? A visual learner will gravitate toward finely detailed pictures of cells in the process of dividing either presented in snapshots or on film. An auditory learner will learn best hearing a detailed lecture about the process. A tactile learner is more adept at mastering the information when playing with models that mimic the cellular process, creating their own artistic rendition of the cell at different stages, or perhaps working with a microscope.

How are learning styles different from the multiple intelligences we discussed earlier in the chapter?

The theory of multiple intelligences looks specifically at how people relate to the world around them and what information and topics they respond to best. In contrast, learning styles consider how individuals best absorb and retain information. For example, a child who shows a high degree of logical-mathematical intelligence and quickly grasps abstract arguments may have an auditory learning style, meaning they are more likely to retain math concepts they hear rather than read on paper. A child with the same aptitude but with a visual learning style will respond better to diagrams and models sketched out on the board or on paper, rather than to lectures. By coupling an understanding of your children's natural intelligence with their learning style, you can further fine-tune your teaching.

Assessing Your Child's Learning Style

As we've discussed, before you can personalize your lessons to your individual children, you must assess which style best suits them. Visual learners need to see things in order to fully synthesize the information. Auditory learners tend to recall exact phrases or concepts that they've heard, sometimes in the same voice and phrasing. And finally, for tactile learners, doing and touching is key.

You may already have a good idea about which style your child prefers. If not, try a few things that will help you assess your child's style. There is ample evidence that learning styles and testing styles are generally consistent for an individual, meaning that a visual learner, for example, will also test better in a visual format, but may have difficulty taking a verbal test where the administrator asks the questions verbally. Some very progressive schools will allow students to take alternative tests that are given in a format that matches their learning style. These schools recognize that the standard paper-based test may not work for everyone and that all learners should have a chance to show an account of their knowledge.

Here's one way to assess your children's learning style using a gentle "testing" method:

1. Come up with a diverse list of questions that you're fairly certain that your children could answer with ease. Divvy up your list into three separate lists, randomly putting an equal number of questions on each one.

2. Take the first group of questions and verbally ask for the answer. Discreetly make a note of how long it takes to get satisfactory answers and with what degree of ease they provide them.

3. Ask your second group of questions in writing. If your children aren't proficient readers or writers yet, draw some simple pictures to demonstrate the questions and explain them. Then, have the solutions drawn and the drawings explained to you. Again, make note of how easily the questions are answered.

4. Finally, for your third group of questions, go outside and play a game of basketball or baseball, and casually ask the questions while engaged in the movement of the game.

5. After you've completed the three different assessments, try to evaluate how your children performed on each type of test: Were they more comfortable answering questions on paper? Did they respond better to questions you asked out loud? Or, were they more inclined when active in the backyard, running from base to base or making three-point shots?

Hopefully, your children will demonstrate which style of questioning they respond to best, and it won't require a great degree of calculation or guessing on your part. If you're still unsure, try emphasizing a different teaching style with different topics and content each week for about a month, closely observing your children's behavior, responsiveness, and attitudes during lessons. Under what teaching modes do they struggle or shine? Also, talk with your children about which week felt like a more positive learning week for them. Once you have an idea of what your children need, adapt lessons to meet those needs.

Adapting Lessons

Knowing how to adapt a simple lesson in order to make it more memorable and accessible for your children is critical.

Lessons for Visual Learners

There are several things you can do help make every subject come alive for visual learners:

- Provide highlighters for passages of reading to add a more direct visual element to what can easily blur into an ocean of words.

- Provide pictures, graphs, and charts as often as possible to reiterate information that you've already covered.

- Encourage the use of tools like brainstorming bubbles and graphic organizers to organize thoughts on paper. Use blank, outline style pages that you can find with most graphic organizers sold over the Web. (These are your best friends if you have a visual learner at home!)

- Encourage journal keeping for drawing and doodling everything from science ideas to illustrations of math problems.

- Incorporate manipulatives into math work for better ways to visualize different outcomes and combinations.

Lessons for Auditory Learners

If you've determined that you have an auditory learner on your hands, there is a lot you can do to make learning more meaningful:

- Balance lectures and reading work with discussion activities.
- Find a local group of homeschoolers and create larger discussion groups where the children can take turns presenting on different subjects.
- Use analogies to link ideas to more easily understood topics (e.g., fractions are like different lengths of a musical beat).
- Compose songs to help remember long lists of items or sets of steps.
- Set passages for memorization to a familiar tune.
- Play online lectures (such as those listed on Open Culture), podcasts (NPR podcasts offer a great variety), and video tutorials (try Khan Academy) in the classroom to supplement your lessons.[4] In general, the Web is a treasure trove of information for auditory learners, who no doubt press the mental replay button when accessing their memory banks.
- Read books out loud or play audiobooks during the school day. These days, many libraries have digitized some of their audiobook collections. Ask your librarian if your library has bought into a state digital library system. If so, you may be able to go online and download audiobooks for free. When the audiobooks are due, they simply disappear from your computer. This is handy for busy parents who might feel frantic over library late fees.
- Reiterate material during discussions and lessons. My husband uses this rule when giving talks and lectures: "First, I tell them what I'm going to tell them, then I tell them, and then I tell them what I told them." Homeschoolers can translate this three-part delivery structure to opening a lesson with a look ahead, teaching the lesson, and then closing the lesson with a look back. For auditory learners, this offers three distinct points of reference within a lesson and helps them recall information better.

A caveat: Because we're predominantly a print-based culture, especially in institutional educational settings where book learning is emphasized, I encourage parents to be mindful of how much you indulge auditory-only teaching. Always be aware of the need to develop other capacities, especially those that need more TLC.

Use a balanced approach: When you encounter something that your children have extreme difficulty with, focus on techniques that accent their natural learning style. But in subjects they find easy to grasp, present the material in other styles. The goal is to offer opportunities for your children to get out of their comfort zones. If your child is a natural auditory learner, try teaching using visual techniques. The bias toward print can make learning difficult for those auditory learners who haven't spent time developing their other latent capacities.

When you encounter something that your children have extreme difficulty with, focus on techniques that accent their natural learning style. But in subjects they find easy to grasp, present the material in other styles.

Lessons for Tactile Learners

Children demonstrate they are tactile learners in two ways: They may simply process the visual and auditory input systems with greater efficiency when they are in motion. Or, they may learn better when information is delivered through movement and physical manipulation. Many tactile or kinesthetic learners share these two styles or may exhibit characteristics of the first type coupled with a highly auditory or visual style.

To harness the power of physical movement, try these activities:

- Introduce information while your children are moving around and being active.
- Use manipulatives and models for math, as they can move materials around to visualize and understand concepts.
- Supplement science reading and discussion with hands-on experiments or model building.

- Use non-traditional testing methods that allow your students to convey what they know while being up and around.

- Take frequent "recess" or physical activity breaks between lessons to work off any excess energy and restlessness.

Enhancing Learning Through Movement

The impact of movement and physical activity on learning outcomes appears promising. In 2007, Canadian teacher Allison Cameron started a "Movement Matters" program at her school, putting exercise bikes and treadmills in high school classrooms.[5] For her language arts classes, she split up the 40-minute class period into two distinct sessions: half exercise and half regular teaching where students sat at their desks as usual. She did this three days a week. The results were staggering. Not only did physical fitness improve, but test scores increased. Another eighth grade class patterned after the Movement Matters program saw its writing test scores improve by 245 percent over the school year.

In 2009, professors at the University of Illinois launched studies that found significant academic benefits from physical education classes, recess periods, and after-school exercise programs.[6] Physical activity increased students' cognitive control and led to better performance results. The general recommendations from researchers included: "scheduling outdoor recess as a part of each school day; offering formal physical education 150 minutes per week at the elementary level, 225 minutes at the secondary level; and encouraging teachers to integrate physical activity into learning."[7]

Multiple studies have also found significant benefits from incorporating physical activity in learning environments for those diagnosed with Attention Deficit Disorder (ADD) or Attention Deficit Hyperactivity Disorder (ADHD). Mark Rapport of the University of Central Florida (UCF) in Orlando discussed some of the potential benefits in a paper published in the *Journal of Abnormal Child Psychology*. He found that movement, specifically fidgeting, which has traditionally been viewed by educators as something that signals distraction, is actually used by students with ADD and ADHD as a way to focus.[8] Stimulants such as caffeine or Ritalin can assist students in sitting still and focusing, but the focus can happen without these stimulants if students are permitted to move and be active during learning.

Researchers have also debated whether some symptoms of ADD or ADHD may actually be innate personality traits. "Our activity level—how much we move around in everyday situations—is one of the most fixed parts of our personalities. If you are a fidgety kid, you will be a fidgety adult, even if you learn to manage your movements with caffeine, stress-reduction, a personal trainer or other adult accouterments."[9]

This suggests that suppressing what's a natural part of our personality in the learning environment could actually do more harm than good. In the case of students diagnosed with ADD or ADHD, some measures to control outbursts of movement may actually distract them from focusing on content.

What these studies and many others have shown is that movement and exercise can be extremely beneficial for *all students*, enhancing learning and performance in the classroom. Educators are catching on, and many schools and institutions are exploring ways to bring more action to the classroom. In "structured learning centers" (SLCs), which are school areas designed for students who need more structured environments, you might find classrooms with students sitting on oversized workout balls behind desks, instead of the usual chairs. Students bounce on their chair balls, and get a chance to work off extra energy.

When I worked in an SLC in Oregon, I took selected students for motor breaks every few hours in the gym. The students rode adaptive bikes, ran laps, and generally shook out all of their bonus energy while we discussed what we'd been learning. Standard classroom students never got these breaks, but I often wondered how many other students in mainstream classrooms could have benefited from regular breaks to be physically active.

IT CAN BE a particular challenge for homeschoolers to make every subject easily accessible for particular learning styles. But there are numerous examples within the five educational frameworks we discussed in Chapters 3-7 that you can look to for inspiration.

To encourage your kinesthetic children, try Waldorf education's emphasis on "joyful movement" (Chapter 4) as inspiration and "act out" the imagery and ideas they encounter in poetry or literature. When teaching math, employ the Montessori method's ideas (Chapter 3) about hand and body connections through number blocks that can be touched and manipulated.

If you have visual learners, a history lesson might go down easier with a trip to the museum to see historical and period pieces, from fine art and furniture, to costume design and the decorative arts. Charlotte Mason education's emphasis on field journals (Chapter 6) will encourage your visual learners to sketch and draw, and provide a wonderful tool for science subjects. When looking at math or science books, be sure to find texts with colorful graphics and models.

Auditory learners will understand math problems that are read aloud and respond better to "hearing" literature as opposed to reading it; audiobooks are priceless in this regard. Utilize the narration techniques in Charlotte Mason education to get your auditory learners to recount material they've learned in a presentation or in conversation, or follow the

Trivium framework (Chapter 5) that emphasizes rhetoric and formal discourse between students and teachers.

With practice, research, and creativity, you can adapt materials and invent activities across different subjects that your young learners—no matter their learning style or intelligence(s) or aptitude(s)—will enthusiastically respond to.

TEN:
Personality and Learning

WE all know children have different personalities; this affects how they learn. Some children are naturally inclined to sit still and can focus on lectures and other sedentary tasks, while others make you suspect a switch at birth with the Energizer Bunny and are easily distracted. Some students are naturally shy in front of a group and cringe at the thought of group activities, while others have no fear in front of audiences and thrive in performance-driven exercises.

Whether personality differences are a product of genetics or parenting style, we can safely assume that all children have natural personality quirks and will respond differently to the learning environment we create at home.

Humorism: From Ancient Theory to Classroom Guide

Just as intelligence can be multifaceted, personality in our children can also vary and shine in different ways. The theory of "humorism" or "the four temperaments," a kind of proto-psychology far older than the theory of multiple intelligences we discussed in Chapter 9, has recently gained attention as a useful gauge to help educators and parents assess how to structure learning environments for children.

The four humors are:

- Sanguine

- Choleric
- Melancholic
- Phlegmatic

Humorism is said to have originated as far back as ancient Mesopotamia. Most notably, the Greek physician Hippocrates explored the idea and applied it to his work in medicine and medical theory.[1] To the ancient Greeks and others, humorism related moods and temperaments to imbalances in different fluids or "humors" in the body.

While this early explanation for differing temperaments is now viewed as a bit crude, it's important to recognize that humorism laid the critical foundations for scientific thinkers examining personality from a biological standpoint. Humorism is often considered the ancient predecessor to modern-day research on brain chemistry, hormonal imbalances, and personality disorders. Humorism also served as the foundation for personality tests, such as the Keirsey Temperament Sorter and Meyers-Briggs test, that many of us took during our K-12 years.

While the study of the four temperaments has declined in popularity among psychologists, and perhaps rightly so, in the halls of teacher education and in textbooks read by preprofessional teachers, the basics of humorism are very much still in use. In the teaching context, teachers use humorism to quickly assess a child's temperament in order to plan activities and structure classroom activities in ways that circumvent routine discipline issues. More than a tool for content delivery, knowledge of humorism helps teachers manage the moods of their students and the tone of the learning environment.

> In the teaching context, teachers use humorism to quickly assess a child's temperament in order to plan activities and structure classroom activities in ways that circumvent routine discipline issues.

Rudolph Steiner, founder of the Waldorf educational framework (see Chapter 4), taught educators to explicitly address these four temperament classifications. However, I want to make clear the distinction between the four temperaments as used by Steiner and Waldorf-inspired education, and how I'll address them here in this chapter. Steiner went further and added features, such as body type, choice in clothing styles, and skin coloration as telling characteristics of each temperament. Those additional traits aren't generally considered in more modern views on temperaments and are more of a throwback to the origins of humorism when things like skin tone were considered an outward indicator of a fluid or bile imbalance. Steiner also followed in the footsteps of Nicholas Culpeper, a 17th century English herbalist and astrologist, and connected astrological signs to the temperaments, which understandably makes many academics uncomfortable.

In this chapter, we'll look at the four humors in a more practical light, as a rough guide to figuring out the psychological needs of your children. Despite being rather simplistic, the four humors provide parents insights into the different personality types and their behavioral dynamics. Once you have a better picture of your children's general temperaments, you'll be more confident to adapt the learning environment accordingly.

Figuring Out Your Child's Personality Type Using Humorism

When assessing your children's temperament, consider their response to everyday situations and get a feel for their habits and moods. Individuals don't necessarily have to fall neatly into any of the four humor categories, but reviewing them here will give you an idea of the different behaviors that you might encounter.

Sanguine

Sanguine children are often the stars of the show, thriving on attention and social situations. Light-hearted and quick to please, sanguine types are often very generous and forgiving, and make those around them feel comfortable and happy. While all of these qualities may appear as positive traits, sanguine children often have trouble staying focused and following through with tasks. As easily as they develop an interest and throw themselves into a task, they drop it by the wayside in favor of the next big thing. Watch out, though: Many young children get mistakenly labeled as sanguine when they might actually have a different personality profile. If your preschooler sings to the checkout lady at the store and then comes home and can't finish a block tower before he's off to race his toy cars, don't automatically assume he's a sanguine child. Many young children show big, flashing signs of being sanguine on the surface, but parents should practice caution until they consider the totality of their child's behavior over the course of time.

Choleric

Choleric individuals are viewed as self-motivated, go-getters, quick to get moving and latch on to a task to finish it. Their remarkable focus also makes them great leaders as they're able to see tasks through to the end, delegating and micromanaging to mobilize and motivate those around them. They rarely lack energy or enthusiasm. On the downside, choleric types with their strong personalities can often inadvertently dominate others. This "bossy" demeanor on the playground or in the classroom can be counterproductive to their social lives and can leave others feeling pushed around and resentful.

Melancholic

Melancholic children are often thoughtful and introspective. Children with this personality have a great propensity for creative work. They're also perfectionists, and as a result, sometimes never feel satisfied with their own work or creations. Melancholic children tend to show great empathy toward others, and their sensitivity can sometimes make them feel overwhelmed by strong emotions. They can fixate on the "dark side" too much, regarding lighter topics or subjects as frivolous.

Phlegmatic

Phlegmatic children tend to be very shy despite their inner reserves of self-confidence. These children are generally relaxed and kind, garnering many close friends, not because they're overly social, but because they're reliable and compassionate. Phlegmatic children, as a result of their shyness around new people and in unfamiliar situations, may appear to be stubborn, resistant to change, or even lazy, but only to those who haven't taken the time to look at them beyond the surface.

Working with Your Child's Temperament at Home

Once you've made a broad assessment of temperament among your children, you can begin to play on their strengths and weaknesses through your daily school routine. Let's examine a few ways that you can take into account temperament and adjust your children's studies accordingly.

I'd like for you to meet Suzie, Max, Alex, and Sarah:

Working with a sanguine child: Let's consider Suzie, who can be characterized as a sanguine child. She loves to chatter and prattle on. She's also known to break out into song and can enchant strangers as she strolls through the grocery store. She has a lot of friends and spends much of her day asking when she can go play with them.

Suzie loves to learn new things, but she often lacks focus and self-discipline. For a moment or two, she'll listen to you tell her about how a seed sprouts; a few minutes later, she interrupts you and wants to know about the sunshine that you mentioned and where it comes from. You decide that you'll follow her bliss, so you start explaining the characteristics of the sun and its position in our solar system. Before you can finish even a few sentences, though, she has wondered off to play with her dolls. How can you possibly teach her?

As Suzie's parent, you can learn to capitalize on her shorter bursts of interest by setting up learning stations where she can touch briefly on different topics. In the early years, this brief, touch-and-go style of learning can suffice, and as Suzie matures, one of two things will happen: Either Suzie's attention span gently increases and she slowly begins to transition into longer periods of focused work, or she remains easily sidetracked. If it's the latter, you'll have to modify the way you teach in order to help her stay focused and master complex material. Modify your existing learning stations into a condensed form of "spiraling" curriculum (first mentioned as part of the Trivium method discussed in Chapter 5).

In this spiraling set-up, Suzie spends 10 minutes on a math sheet. Then, she gets up and moves to the spelling station where she memorizes spelling words for another 10 minutes. Next, she moves on to the final learning station for a science lesson. The next day, Suzie spirals back through the same learning stations in the same order. First, she visits the math station and wraps up any loose ends with her math sheet. Then, she moves on to spelling. Finally, Suzie heads back to her science program at the last learning station. For each successive visit, the material advances and becomes more complex.

This format may help your young sanguine learner like Suzie stay focused. By spiraling Suzie's day through repeated rounds of the same set of subjects, you're working with her temperament to better teach her. This is just one of the many ways that a creative parent can use her knowledge of her child's temperament to expand learning potential.

The Duration and Frequency of Learning Sessions and its Impact on Knowledge Retention and Memory

How do bite-size sessions affect learning? Many parents worry that short bursts of teaching may result in scattershot knowledge retention. Researchers, however, have found that breaking long stretches of learning into shorter sessions may actually increase knowledge retention for some students.

Studies on memory show that people are most likely to recall first and last items on a list. In the classroom, students often remember the first and last spelling words that they've learned, or the initial and final math facts that they've studied. Not only do we have better recall of these bookend points, but we also have greater trust in the first and last things we read or hear. This phenomenon has come to be called the "serial position effect" and has been explored in numerous studies in psychology.[2]

With the scope of research conducted in this area, it's hard to ignore the evidence: Short bursts of learning can encourage memory retention. Students are more likely to retain informational tidbits that are introduced to them in a steady progression than as sizeable, one-time chunks. But even if short bursts are helpful, how many times should information be repeated? If you're doing a science lesson, for example, how many times should you revisit the states of matter before moving on?

Hermann Ebbinghaus, the man who coined the term "serial position effect" and a research pioneer in memory and learning, has explored this question in his book, *Memory: A Contribution to Experimental Psychology*. From a battery of self-studies exploring repetition and recall, he found that "[r]elatively long series of ideas are retained better than relatively short ones."[3] Ebbinghaus went on to find that essentially more repetitions meant better memory retention though only after a certain threshold. He writes: "When the series were repeated eight or sixteen times they had become unfamiliar to me by the next day... But with fifty-three or sixty-four repetitions I soon, if not immediately, treated them as old acquaintances... I remembered them distinctly."[4]

Obviously, students would never have enough hours in a day to come back to the same content 53 times, nor would anyone want them to. So, what does this mean for you as a homeschooler?

Experiment and see what works. If you see an increase in knowledge retention— fantastic. If you don't see a bump in retention, but your relationship with your child has improved because he or she feels comfortable in this spiraling format, that's great, too. However, if you find that with short bursts, your child isn't getting the prolonged exposure that he or she needs to learn and progress, you may want to try alternatives. Go back and re-consider an instructional approach like Waldorf education that encourages longer learning blocks (Chapter 4).

Working with a phlegmatic child: Now, let's consider Max. As a phlegmatic child, Max prefers to work independently and is shy and tentative about trying new things. While he's generally a good worker, once he's mastered a topic, he resists moving on to more advanced material because he doesn't like relinquishing the feeling of mastery. He often feels anxious with new material and abhors the possibility of failure. For this reason, you feel stuck. In an effort to avoid any trauma or confrontation, you've allowed Max to stay at a lower grade level of content, despite his obvious intelligence or aptitude. You hope to develop a systematic plan that will protect his feelings and dignity while helping him realize the value of challenging himself. What can you do to help Max move out of his comfort zone?

Start by sitting down with Max and having him make a list of what he likes and doesn't like about his school work. This isn't the time to be vague. Let's say that Max insists he likes math worksheets. Encourage him to think about why he likes worksheets by asking: "What is it that you like about the worksheets?" or "How do you feel about yourself when you are doing your worksheets?"

With any luck Max will reply with something along the lines of, "I like how fast I can do them," or, "I feel good because I almost never get anything wrong!" You know, of course, that he always gets high or perfect scores because he's stuck on worksheets that are too easy for him. Still, you want to take into account his feelings.

To spur Max out of his comfort zone, devise an incentive plan to help him learn new math facts. Start by proposing, "I wonder how long it would take for you to memorize the next set of facts. A year, you think?"

Max may feel a little insulted and challenge you by saying, "Are you kidding? A year? No way! I could do it in less than a year for sure. Maybe a month."

To which you might reply, "Let's see. Here's the new set of flashcards. If you can really learn them all in one month, I say we celebrate with a family game night!"

So, Max sets his own timeline for progress, and the usual anxiety he feels about approaching new skills is significantly diminished. How did this happen? By shifting his focus away from a fear of failure to specific goals that Max can work towards. With goals in mind—goals Max sets himself—there's no outward risk of failure. If he doesn't meet his original goal, he revises his timeline with a new goal. In addition, you can make sure you set him up for success by giving him content that he can easily master in even less time, say two weeks, rather than the month he gave himself.

As you slyly go through this sort of plan for different subjects, Max builds up his self-confidence and works through his fear of failure. Will he cease to be a phlegmatic child and suddenly be rocked with confident enthusiasm for every subject? Probably not. Remember, you're not there to radically reconfigure his personality, but to work with his innate disposition to help him better face challenges with confidence. Through your staunch support, he'll hopefully gain quiet self-assurance and be less likely to stagnate in his work and hold himself back.

Working with a choleric child: Alex is a take-charge kind of fellow who knows what he likes and expects everyone else to agree with his tastes, too. He's not fond of being told what to do, and this makes school time a bit difficult. He's prone to highly emotional outbursts, especially during instructional periods. As Alex's parent, you can feel overwhelmed, perhaps even held hostage by his mood swings and temper tantrums. How are you ever going to teach him when every time you sit down for a lesson, he crosses his arms and refuses to participate, eventually screaming and storming out of the room?

While the choleric child certainly isn't the easiest to deal with, you have some options. First, accept that his temperament is what it is. His young age is also going to exacerbate the downsides a little more. As he gets older and with proper training, his moodiness may become less severe, and he'll gain better self-control. It's clear that his emotional flare-ups happen when Alex feels a lack of control. To mitigate this, find ways to structure the day so that Alex feels like he's coming up with his own plan. Rather than telling Alex that it's time to do his math, for example, offer him a choice. "Would you like to do reading next or math?"

Create a checklist of things that need to be done over the course of the school day and allow Alex to complete those tasks in any particular order he chooses. This gives Alex the sense of ownership to decide his own class time and ensures he gets things done. The odds are good that with a checklist to choose from, Alex will eventually tire of the choice and just check things off in the order that they appear. It's the sense of having a choice that you're aiming for here. But make sure that you don't offer any choices that you, as the parent, can't live with. Alex is great at calling your bluff.

In subjects that are less linear, such as science, let Alex decide what he most wants to study next. Does it really matter that space and astronomy came next in the textbook if Alex really wants to learn about ecosystems first? Alex will feel reassured when he's given some flexibility on the sequence of topics to be learned. By granting him some independence during school time, you won't trigger his rebellious side. Eventually, once he trusts that you give him choices when you can, Alex will likely be more understanding when situations arise where he has limited or no choices.

Even with every effort to grant free rein to Alex's bold personality, you may find that his emotions still flare up from time to time. Don't panic. He may swing between intensely happy and intensely disappointed with a fair degree of frequency. One of the best things to do is to resist the urge to clamp down. If Alex needs to rage a little, take him to an area where he can rant and wear himself out without disrupting the rest of the family. When he's done, happily welcome him back to the group. Don't hold a grudge, even for a while. Your unconditional support and acceptance of his personality are of utmost importance.

Sometimes, you'll need to have a brief talk about his reactions and behavior, but recognize that spending too much time in disciplinary mode can backfire with cholerics like Alex. More likely, you'll be spending the day feeling angry instead of helping Alex settle down and move on with his work. Staying calm and moving on as quickly as possible can have a more positive impact on his behavior and resolve disciplinary problems sooner.

Alex's bold personality makes him a great leader, so it's important to spend time on character building and positive leadership skills. Bullies are thought by some to be choleric children who've been allowed to run rampant with their strong personalities. Among peers, it's easy for such strong-willed and dominant personalities to come across as brash and mean. With a focus on positive leadership and virtuous behavior, and by using a firm but nurturing hand, you can teach Alex to be an empathetic leader who's admired and not feared by other children.

One last thing that may help Alex: Choleric children tend to respond better to tasks with a clear end. Tasks that are vague with no clear goals will quickly frustrate and prompt outbursts, while tasks that are concise and doable should be less problematic. For instance, telling Alex, "Go organize your room," will set his head spinning. In contrast, saying,

"Please take out the trash and put a new bag in the can" will generally be met with action. Try breaking down larger tasks into smaller ones and only give specific instructions. You'll keep Alex from feeling overwhelmed.

Working with a melancholic child: Sarah worries you. She's always so serious, and you wonder if she ever has any fun at all. Sarah quickly does chores and school work when asked, which you appreciate. You also wish she found more joy in her everyday activities. Even her hobbies, which she says she enjoys, are serious endeavors. She enjoys writing poetry, but the subject matter is often on the morbid side for someone of her age. She's a good listener and she takes her friends' problems seriously, but while her friends quickly get over their problems, she dwells on hers for days.

To balance Sarah's melancholic intensity, find ways to encourage her to lighten and brighten her daily experiences. It takes diligent effort to genuinely accept her mode of self-expression, while at the same time exposing her to the joys of life, without devaluing her intense feelings.

In school, she'll do the absolute best work, but her perfectionism makes her feel like a failure no matter how much gratitude and praise heaped on her. Sometimes you wonder why you bother doling out recognition since her reaction is so lukewarm. But you know it's absolutely essential to continue acknowledging her accomplishments; Sarah is even harder on herself when no one acknowledges her efforts. How do you create a learning environment for a melancholic child like Sarah?

Make an effort to alternate intense subject matter with lighter, more uplifting topics. Allow Sarah to study the morbid stuff she likes, but balance it with spending time on lighter material. For example, if you're doing a lesson on the Titanic, Sarah may fixate on the tragic loss of lives and undoubtedly want to write volumes on it, or write poetry about the unfulfilled potential of the young victims who never had the chance to grow up. Maybe she'll focus on the economic disparities among the passengers and the unjust class system of the time.

Unlike other students, Sarah won't need any guidance to consider the deeper meaning of tragic events like the Titanic. What you'll have to guide her towards are the other facets of historical events. Maybe a look at the individual acts of heroism on board the ship, the happy activities that took place before the ship sank, and the exciting lives of the lucky survivors. Balance the dark stuff with more joyous experiences.

As a student and member of the family, Sarah is about the easiest child you could ask for. It's her intensity that can be challenging. Highly emotional and sensitive, her feelings and ego are easily bruised, and she doesn't readily forgive. Her response to the slightest of injuries can seem vastly out of proportion. As Sarah enters adolescence, her friendships will become as intense as her self-expression. She'll be deeply hurt by small offenses from friends and family members.

Resist the natural inclination to leave her alone to deal with her intense feelings. While Sarah will do everything in her power to make you believe that she doesn't want your advice, she'll want to tell you about all of the horrible things her friends or siblings did. Be a patient listener. Sarah may seem aloof and disinterested in your advice, but she deeply appreciates the chance to share her feelings. Try not to judge or interrupt when she pours out her emotions and lists her grievances. What you can do is provide the reality checks. For example, dissect overwhelming social interactions and help Sarah find perspective about perceived slights.

Give your melancholic child like Sarah solitary activities that allow her to be alone with her thoughts, while also providing opportunities to be productive and helpful. Practice caution, though: Many families make the mistake of heaping responsibilities on melancholic children because they seem so responsible. It's easy to give Sarah more school work and chores simply because she does them willingly, while you inadvertently give her brother fewer tasks because he always complains about them. Parents should also watch out for the "black sheep" syndrome, inadvertently singling her out for being sullen compared to her sunnier siblings or peers. This may lead to feelings of resentment and push her to be more antisocial and aloof around others.

If you remain lovingly available to Sarah as a mentor and appreciative audience for her sometimes fringe interests, she'll learn, through those interactions, to open up to others and come out of her shell.

Temperaments Aren't Fixed

It's important to keep in mind that there are no absolutes when it comes to temperaments. Rarely do children exhibit signs as clearly as the characters of Suzie, Max, Alex, and Sarah. No one individual is a singularly "pure" personality type. Some people can even be shades of all four temperaments, even if one or two types dominate.

We can also grow and change depending on our environment and the people around us. Parents often make the mistake of pigeonholing their children early on. One parent might think, "Oh, Anna is just shy; we shouldn't push her to make presentations in front of her siblings." Snap judgments and entrenched ideas about personality can have devastating impacts on child-parent relationships.

Suppose a child showed a cranky demeanor as a toddler. The parents quickly decided their child was just innately bad-tempered. Then, as the child matured, she grew up to be a ray of sunshine on earth—liked by her peers, often described as someone with an upbeat disposition by other adults. Because of built-in expectations at home, the child gets conflicting signals from her family.

> Remember that children may change as they mature. As parents, we shouldn't be too quick to judge our kids based on personality quirks we see up front, and we should learn to adjust and adapt to them as their personalities develop and change.

It's hard to feel like sunshine around people, especially family members, who cling to a particular view of you. The parents might make comments to appease their daughter's moods; if the child shows a grumpy side, the parents overreact.

Remember that children may change as they mature. They could outgrow their quiet demeanors and become more outgoing and forceful, or the opposite. As parents, we shouldn't be too quick to judge our kids based on the personality quirks we see up front; rather, we should learn to adjust and adapt to our kids as their personalities develop and change. Use the humors system to help you accommodate your children in the present. Rather than labeling your child as inherently one personality type and letting that define how you interact with him or her on a permanent basis, observe that, at the moment, he or she appears to be in this personality mode and accommodate your child accordingly. A few years later, if your young learner rounds a corner and seems to have other needs, adapt your thinking and response.

Motivation: What Works and Doesn't Work

In studies aimed at exploring the effectiveness of positive or negative reinforcement, it's been found that both are, on average, equally effective.[5]

Use the right type of motivation. With negative motivators, however, parents should be discerning about what they use. Negative incentives, like loss of privilege, money, or points, as was the case in the various experiments deployed to study motivation, seem to work. In contrast, outright criticism just doesn't. Belittling or assigning blame to a child, for example, is drastically different from simply taking away his or her privileges. Shirley King, a researcher at the University of Calgary, found that "verbal abuse is even more likely than physical abuse to damage children's self-esteem."[6] She found that harsh criticism actually acts as a de-motivator and lessens the desire to try new things.

You get only short-term gains from criticism. Negative motivators, specifically criticism, may motivate children in the short term, but only dampen intrinsic motivation and self-esteem over the long run. In the case of Max, who didn't want to move on to more challenging material, his family used positive motivators that challenged him to set his own goals. They said, "I wonder if you could..." and provided an attainable goal, rather than saying, "I'll bet you can't..." and setting the challenge for him. They gave Max the means to test his own limits and progress forward on his own terms. Max's family helped him learn to find his own motivation. That lesson will certainly last into adulthood when the cheerleaders and coaches in his life are replaced, one by one, with peers and contemporaries.

I hear negative motivators in the form of criticism all the time and, frankly, it drives me crazy. Kids see right through it; I've never met children who genuinely felt motivated by adults telling them they couldn't do something in that contrived way. What it does is simply belittle the child by using the fear of failure to force action.

My system of positive and negative reinforcement: In our home, we employ a system that harnesses both positive and negative motivators to reinforce good behavior and discipline bad behavior. For rewards, I didn't want to lavish my kids with junk food or meaningless stickers. I did want to develop some sort of system that was easy to understand, made a visual impact on my younger kids, and was meaningful enough to work. So, I came up with a system I've dubbed "bead cups."

Bead cups are little clear cups that bear each child's name. When I catch my kids doing something great, I compliment them and add beads to their cup. For good manners without prompting, I add one bead. For sharing a coveted toy with their siblings or friends without me having to guilt them into it, I add about three beads. The kids even nominate each other for beads and do the dirty work of positive reinforcement for me sometimes.

Punishments involve depleting the beads. When they whine after a verbal reminder to be positive, a bead gets taken out. If they throw a fit, several beads are taken out based on the duration of the negative behavior. And if they tell a lie, I dump the cup out completely. Every family ranks values differently, so maybe a little fib in someone else's home would just be a loss of a single bead. Honesty is a big deal in our home, and we can't very well thrive together all day every day if we can't, at a minimum, trust one another.

What's a bead worth? Each bead amounts to the equivalent of one minute of frivolous screen time, whether on the TV or computer. It doesn't have to be educational, but it does have to fall within the family's framework for acceptable viewing. beads can be redeemed for an old episode of *Bewitched* or the *Andy Griffith Show*. Any amount of beads can be redeemed for a comparable amount of videogame or appropriate web surfing time.

The upside to this reward/punishment system is that it's easy to manage and the kids respond well to it. In our minimal screen-time household, where the kids maybe get one show per week without earning it, they're thrilled to get beads and devastated to lose them. In homes where TV isn't the forbidden fruit, parents can certainly find other motivators that are just as effective.

What also really works with this reward system is the law of small increments. My children can see their bead cup banks building up, so it's immediately satisfying as beads are added, or devastating as beads are depleted or taken away. They know they can earn beads through good behavior and habits, and that the rewards can only be redeemed when they accumulate enough beads; this teaches them the intrinsic value of delaying gratification.

As parents, we want to reward positive behavior in our children, but we also want to immediately discourage bad conduct. A system where points are earned or removed in increments motivates children in an easy and effective way.

On the down side, the bead cup system isn't very portable, so I find myself virtually docking or adding beads while on grocery shopping trips, but then forgetting to actually do the necessary accounting when we get home. The kids know this, and so the incentives are less effective when we're in public. I tried taking the bead cups on vacation trips, and that also proved to be less effective. In hotels, there's easy access to TV, so that motivator is diminished. Plus, on vacations, we aren't eating our regular healthy food, and we're never in bed on time, so everyone is a little stressed and irritable, and the more emotionally-taxed child responds less to the motivational scheme.

Still, I love my bead cup system because it consolidates both positive and negative reinforcement.

THERE ARE ENDLESS possibilities to how you can adjust your teaching strategies to accommodate your children's personality quirks. Temperaments clue you in on special considerations that need to be made so that you can adjust how you teach to meet your children's needs at home. One of the major goals of schooling at home is that your children not only absorb information better, but that they also develop personal coping strategies. In our stylized examples, Max, Suzie, Alex, and Sarah learned how to meet challenges with fewer struggles and more success thanks to the assistance of their loving families. The families recognized the children's different personalities and adapted their teaching styles accordingly.

Having a good grasp of your children's unique brand of intelligence, learning style, and temperament allows you to anticipate problems and forge better schooling plans at home. You can begin to look at their unique needs and launch a homeschooling plan that not only meets your children's academic needs, but also lays a solid foundation for their emotional development. If you can teach your children how to learn *and* to take advantage of their own strengths, you'll have met your parenting and teaching goals.

Now, all that's left is to put everything we've learned to practice at home.

ELEVEN:
Designing and Planning a Tailored Home Education

Homeschooling allows education to fit into your life rather than trying to force your life to fit into the education system. That's the home field advantage.

NOW that you have a good grasp of several core teaching methods and frameworks, as well as a better handle of who your young learners are, their aptitudes, learning styles, and general temperaments—it's time to put everything together. At the heart of how we'll do this is a "whole-child" approach to create real learning experiences for your children at home.

The Whole-Child Approach to Tailored Home Education

You've set out on this homeschooling adventure because you want the best for your children. Not only do you care about your children as students who will thrive academically, but you also care about them as spiritual, social, and intellectual beings who will grow up to be happy, fulfilled individuals. Your reasons for homeschooling are no doubt complex because you realize that your children are themselves wonderfully complex, too. You recognize that they're multidimensional beings, not just columns in a grade book.

No two kids are exactly alike. I came to that realization over time after much soul-searching and trial-by-error. With the birth of each of my children, I would often find myself reading a slew of new parenting books. Surely, you can recall that earnest feeling; I refer to it as "new parent desperation," when sleeping patterns change, nursing schedules seem off, and you feel like you're drowning in the day-to-day of life. Whenever that feeling would grip me, I'd consult a stack of new books, hoping to find comfort in some miracle parenting technique or solution.

Each book on my nightstand had boasted of surefire solutions to all of my mommy problems. Attachment parenting advocated for me to be ever responsive to the needs and wants of my children, putting their comfort above all else. The books on scheduling made me believe I could master all of the challenges of parenting and childcare through meticulously planned days full of task lists and calendars, and that my children would be more secure this way than if I catered to their every cry and desire. Over the years of flipping endlessly through those books to find that one perfect schedule for my restless baby so that I could find some modicum of peace—I stumbled on a pearl of insight: Even as different authors advocated for different solutions, there really was no one right answer.

When Haven was born, I decided to let all of those books gather dust on the shelf because I realized that the experts don't know my children the way I do. Not one of them has ever looked into my children's eyes and asked, "What do they need today?" While some families are lucky, it's more likely that families don't find all the answers they need in a single book or even in several books.

I don't want to tell you what's best for your children. What I do want is to teach you how to be more confident in evaluating your children for yourself and assessing their needs before responding. That's why I advocate that parents approach homeschooling with the whole child in mind, just as the educators and founders of the methods and approaches we've learned in this book have. The best thing to do is to learn how to tailor your parenting and homeschooling to each child individually.

Let's get started with creating your own educational plan.

Creating Your Homeschooling Plan: Putting It All Together, Step by Step

You can bring some order to the chaos of the homeschooling journey and still personalize the experience with these steps:

1.   Do a family financial check-up and set a budget.

2.   Define your educational goals.

3. Pick your subjects and design a customized schedule (daily and weekly) for you and your children.

4. Personalize your teaching style to each child.

5. Choose (or design) the best curriculum for each subject.

6. Shop smart and consider cost against quality.

Step 1: Do a family financial check-up and set a budget.

Many friends over the years have said, "I'd really love to homeschool, but our family can't make ends meet with just one income." In response, I've found ways to gently say, "If you're just being kind about my choice to homeschool, thank you. If you genuinely want to switch to homeschooling, and finances are all that's holding you back, let's look at that."

To outperform institutional schools, parents need to be able to access at least as many resources as the schools can, and it's likely that they'll have to do it on a fraction of the budget. So, let's have a candid talk about the very real concern of finances and homeschooling.

Aligning Your Finances with Your Core Values

By using three simple lists, I've found that most issues regarding finances can be addressed. Head over to the "Resources" section at the end of the book and complete "Worksheet 1: Financial Planning" (page 253) There you'll find three lists that will help you plan your family budget and assess your finances to make room for homeschooling:

▪ **Family priorities:** First, make a list of everything you value and want most for your family. Often this will include things like more family time, time spent within your particular religious community, happy kids with strong sibling bonds, strong husband and wife ties, and so on. That list is the easy part. Take a moment and jot down a list ranked in order of importance. Then, set this list aside and wait a few days. Revisit the list and update it as needed.

- **Time accounting:** Make an honest assessment of where your time is spent. This list is where it's easy to fudge or justify misallocated time, so try to be honest. If you're like most families, you'll see more time than you'd like spent on watching television, web surfing on the computer, and commuting in the car. Got your list? Okay, that might have stung a little, but be strong. We have one more list to make.

- **Expenses:** Track your expenses for the month. If you're like most people and pay for things predominantly with debit or credit cards, it'll be easy to look at a statement and see where your money is going. Many banks also have online features that give you a spending report on where your monthly spending is going. After paying your major bills like rent/mortgage, utilities, and the like, do you find that quite a bit of money is spent on dinners out or at Starbucks? And what are you considering basic utilities? Maybe cable or extended cable packages? What about gas for the family vehicle or insurance for a spare vehicle that rarely gets driven?

Often the actual money we spend and the time we devote to certain activities tell a different story about what we value and prioritize. The results may surprise you. I often find that when our time and money are spent on what we actually value, we really can afford to live on one income and still not live like paupers.

Don't forget what you also save by staying home. If you're homeschooling, you're around to make the family meals, which not only saves you money, but also provides the kids opportunities to help with the cooking and cleaning. This gives you more family time and lets you impart important lessons on responsibility. You can then skip the nutrition lessons if you talk about the food choices you're making while you cook together. If you drop cable, you're buying more time doing things as a family and less time sitting near each other and tuned in to the screen rather than to each other. If you're not driving to work during rush hour, picking up and dropping off the kids at school, and driving to that restaurant for dinner, your gas bills will plummet. You may even find that you can drop one of the family vehicles and save on insurance costs. For years, we were able to be a one-car family, and only added a vehicle when we inherited a truck from my husband's family. Being a one-car family isn't glamorous, but if it gets you where you want to be, who cares what the Jones's think?

Now, I don't mean to imply that homeschooling and family budget cuts are for everyone. Some people really don't want to pass on their Starbucks lattes and dinners out. They and their children love their childcare provider. And that's absolutely wonderful! There's nothing at all wrong with having found reliable care and enjoying some luxuries. The three lists in Worksheet 1 I've discussed here are meant to help those who have the longing to homeschool but have a perception that time and money stand in the way. In reality, when our finances and energy are aligned with our actual core values, there's usually a way to make ends meet and stay home. If homeschooling is where your heart is, don't let finances stand in your way.

Family Attitudes About Financial Sacrifices

Despite the things that you can do to increase your family budget for homeschooling, financial sacrifices can still be a sensitive issue, not only for families considering homeschooling, but also for those who are already homeschooling. While all of our children love homeschooling and my husband can see the clear benefits of it, there are still times that he daydreams of what it might be like to have that second income. We bought a real fixer-upper of a house and decided to do one major project per year, doing things as we could afford them. Last year, it was the yard; this year, the kitchen and roof (because that couldn't wait); and next year, it'll be the bathrooms. It's fine to take our time like this, but when the run-down bathroom starts to get to him, he can't help but think: *If we weren't homeschooling, we could afford to get that new bathroom and maybe take a vacation. And our retirement account would look even better than it does.*

I've heard a lot of parents report the same low-level resentment within their families. But I'm also sure that if the same moms worked and weren't home to cook or tidy up, and the kids spent their evenings doing homework instead of spending quality time with the family, there might be some resentment or regrets about that, too. Keep in mind that there will always be waves of "what-ifs" when it comes to finances. Just make sure that the entire family is happily on board before taking any drastic actions.

Believe it or not, I knew a mom who got a call from the school to come pick up a child who was in trouble, and right then and there, she just decided that her kids were done with school altogether. She pulled them all out that day. On the drive home, she called her husband and informed him that they were now homeschoolers. I can only imagine what a shock that must have been for him. That, dear friends, is not the way to decide about homeschooling! Homeschooling is a family decision, and no matter how much you may want to homeschool, if your husband or your children aren't on board, you'll never have the happy homeschool experience that you envision.

Let me highlight one final point concerning family finances before we move on. The discrepancy in costs to educate students at home and in public schools is huge. One study finds that the average cost per homeschool student was $546, while the average cost per public school student in that same year was $5,325.[1] And yet, on nationally standardized achievement tests, home-educated children averaged in the 85th percentile, while public school-educated children averaged in the 50th percentile.[2] Sure, your taxes won't cover your schooling expenses, but look at how affordably you can school your kids at home. You don't need all of the physical resources that schools have, such as computer labs and libraries. Take heart in the reality: Even spending a small fraction of what the schools spend, you're likely to have better educational results (for an extensive discussion on this, see Chapter 1).

When you're confident about your finances, move on to Step 2.

Step 2: Define your educational goals.

In your enthusiasm to start building an educational plan for your family, you might be tempted to make decisions too quickly. "Oh, that's Johnny," you decide. "Yup! Now I know exactly what kind of kid I've got. Time to go curriculum shopping!"

Hold on, dear readers. The first step in tailoring an educational plan is to reflect on what you want your children to get out of their schooling experience. Take out "Worksheet 2: My Homeschooling Vision and Mission" (page 255). Fill out the first section: How do you define an education? What do you hope your children will take away from class time? What are your educational goals for them? In effect, you want to write about your overarching goals as a homeschooler and parent.

After you've completed the Worksheet 2, take a few days to reflect on the other basic areas that we've touched on so far in the book:

- Your children's educational and emotional needs: How do your children best learn? What are their learning styles? Do they have special needs you need to account for?

- Your children's aptitudes: What areas or subjects do they excel in and where do they need extra TLC? How are you going to approach those less desirable subjects?

- Your children's personalities: What are their general temperaments? How do they react to rewards and discipline?

Finding the Right Blend

After a careful reading of the available educational methods and a more holistic picture of your children's innate traits and abilities, you should begin to realize that your children aren't cookie cutter molds for any one educational framework we've discussed, whether it's the Montessori method, Waldorf education, Trivium, Charlotte Mason education, or unschooling. Be ready to recognize that your child may likely benefit from a *blend* of those methods. What particular "blend" you gravitate towards depends on your preferences and your children's particular needs. Children's cognitive receptivity is based on a variety of factors, and it takes planning and effort on your part to find their learning "sweet spot."

> What particular "blend" you gravitate towards depends on your preferences and your children's particular needs. Children's cognitive receptivity is based on a variety of factors, and it takes planning and effort on your part to find their learning "sweet spot."

Think of the various combinations: Do you do a blend of Montessori and Trivium for math and science subjects, and switch to a hybrid of Waldorf and Charlotte Mason to study literature and history? How do you structure classroom activities to appeal to your sanguine, interpersonal learner, or to your choleric, naturalistic learner? You might explore social, group activities and presentations for the first child, and outdoor-based, field study for the second child. The possibilities are endless and what "blend" you decide on all depends on how you define your overall homeschooling goals.

Different "Blends" for Different Kids

Some families may find that all of their children's needs are similar, while other families juggle very different needs. For example, imagine that you have two very different kids: Your eldest is a phlegmatic, tactile learner with strong mathematical aptitude, while your youngest is a choleric, auditory learner with a great knack for speaking and writing. How do you design a schedule, pick a curriculum, and create lessons that meets their individual needs, while playing up their strengths and compensating for their weak spots? Finally, what educational frameworks appeal to your personal values as a family?

When the needs of a child conflicts with the needs of another, families can feel at a loss on what methods and teaching techniques to try. Stay calm; this wonderful adventure called homeschooling often requires a bit of trial-and-error. For homeschoolers, the cardinal rule is actually about not feeling bound by the rules. My advice: Blend, blend, blend.

Think about how a patchwork quilt is made. When you set out to design and make a quilt, you first decide on a pattern. You find something that's appealing at a glance. Then, you choose fabrics and threads that will make that pattern your own. A hundred people may have used that same pattern, but their quilts vary greatly in color, print, and stitching. As you carefully put the pieces together, you improvise a little here and there to make things fit together just right. In the end, it's worth the effort because not only are you warm and snug under that handcrafted quilt, but you've created something that reflects your own sense of style and satisfied your creative appetites.

> This wonderful adventure called homeschooling often requires a bit of trial-and-error. For homeschoolers, the cardinal rule is actually about not feeling bound by the rules. My advice: Blend, blend, blend.

Step 3: Pick your subjects and design a customized schedule (daily and weekly) for you and your children.

Designing a schedule lets you plan what you want your typical school day and/or school week to look like for your family. By starting with a schedule, you can honestly answer what academic subjects, skill-building activities, and teaching styles are most in line with your core values and educational goals for your children.

Let's go back to Worksheet 2. Maybe your overall goal is spiritual development and creative independence. If that's your vision, then you'll probably want to carve out more time in the school day for spiritual practice, as well as independent projects and activities across a range of subjects your children naturally gravitate towards. Or, perhaps you really want your child to have a broad base of knowledge in a range of core academic subjects, like math and reading. If so, you'll favor designing a schedule that allows for more rigorous, academic learning.

Selecting the School Subjects

As you start building your schedule, first consider the particular subjects your children will study. Math and reading, of course, are the usual core academic subjects institutional curricula emphasize, but at home you have more options and can devote more time to subjects that complement those core areas. For example, learning science or music can complement math topics, while literature and social studies work well with reading lessons.

Now, take out "Worksheet 3: My Homeschooling Goals, By Subject" (page 257) and consider your goals for specific subject areas. Using your previous responses back in Worksheet 2, define what areas you want to emphasize. If you wrote that you want an education that's spiritual in focus and motivates students to be creative, free thinkers, you may want to schedule core blocks of time on spiritual studies and on social studies, where readings focus on the biographies of community and social justice leaders. If you jotted down a desire for your kids to have an academically-rounded education, with a focus on science, you may want to spend more time on specific science subjects, like biology, ecology, or chemistry, alternating on different days of the week. If your goal is to motivate your children to be more artistic and to hone their sense of self-expression, you may decide to focus your subjects around creative activities, such as design, art, music, or writing. Together, your homeschooling vision (Worksheet 2) and subject list (Worksheet 3) will form the basis later for choosing a homeschooling curriculum for each child. We'll get to how to select a curriculum later in the chapter.

As you complete Worksheet 3 for each of your children, remember that each child may have wildly different plans, following different subjects. Sure, it would simplify your life if you could just clone one program for every young learner in your family, but most likely—especially in the later grade levels—their programs will vary and change as your children mature and begin to follow their own paths.

Different Schedules for Different Kids

When you first set out to design a school schedule for your children, you'll no doubt consult experts, read countless books, scour numerous blogs, or talk to other homeschooling families for ideas. As you do your research, you'll likely meet a few people who swear by their schedules and plans, who claim that they've found the perfect school routine for developing little geniuses who could beat Ben Stein in a game of chess, or that they've discovered the secret to nurturing young Gandhis. You know what? I feel that way about my own schedule, too. Eventually you'll feel that way about yours.

Be bold and dare to customize. For example, your schedule may be highly structured, listing specific subjects that need to be covered each day, or it may be loosely structured, listing the general topics that should be covered each week. You may find yourself using a schedule that you've seen others use, or you may plan one out that's finely tailored to your children. Avoid the inclination to follow every move of homeschooling families you admire. Glean inspiration from them, but first focus on understanding the value of the individuals in your home and devise a plan that fits them, not others. Also, keep in mind that your schedule may change every few months to accommodate the changes in your children and their lives.

> Avoid the inclination to follow every move of homeschooling families you admire. Focus on understanding the value of the individuals in your home and devise a plan that fits them, not others.

It's time to work on "Worksheet 4: School Day Schedule" (page 261), which divides a school day into 30-minute segments, from 7 a.m. to 4 p.m. Sketch out what you envision for a full school day routine. Maybe you know that no one in your family is a morning person; if so, don't block in any class work before 9 or 10 a.m. Or, maybe you break up subjects by blocking in chores, so that your kids can get up and move around throughout the day.

In our home, I let our kids each add one special thing to the schedule, usually morning yoga and tea time in the afternoon. On these school-only days, when no obligations make us leave the house, we start the day with a centering activity, like circle time, that brings us together as a group and gets our minds and bodies ready for an academic focus. Sometimes, we throw a little party in the afternoon to wind down the day.

Setting School Hours at Home

Many homeschooling parents feel that every school day should look the same. This often happens when parents try desperately to mimic the public school day. And yet most parents have no idea just how flexible and varied the public school day can actually be. They hear the mantra, "Children thrive on routine," and immediately think that routine should govern their school time at home, too; or rather, a certain type of routine based on repetitive activity with no room for flexibility or variety.

In my experience as a teacher in institutional classrooms, school routine was actually a planned combination of flexibility and variety built into teaching schedules. As a public school teacher, I planned for the unexpected by staying flexible. In the elementary classroom where I taught, I built little time buffers into my day by budgeting for extra time for individual lessons or trips to the bathroom. This ensured that I would always have enough time to get through my core lessons even if there were disruptions or unexpected events during the day.

For example, maybe a kid threw up in the hallway, and we needed to address that with a flurry of nurses and janitorial staff and a little time for the other students to get the "Eeeew! Grooooosss!" stuff out of their system. Or, maybe we had an unexpected school visitor drop by the class to give a presentation.

Most days, that buffer time was consumed either by unexpected events or simply by the dawdling and distractions. On rare occasions, when the day went smoothly without interruptions, we'd be lucky enough to have accumulated what I liked to call "bonus time." Bonus time was a period at the end of the day when I'd be able to squeeze in a novel activity for the students outside of our planned lessons, or when I'd give the students "free time" to use as they pleased.

Each day at institutional schools also didn't look just like the next. Mondays wouldn't go down exactly like Thursdays. There might be extra classes for music, computer lab, or foreign language training for which the students would see a different teacher and leave my care and classroom. These classes were considered extras outside the mandated daily curriculum and often took place at different times of the day.

> Think of your schedule as a list of guidelines to ground your daily rhythms, not inviolable rules. Save yourself (and your kids) the stress and avoid setting a strict daily regimen unless you have a special set of needs that necessitate rigidity.

Flexibility and variety doesn't mean that these public school students didn't have a routine. It just meant that they had an *irregular* routine.

As a homeschooler, I define the idea of children thriving on routine this way: Having a routine isn't about doing boring, repetitive work that's planned out like clockwork. Instead, it's about setting patterns and rhythms at home. The concept of routine we prefer to use at home is similar to the Waldorf way of looking at time: a "low pressure, high enjoyment" view of schooling and life. Nature has seasons that flow naturally from one to the next, and most families, too, have their daily, weekly, and monthly rhythms. In our home, these rhythms aren't strictly structured but are still predictable enough that my kids have a safe, stable sense of their day or week.

Think of your schedule as a list of guidelines to ground your daily rhythms, not inviolable rules. Save yourself (and your kids) the stress and avoid setting a strict daily regimen unless you have a special set of needs that necessitate rigidity.

Many homeschoolers also feel unsure about how long a typical school day at home should last. A typical school day at an institutional setting may feel like a long day, with drop-off around 7 or 7:30 a.m. and pick-up around 3 p.m. or even later. Do you really need to make your school day at home last eight whole hours?

In institutional settings, the logistics of managing groups of kids can eat up precious instructional time. At the elementary level, students line up when the bell rings, walk in a slow and orderly fashion from place to place, and go through roll call when they arrive at their classroom or attend an event at the auditorium. In middle school and high school, students spend time "commuting" from class to class, watch videos that teachers put on to fill in class time while they play catch up and get a much needed brain break, and also attend assemblies, pep rallies, and all of the other fun though unnecessary events that are a part of school life. At all levels, the discipline issues of a few unruly students can also eat up teaching time.

Comparable School Hours—in Less Time

With the right schedule, your kids can accomplish and learn more in less time or in more efficient ways. In fact, you don't need to teach from 7 a.m. to 3 p.m. every day as they do at institutional schools, and you can cover more subjects or subjects with more intensity. For example, some families only do formal schooling on the traditional subjects four days a week, or only until noon, or some other variation of the traditional schedule. Some save up a whole day to devote to a subject. Social studies might be an entire Friday of immersion in a culture or time period, with related activities, such as meals, music, and literature.

Devote as much time to subjects you find important: no more, no less.

At home, you also get the luxury of bonus time—time to devote to subjects that would be considered peripheral studies at schools. In our family, we practice our foreign languages, computer skills, and music lessons daily; other subjects, like health and community service may or may not get scheduled attention, and probably not on a daily basis.

What about state-mandated school hours? In many states, mine included, homeschoolers must sign an affidavit promising to provide the same number of instructional hours at home as your child would receive at an institutional setting. My thoughts on this are controversial considering the strict guidelines that many states set out regarding homeschoolers. I say that you should devote as much time to subjects you find important: no more, no less. You can do this at home because your children are getting exposure to certain subjects in a nontraditional way that you may not be able to quantify for the government, but that I argue, still counts as learning.

So, how do you manage a school day given your state's required hours of instructional time?

In our home, we've creatively worked around the time requirement with the idea of "alternative lessons," where everyday chores and routines become teachable moments. Consider the time I devote to teaching my children a health lesson. In my home, health doesn't make the cut for daily, formal planning. Is it important? Absolutely. But my kids don't need a separate, structured lesson on healthy eating or exercise because I make it a point to turn family activities into moments of hands-on learning. I discuss the benefits of a balanced diet when we cook and prepare meals together. We talk about the importance of exercising when we do yoga in the mornings or walk the dogs. And we get our fill of intense, physical activity through the manual labor and daily chores we do as a family to keep our little farm up and running.

At institutional settings, where students sit behind a desk all day and eat in cafeterias where food is handed to them on a tray or in a fast food wrapper, you can argue that students definitely need formal instruction in health. At home, where my children cook their own balanced meals or do manual chores every day, they aren't disconnected from healthy choices; a healthy lifestyle is already integrated into the day. Because I make sure my children are mindful of our daily activities that relate to healthy living, and because I'm there to lead discussions, I count our daily household routine of meals and chores as "school hours."

Now, I know many families might balk and say that tossing hay or rounding up sheep are examples that don't apply to them. That's fine. There are other creative ways to turn everyday routines into lessons—no matter what your home environment. Maybe you live in a city apartment and cook all of your children's meals in a small kitchen. We have friends in just that scenario who turn hobbies or projects into lessons. For example, several families teach math and computer science through alternative lessons. What do these creative homeschoolers do? The children run their own crafts and jewelry business, designing and constructing bracelets and magnets that they sell at local stores on consignment, from their website, and at tables set up at Saturday markets or near the bus stop where the public school kids are dropped off. The kids design their own products, keep records of sales, maintain a professional website, and pay business taxes. What better math and computer class could you have than one in which children no longer have to ask, "When will I ever use this in the real world?" I'd definitely count these business ventures as school hours, too!

Another way we've made more efficient use of "school hours" in our home is through online classes. From time to time, my children attend online public school for a handful of courses here and there. In the particular program we do, when a lesson is finished, attendance is marked. No matter how fast or slow my children work through a lesson, the program marks them as spending 90 minutes on language arts and 60 minutes on math.

Even if they complete an activity or lesson in less time, the full time is always marked automatically by the system. I can safely say that we've never ever spent the full 90 minutes on language arts. It seems the designated times are fashioned for public school curricula, which specifies that an hour and a half is adequate time. While an hour and a half might be an accurate estimate for a class of 30 or so kids, it's probably more time than you need for a few kids working at the kitchen table.

Breaks and Downtimes

Be mindful of your children's daily ups and downs during a typical school day, as well as your own (make the necessary adjustments to your daily schedule on Worksheet 4). Just as you have a "witching hour" when you know you aren't going to be good for much of anything for the rest of the day, so do your kids. You certainly want to allot for enough time to cover the essentials and get things done before their witching hour (and your own) arrives to knock everyone out. I find that I'm completely worn out by 4 p.m. Even if my kids could go on, I'm mentally spent and I don't have the focus for much during the late afternoons. So my kids know that they'll be on their own with whatever didn't get done by late afternoon.

Sometimes too much energy can be a distraction as well. Recently, we found that our surge of energy in the post-breakfast morning hours was making it difficult for my boys to focus on our circle time activities. I had always suspected that if I let Hunter and Haven have playtime in the morning, right after breakfast, then I'd never be able to reel them in for school work. It turned out that I was wrong. When I started letting them stay outside to play for a full hour after morning chores, our morning school time was radically improved. They came back inside with more focus for their school work. I believe part of the reason was that they got their daily dose of fresh morning air and worked out some of their restlessness, which made them much more receptive to their school work. Without letting out some of that pent-up energy, they would be sitting at their desks, feeling distracted and pining for playtime.

So, don't be afraid to play things by ear. Don't assume, as I once did, that giving an inch will result in your young learners taking a mile. Watch out for those times in the day when your kids need to get up and move around, and allot for that.

Beyond the 'Regular' School Day

Now that you've already designed your ideal full school day schedule in Worksheet 4, we're going to look at how to plan those other days—special days when you deviate from the set school-only schedule to take into account other activities. Take out "Worksheet 5: Weekly Activities Calendar" (page 265) to help you take into account any weekly recurring activities and obligations. For example, consider your weekly obligations, such as errands, co-op meetings, or your children's music lessons or gymnastics classes. (Consider it a weekly variant of your daily schedule you devised in Worksheet 4.)

On those days, you'll want to implement what I call "skeleton school," a bare-bones, minimalist schedule. If you have soccer practice at 3 p.m. on Tuesdays and Thursdays, maybe you decide you won't study any of the core subjects on those busy days, but instead cover things that usually don't make the cut in daily instruction, like community service or art projects. Or, maybe you only cover the core subjects and those more frivolous areas of study take a back seat.

In our home, these activity-packed, light school days still cover core subjects like writing, grammar, and math, but I scale down each of those subjects into a single worksheet divided up into several sections. For example, for the grammar and handwriting portion, I'll have my children copy a sentence and then work on diagramming that sentence for grammar work. Then they'll move on to a math section with several problems that reinforce concepts they've been learning that week. For my youngest, it might be basic addition and subtraction, for my middle guy, it's addition and subtraction with regrouping (carrying and borrowing), and for my eldest, it's generally geometry with missing angle measures and a few equations to be balanced. Finally, they complete an essay section where they're asked to write down a paragraph or two about some broad topic that interests them. These free-style paragraph essays give me hints as to how their interests are shifting, which I can then use to design lessons for the following week. It also gives me a chance to evaluate their writing mechanics.

If we're *really* busy, then that one sheet covers enough material for the day. The worksheet is also versatile. If we're on a road trip, then that one sheet can be done in the car. If the children never ever did anything but that one, mom-made worksheet and maybe some reading for the day, they'd meet the minimum requirements for a school day.

Of course, we only do those skeleton worksheets and nothing else on super busy days. On most days, we do a program with more in-depth content and include the skeleton worksheet as a supplement to their core work or as a review activity.

Step 4: Personalize your teaching style to each child.

As I've emphasized throughout the book, no one knows your children better than you. You're the expert when it comes to what will best meet their educational needs. Again, this comes back to why you chose to homeschool in the first place, and what your goals are for your child. When designing your children's schedules, you should always take into account their individual strengths and weaknesses, as well as their personalities. We'll use "Worksheet 6: Student Assessment" (page 271) to guide us through this evaluation.

Focus on Student Strengths or Weaknesses?

Some parents like to customize a schedule and program that empowers their children by focusing on strengths. Others look at their children's weaknesses and try to formulate a plan that bolsters areas where they struggle. Which approach works best? The choice is yours. If you want your children to grow up to be confident discussing a variety of topics and be moderately well versed in just about everything, you'll probably want to strengthen areas of weakness. However, if your desire is for your children to be super stars in their favorite area, you'll likely play to their strengths. Of course, there's also a strong case for a balanced approach, blending these two together so that your children get to explore their natural gifts and aptitudes, while also learning how to boost areas where they struggle.

Don't forget to consider your children's temperaments (discussed in detail in Chapter 10). Are they finicky when it comes to school time? Are they cautious about new topics? Is one child gregarious, while the other more introspective and quiet? All these personality quirks will impact how you tailor your school schedules. Also, try asking your children what they want. Some children prefer to control their day, but would seriously lack the focus to power through if they weren't on a strict schedule. On the other hand, some children will insist on giving their input and opinions about what they like and don't like and want more control. Also, remember that children aren't fixed in their temperaments and preferences. One year, your child may be happy taking the lead; the next year, he or she want you to take charge.

For a long time, my daughter and I worked together to plan out the day's activities: I specified the list of activities, while Hannah Jane determined the order they were to be completed and the duration of time spent on each activity. This freedom to set her school day prompted a surge of enthusiasm in her school work. But after a period of time passed, the novelty of choosing how to sequence her day waned, and she lost focus. Once I observed her disinterest in taking the lead, we promptly moved on to a different schedule. I took over setting the time and order of her activities—but shuffled things around a little every day to surprise her. As many children are, she's a novelty addict and thrives on surprises. I know this is her temperament, so I adjust her schedule accordingly.

Make sure your children recognize that part of the adventure of homeschooling is exploring different ways of learning. You might explain to them, "We're going to try out three different ways of schooling. We'll give each one a week, and we'll really give it our all for that week. At the end of the three weeks, we'll sit down together and figure out what worked best. You can help decide what we do." By emphasizing experimentation and flexibility, you and your children don't need carefully orchestrated schedules that fit perfectly from day one.

Plan for the unexpected, and expect change and transformation. Homeschooling is a dynamic process and most years will start off in this tentative way, where you and the children "feel your way through" and figure out what works best for that particular month, "semester," or school year. As your kids mature and develop, there's no reason to think that their needs or appetites for learning won't change over time, too. In fact, every new school year or grade level might be a time for re-evaluation and discovery. If you've had kids at institutional schools, you probably noticed that sometimes just being in a new class with a new teacher with different ways of doing things becomes a real pick-me-up at the start of the school year. View the gift of change as part of the fun of homeschooling.

> Plan for the unexpected, and expect change and transformation... View the gift of change as part of the fun of homeschooling.

Individual vs. Group Work

Now, consider how much of your teaching time for each child can be divided between individual one-on-one time and group work. By second or third grade, for example, you may find that your role shifts from being an instructor to being more of a facilitator. I heard one educator refer to this as being the "guide on the side" rather than the "sage on the stage." As your children get older, they may be studying on their own for the better part of the day, and you'll merely be there to mentor them when they need some extra attention. For each subject you plan to teach, note how much time you'll need to devote on an individual basis and which subjects require mostly self-study.

As educational plans diverge for each child in the family, timing becomes a central issue. How can you teach each child individually according to a tailored plan and schedule without overstretching your efforts? One answer: By staggering and coordinating each schedule so that your children work individually with you on a one-on-one basis, as well as alongside each other in group work.

The first few weeks of each school year or each new shift in school scheduling usually requires a lot of mom-intensive time. I give the kids a lot of personal attention in those early days to help them adjust to the new schedule, the pace of their new books or programs, and the rhythm of my rotating attention. It's not unusual for me to feel overwhelmed and intimidated during this period because the kids aren't yet able to progress in their studies without me. At that point, they still need my undivided attention every minute of the day. After a week or so, they get the hang of their new curricula and get a sense of when I'm free to answer questions. Before I know it, they're capable of moving themselves through the day without much guidance, freeing me up to make the rounds and oversee their individual progress. Until that magical moment arrives, though, you really must stagger your work times and offer one-on-one attention as best you can.

The advantages of staggering individual work are that each child works on subjects that require extra parental input at different times. If all of your children are having the *same difficulties* with the same subject, then staggering is far more beneficial than having everyone work on the same subject at the same time. Staggering your one-on-one teaching time assures that no one falls through the cracks, and that you're able to work with each child without becoming overburdened.

On the flip side, if your children all have *different areas where they excel or struggle* on a particular subject, following the same schedule for that subject may improve learning. How? By allowing for group work and sibling mentoring. For example, while learning biology, one child's affinity for remembering scientific terms can complement his or her sibling's aptitude for grasping cause and effect. If your children are close enough in age that working together isn't a problem, then following a similar schedule can be convenient and effective. Also, if it turns out that you have several subjects that you can teach to everyone at once, then consider blocking those subjects together in your daily school-only schedule (head back and revise Worksheet 4). Don't be afraid to make changes.

Step 5: Choose (or design) the best curriculum for each subject.

With a tentative school schedule in place—one that takes into account your children's individual strengths, weaknesses, personality, and teaching preferences—it's time to choose your curricula. For homeschooling parents, this is usually the fun part. This stage in the planning process is where you get to personalize homeschooling for your family, much like selecting the colors and print patterns for your quilt. The "texture" and "color" of every member of your family is special and unique and your choice in curriculum(s) should reflect that.

Choosing curricula for your children can be overwhelming if you just dive in with no idea of what's out there, or what you're looking for. Luckily, we've gone through the core educational frameworks in Chapters 3-7, many of which have been adapted for homeschooling. When you start shopping for curricula, you'll already be familiar with some of those popular educational methods that guide many of the products on the market.

> **Tips for Choosing Curricula:**
> * Create a short list of the curricula that you like.
> * Weigh the upsides and downsides to each curriculum.
> * Try the 'wonder box' approach.
> * Explore using your local libraries or creating your own materials.

Shopping for curricula is a little bit like detective work. First, let's revisit your educational vision and goals. Take out Worksheets 2 and 3 and look over what you wrote down for what you want to get out of homeschooling and what subjects you want to focus on. Second, take out Worksheet 6 and review your children's strengths, weaknesses, preferences, and special needs.

As we move through this section, you'll be asked to make a short list of curriculum options and complete "Worksheet 7: Curricula Comparison" (page 275) helping you evaluate your options and more effectively comparison shop. While there's no practical way I can weigh the pros and cons for all of your curriculum options, I can provide you several tips to help you hand-select what curricula will work best for your family.

Use these tips as a loose guide and follow your heart:

Tip 1: Create a short list of the curricula that you like.

Check out the product reviews. Pick one subject from your list. Let's use math as our example. First, hop online and run a web search for "homeschool curriculum reviews." You should get plenty of results. What you're looking for are websites that allow registered members to post their thoughts on any purchased curriculum that they, themselves, have used. I've found Homeschool Reviews (homeschoolreviews.com) and Homeschool Curriculum Reviews (homeschool-curriculum-reviews.com) to be useful.

At the site, head over to the math section, and you should see a list of math curricula. You'll probably see things you've been curious about, as well as things you've never heard of. Start browsing. Read at least a few comments on every available curriculum. Don't be put off by a curriculum just because it only has four reviews, while others have 80. That may just mean that the curriculum is new, which isn't always a bad thing.

Be on the lookout for sneaky self-promotion. Just like everything else, homeschooling is a business for the publishers, and it's not unthinkable that these companies compensate homeschoolers for submitting rave reviews, or that they even register as homeschoolers and write their own glowing reviews. I've read a few reviews that sounded suspiciously like they were paid endorsements or staged reviews by reviewers posing as homeschooling parents. The same is true of your favorite homeschool bloggers. If you love them, and they love a particular curriculum, browse their blogs for something that tells you whether they accept payment for endorsements. Many do, and if they don't, they'll usually tell you in their endorsement that they're not being compensated in any way for their positive opinions.

Review both negative and positive reviews. When parents take the time to give a review, negative or positive, it's usually with the intent of helping other families. As you browse the reviews, make sure you read as many negative reviews as positive ones. Criticism can often be more telling than praise, but weigh them carefully. Negative reviews generally come in two flavors: one that invites you to do more investigation and reading about the product, and one that raises red flags and tells you to walk away. Both should be honest and truthful.

Here's the first type of review you might stumble across:

> We heard so many great things about _____,
> so we couldn't wait to start using it with our kids. When
> it arrived we realized immediately that the pace was a
> little fast for our daughter, but our son loved it. We
> decided to stick it out for the year because we had just
> shelled out a ton of money for it, and we were hoping
> that by the end of the year our daughter would get the
> hang of it. But by the end of the year we were just really

frustrated. Even though our friends had found great
success with it, it just wasn't a good fit for our family.

Here the reviewer isn't critical of the curriculum itself, but is
providing a balanced perspective that indicates that it wasn't a good fit for
her family. The negative review doesn't criticize the curriculum outright,
but provides some context for why it didn't work. When you read a review
like this, don't assume that just because the curriculum didn't work for
this family that it won't work for your family. Rather than ruling out this
curriculum as a possible choice, read a few more reviews for more specific
detail about what types of learners are having success with the program or
having problems.

The second type of review often reads like this:

> We were excited about using this program because the
> representative at the homeschool faire made it sound like
> exactly what we were looking for. I also looked at their
> web site before ordering and they had all sorts of
> percentages and graphs to show student improvement
> after using the system. But as we used the program we
> began to find a lot of typographical errors, missing pages,
> and lines of reasoning that just didn't make sense. I
> called the help line that they offered, but I could never
> get through to anyone and they never returned my calls.
> This was a complete waste of money!

That type of review should raise red flags. Read a few more reviews to
see if the criticism is consistent. When a product is full of typographical
errors and the company seems to have a reputation of bad customer
service and offers no support, it's usually a sign to walk away.

My family fell victim to a flop: a Spanish language program we found
online. Everything on the website looked great, the price was right, and it
came with audio material that the company claimed was recorded by
native Spanish speakers. The program boasted that the speakers used a
variety of regional dialects from the Spanish-speaking world, ensuring that
your child would be able to effectively communicate in Barcelona, Mexico
City, or Buenos Aires. Unfortunately, we didn't reap the rewards of this
supposed benefit. What we found was a hodgepodge of inconsistencies.
The same phrase would be spelled differently on different pages of the
book with no preface or explanation as to why. I assumed that we were

seeing those regional differences in action, but these differences could have easily been the result of sloppy editing. Not being a Spanish speaker myself, there was no way for me to vet which words were different because of differences in regional use or because of outright errors. The experience became too stressful, and we soon abandoned the program.

Once you've read a balanced amount of reviews on each curriculum and decided which ones sound like they might work for your children's learning style, it's time to make a short list of candidates. The length of your short list will vary depending on the subject. Math might have 10 options you really like, while German language might only have two. The less universal subjects tend to have fewer powerhouse players, which makes the vetting process a little more difficult. You may see only a dozen German curricula with only three reviews each, and none of them very illuminating. In those cases, sometimes you'll have to take the leap of faith and go with your gut instinct. In general though, you'll have enough options to wade through to create your short list.

Tip 2: Weigh the upsides and downsides to each curriculum.

Visit the website of each company that produces the curricula on your short list. Since you've already read a few customer reviews (see Tip 1), completely ignore the posted testimonials. These are usually less balanced than the evaluations on review sites. Glance through the statistical information, but keep in mind that there's no way for you to assess their accuracy without any access to sample size or margin of error. You also don't know how the questionnaires were worded to gather the statistical data. While numbers don't lie, they can be skewed in a way that distorts the full picture; the impact of a program can be exaggerated or made more dramatic. In general, companies only publish information that casts a positive light on their products.

Instead, take stock of the following; this is where you should focus your consumer scrutiny:

- Virtual communities
- Customer or technical support
- Lesson plan support
- Trial periods

- Sample units

- Money back guarantees

Virtual communities: Many power players in the curriculum business have created virtual communities where users exchange their own ideas and support. Sometimes these online communities become localized and the users in a particular region will start their own local groups. Support groups are great resources. For example, an online community for a math curriculum you're interested in might be a place where you can find families sharing ideas on activities to supplement textbook learning. Communities around your particular curriculum can be wonderful resources to find novel ways to work with the curriculum materials.

Since most of these communities operate on public online forums like Yahoo Groups or Google Groups, you can often join without purchasing the curriculum. This gives you a chance to explore what parents are discussing and even ask questions that will help you determine if the curriculum is really the right choice for you and your family. Request membership to any forums and see what people who are presently using the program are saying. You may find that everyone loves it. You may also be able to tell that the curriculum will be more planning-intensive than you feel up to, or that the approach seems too baby-ish for your children. All sorts of things can be brought to light by exploring these online networks and communities.

If the company site doesn't feature online communities, don't assume that one doesn't exist. Do a web search on your particular curriculum and you might find informal communities that have formed. And don't worry if it's a local group on the other side of the planet. You can still read what they post online and get ideas from them. Our favorite history program, "Tapestry of Grace," has local and worldwide online communities for different age groups. It's been inspiring to log on and see how parents in different countries are customizing the curriculum or taking the Tapestry of Grace content and running wild with it.

Customer or technical support: Customer support usually takes the form of the company offering a hotline where you can speak with a certified teacher or program designer during specific hours. If you're seeing this as an option for the curricula on your short list, then the next step is to go back to the reviews and look for specific feedback on people's experiences with the company's support and customer service.

Remember, a company having a support line for you to call doesn't mean you'll find it easy to speak to someone who can answer your questions in a timely and professional manner. If you can't find any reviews specific to user support, surf the company's site as a "product user" and look for the support line to call yourself. If they answer, just say, "Great! I was just making sure that there was actually available support before purchasing your product." They will understand and be happy that you're considering buying.

On the other hand, you may call and find that you're directed to voice mail or prompted to send an e-mail. If you're sent to voice mail, I would encourage you to make a call at various times of the day over the next few days and see if you ever get through. Some companies are family-owned, small-time operations, and you may never get an answer because they just don't have staff to field phone calls. They may be busy, but hopefully the next day or so, you'll get through to a live person. High call volume can delay the process of getting through, but watch out for companies that perpetually experience "high call volume." With those companies, your chances of getting timely support won't be good.

If you do get through to an agent, be aware of whom you're speaking to. Sometimes, you'll get through to a very friendly person who sounds competent enough, but if you ask a content-related question it immediately becomes clear that you're speaking with someone who's better at entering in credit card and billing information than discussing the finer points of chapter twelve's biology activity. It's good to know what is meant by "customer support." Let the agent know you have content-related questions and find out if you can get access to certified teaching specialists or instructional designers to answer your questions.

If you're a homeschooling parent who's new to a particular curriculum, or who has little or no background in education, the odds are good that eventually you're bound to have questions about the material. In fact, you may be faced with a situation where you reach an impasse in your lesson and need to speak to a specialist in real-time. What will you do when your children look at you with those big eyes, asking, "Well, Mom? What are we doing here?" You may ask them to wait while you call up customer support to get some clarification. It can feel frustrating if you're sent to voicemail or are prompted to send an e-mail and wait. Your children will soon get impatient and their enthusiasm for learning will be momentarily lost. This is just the type of galling situation that many homeschoolers hope they never find themselves in. So, please do your support system research before committing to a curriculum or program.

Lesson plan support: Many curriculum companies provide lessons plans to accompany their materials. While a curriculum is simply guided content, a lesson plan serves as an outline of how to deliver that content to students. Plans may include activity guides, as well as teacher scripts and sequences. Some curricula are inseparable from the lesson plans. For example, Saxon math has every element entirely scripted. In contrast, other curricula simply recommend a sequence of topics to be taught without dictating how you teach them.

Whether this feature is a priority in your evaluation depends very much on you and your needs. Are you a pretty creative parent with a lot of ideas about how to make ideas more meaningful for your children? When your children ask you to show more details about a concept, do you immediately have an idea for an activity that they can do to reinforce the ideas in the curriculum? If so, you won't want to make your decision to buy a curriculum based on something like free lesson plans. Why? Because the free plans that come with the curricula are typically basic and no-frills. If you're the creative and inspired type, what you come up with will likely be better than what you get from the company. On the other hand, if creative ideas aren't your forte, you'll find that built-in lesson plans are invaluable, and you'll want to make sure the company offers them.

Better yet, turn to your online support communities. Parents are constantly posting new ideas for lessons and activities that you can adopt for your curriculum. You'll be hard-pressed not to find something inspiring and useful. In my experience, community sites usually provide some stellar alternatives to what you'd normally find in the included lesson plan. Homeschoolers are some of the most community-minded people you'll meet and are usually more than willing to share their know-how.

Trials periods: Many companies will offer you a trial version of their program, usually a week or two of lessons for free or for a prorated cost to test-drive the curriculum and see if it's a good fit.

Trial periods can be quite a money saver if approached carefully. But many times, parents are so excited about a program, they want to skip the trial and go right for the full program. Try to resist the urge to buy on impulse. It's sort of like when you decide to paint a room in your house a new color. Even though I know it's smart to buy the sample jar of paint and try it on a wall before buying the full 10 gallons, I tend to just dive in, sometimes with just a color swatch in hand. (For this reason, my hallways are regrettably the color of the inside of a pumpkin.)

Throwing caution to the wind can lead to bad choices with curriculum purchases, as well as to unusual design choices (though I've grown to love the color of our hallways!). Since the financial investment of choosing a curriculum is much more nerve-racking than redecorating, I encourage parents to give the trial runs a shot with a few caveats in mind:

- Make sure that if you end up buying the full curriculum, any price you paid for the trial version will be deducted from your total purchase price. Most companies will do this when asked, even if they don't volunteer it on their website.

- Confirm the shipping terms for the materials. Find out who's responsible for shipping each way (typically, you'll be charged for all shipping costs) and be clear what the charges will be. Shipping heavy textbooks and other printed materials isn't cheap. Knowing these costs will help you evaluate the real potential costs before you fork over your cash.

- How many days do you have to review the materials before you have to return them to get a full refund? Some companies charge a prorated fee for the duration of time that you possess the curriculum materials on a trial basis. If you decide to return the curriculum, make sure that you don't put off shipping it back because you may be charged for each day that exceeds the designated trial period. The penalty is uncommon, but some companies may have it as their policy. Always check.

Sample units: Reviewing sample units or lessons can be a great way to determine if a curriculum is what you want. One time, I found a very exciting curriculum that was structured in a "unit study style," weaving language arts, history, and art together into one comprehensive wonderland of learning. The company that designed the unit offered a free week of lessons, no obligation or hoops to jump through to view them. I simply downloaded the lessons and all of the bonus content.

We were in heaven! Never had our class time been more exciting or hands-on. I was sold! I promptly forked over the debit card information and waited very impatiently for our box to arrive. Once we received the full curriculum with all of the lesson units, the thrill faded a little. While I don't regret my purchase at all, it was clear that the free sample unit was the most creative and exciting of the whole year of curriculum. The lessons are still some of the best we've used, but they don't come anywhere close to the level and quality of those sample lessons.

Here are a few other ways to better evaluate those sample units:

- Be realistic and adjust you expectations, accordingly. Sometimes the sample units of a curriculum seem too good to be true.

- Seek out families who use the curriculum and ask how the free units measure up to the full package.

- Call the company and speak to their content consultants. Ask them to explain how the sample units stack up to the rest of the units in the curriculum. Be specific with your questions: What is the average number of hands-on activities per week? Is there variety among the activities week to week, or is there a lot of duplication? Again, don't be afraid to make these calls. The companies won't be irritated by your questions, and the people on the line will be more than happy to facilitate the sale if you decide to buy.

Money back guarantees: Money back guarantees come in all forms. It can be tricky to know exactly what you're getting. When I speak with sales representatives, I like to do a few things to make sure that things go smoothly if I decide to make a return. I always start out by asking the sales rep's name and using it often as we talk about the terms of the guarantee. This tells reps that I know who's responsible if there's a misunderstanding, and it encourages them to make sure that I'm clear on the terms and that my questions are carefully answered. The last thing reps want is for me to come back dissatisfied and identifying them by name as the person who led me astray.

Always ask specific questions about return policies. Before I buy, I think of all of the reasons that I might want to return a product and ask about each one specifically, and how the money back guarantee applies. Some companies have a "no questions asked" refund policy, while others require that you return a program within a certain period of time, or that you prove that the program was deficient in some way in order to get a refund. Before concluding your call, ask the rep to send you an e-mail with the specific terms of the guarantee for your own personal files; don't rely on the posted guarantee on the website, which may be changed without notice. Read over the e-mail, examine the language carefully, and only then decide if it feels safe to purchase the material on a trial basis.

If you decide that it's not working for your family, have on hand a copy of the money back policy and the name of the sales rep that explained it to you. Gather all of your e-mails. It can be helpful to request your original representative if you call to initiate a return. The odds are good that when reps realize that you've dealt with them from the beginning, they'll make sure that you associate their name with a positive experience.

If you attempt to use the money back guarantee and the company is reluctant to give you the refund even though you feel you're within the bounds of the agreement, review your paperwork, ask to speak with a supervisor, and just be calm and clear about what you were told and were led to understand about the terms of the agreement. In general, if you're persistent, you'll find that the company would rather part with your money than deal with the ongoing aggravation of a dissatisfied customer and a public relations disaster.

Tip 3: Try the 'wonder box' approach.

If you find the prospect of buying textbooks, activity books, and all of the necessary materials daunting, there's a surefire solution: You can opt to buy a "wonder box," a pre-packaged curriculum that covers several or all of your core subjects. Shipped to you in a box with a bow on top (well, there's usually no bow, but there should be!), these wonder boxes remove all the guesswork to putting together a complete curriculum.

Here are several reasons why you might find a wonder boxes a useful way to purchase curricula:

Wonder boxes can be a safety net for newbie homeschoolers. You're probably thinking that this boxed approach is exactly what you wanted to avoid when you decided to homeschool your children. But if you're just starting out, feeling inexperienced and insecure about your choice to homeschool, a wonder box can be just the "training wheels" you need to transition you into homeschooling. Your children certainly won't suffer any ill effects from working on materials from these boxed sets of educational goods.

Of course, if you've read this far, my guess is that you have a healthy appreciation for the value of tailored education, one that meets the multifaceted needs of your children. The companies that produce wonder boxes may have outstanding materials for each and every subject that they offer, but they'll likely address every subject in the same way. There's no guarantee that their system will be the optimal one for all of your children. Wonder boxes are simply safety nets; the materials are no better or worse than the materials kids get at standard institutional schools.

For new homeschoolers, I think it's a fine place to start, especially in those tentative, first years of homeschooling when you need the most support. Over time, you'll begin to get a feel for how homeschooling will work for your family and gain the confidence to be a little more creative in future school years.

Wonder boxes can be found for most educational methods. Wonder box curricula are available for all sorts of approaches. With some web research, you can easily find wonder box companies that follow specific educational frameworks. There are wonder boxes that present material through a deeply religious lens. There are Charlotte Mason education kits, as well as various Montessori method boxes for those with younger students. Even methods that are usually seen as anti-textbook, such as Charlotte Mason education (with its preference for "living books") and Trivium (with its heavy emphasis on classic texts and original sources), offer wonder boxes.

Watch-out: Wonder boxes are usually textbook-based. That brings me to one of the main drawbacks in buying wonder box curricula: The materials are primarily textbook-based, with only a few exceptions. If one of your homeschooling goals is to rid learning of rote textbook style reading, memorization, and testing, it can feel a bit restrictive to work with wonder box curricula.

Just because materials are presented as part of a wonder box, it doesn't mean you have to use those materials in that way. From time to time, I've elected to choose only one or two subjects from a wonder box made by an educational company. Maybe you've heard good things about a company's reading program, but you don't feel like their entire fifth grade kit is for you. Check to see if there's a way to buy *a la carte*, where you only buy by the coveted subject. Very often, companies are flexible and can sell you only the subjects you want. If you don't have the option to break up a box set, the odds are good that you can find gently used pieces from a wonder box on Amazon or eBay. I've purchased a ton of curriculum guides this way, and it's saved me time and money.

Explore online public school options. While you can buy most wonder boxes online, you can also find "free" wonder boxes through online charter schools in your area. These "public school from home" options are generally no-cost resources, such as classes you can take at home on the computer, materials that you can download and print out, with accompanying textbooks mailed straight to your door. Parents can even get support, such as access to trained support teachers.

A word of caution: Many hardcore homeschoolers turn up their noses at these publicly available materials. When I started using online public school resources for our foreign language and art lessons, I received a slew of criticism. My blog readers and dyed-in-the-wool homeschooling friends wrote critical e-mails, "unfriended" me on Facebook, and posted negative comments about my decision. I couldn't believe the reaction. "Be mindful of what you are giving up just to get free stuff from the government," one person wrote in an e-mail. "We thought you were a homeschooling hero. It's so sad that you're selling out..." another parent wrote.

Even at the risk of inciting more criticism, I have to stay true to my fundamental beliefs about homeschooling: It's all about having the freedom to do what works for you. If you're a parent who's not completely sold on home education yet, who doesn't have a ton of money to plunk down on a trial year, or really wants some formal support, opting to use public school resources can be a great place to start. As you develop your confidence and surefootedness in your homeschooling and teaching, you'll venture down your own path, using what works for you and your family.

If using online public school materials interest you, then I recommend K-12 (k12.com). Through their website, you can find out if your state offers a free program for in-home use. Some states require you to take all of their classes, while other states let you choose which of their courses you'd like to use or pass on. Luckily, the state of Utah, where we live, gives parents the choice.

There are also online charter school options in many areas that may reimburse parents for the cost of their chosen courses, giving families the freedom to choose what they want to teach at home on the taxpayer's dime. Other schools may loan out material from a central library that boasts a variety of resources for homeschoolers to choose from. I recommend searching for "online charter schools" in your state, as well as posting a query on a local homeschool forum about your local options.

Exploring the online public school in our area, my kids have found a few courses that they like, and we've enjoyed getting those resources for free using the format. Some of the courses, however, haven't worked for us. If we had to take the bad to get the courses we did want, we simply avoided using any of the unwanted material. Every state is different in its public school wonder box offerings for home use. Check them out and ignore the critics if it feels like a good fit!

Tip 4: Explore using your local libraries or creating your own materials.

Putting a curriculum together yourself sounds easy enough, but a word of caution: This D-I-Y approach isn't for everyone because it's time-intensive and requires a lot of research savvy. I've always felt confident in schooling my children, and yet there have only been a few years that I was brave enough to design curricula entirely on my own. I'm also not always willing to put in all of the hours that it takes to pull it all together.

Still, there are several ways to design your own programs just like the instructional design pros do. For example, if you're diligent in your research, you can easily find tables of contents for textbooks online to give you an idea of the sequence of topics and how information is presented in formal curricula. Visit the local public libraries and gather the necessary books on the appropriate topics. Libraries can be great resources for curriculum materials. I know many homeschooling families who find everything they need at the local library.

When I started homeschooling, I wasn't quite that confident that I could pull it all together. I was worried that I'd miss an important foundational skill, so I went with a purchased curriculum in most subject areas. After years of homeschooling, when I finally got the knack of it, I found that I was buying less and less from curriculum companies, with some years only purchasing a formal curriculum for a subject or two.

A caveat: Don't fall prey to books that claim that they can show you how to homeschool for free. They are usually full of irrelevant websites and mailing lists, half of which are inactive by the time the book was published. If you can't resist the draw of such claims, check out a copy at the library and see for yourself before buying your own copy.

Step 6: Shop smart and consider cost against quality.

I've had my share of epic flops when it comes to making decisions about buying homeschooling supplies and materials for our family. With the plethora of options out there, you're bound to make some mistakes. I'd like to reassure you that it's not the mark of failure as a homeschooler if you find yourself stuck with a less than stellar curriculum or with materials and supplies that don't deliver.

In this section, we'll go over some common shopping blunders to avoid, and review some tips for evaluating costs and quality:

Shopping Blunders to Avoid

Here are several of the most common regrets parents have when they purchase homeschooling supplies and books—and how to avoid them:

Inaccurate testing and assessment for curriculum materials: Testing is always a touchy subject for homeschoolers, but if you live in a state where testing is mandatory, then you'll need to make sure that your curriculum has an assessment process that's easy to understand and implement. Not all assessments are created equal. I once used a phonics program that

> Shopping Blunders to Avoid:
> * Inaccurate testing and assessment for curriculum materials
> * Giving in to sales tactics like upselling
> * Buying software that isn't compatible
> * Giving in to the impulse buy

my children adored. When the company released an online version of their wildly popular workbooks, we were on board.

Not three days into using the online program, my daughter started to complain. "Mom, I'm giving the right answer, but it's telling me I'm wrong." These apparent discrepancies continued, so one night I sat down to take their kindergarten level phonics lesson to see what the deal was. I then took the assessment portion, which checks for comprehension and mastery. The result: I had failed the test! The next day, I called the company to complain. I thought there might have been a software glitch causing correct answers to be scored as incorrect. Here was an example:

Phonics question: "Can you catch a crab in a net?"

My answer: Yes

Assessment: Incorrect!

Apparently, the designers for this program thought you couldn't catch a crab in a net. The guy on the phone politely told me I was a moron. (Okay. He didn't say it like that, but he might as well have.) He told me that while my feedback was appreciated, the program was what it was—and obviously a crab could clip its way out of the net.

Hannah Jane had done so well with the workbooks because I was the one grading them, and she and I had a similar frame of reference. Anyone who is even slightly familiar with crabbing knows that fishermen use nets or cages made out of netting to catch crabs. We've spent hours at the pier watching nets being pulled up with crabs in them. Unfortunately, the program writer had apparently spent all of his time behind a screen, imagining ingenious crabs clipping away at the netting to escape. (A creative scenario perhaps, but not an accurate one at all.)

So you see, the program's feedback about my child's phonetic awareness was based more on whether we could agree on what animals could or couldn't be caught in various traps, than on what she could read. It assumed that if she answered, "Yes," it was because she couldn't decode the words in the question.

The moral of the story: Check the tests and assessments! Make sure that the style of questions is measuring the skills that you want measured. There are actually many assessments that do a very poor job of measuring student abilities in the subject it claims to test. I would advise taking a few lessons and assessments yourself before buying.

Giving in to sales tactics like upselling: Have you ever been at a restaurant and asked for water, and the waiter responds by asking if you'd like a soda or bottled water instead? Have you ever experienced a server try to encourage you to tack on a piece of pie, or even a whole pie, to take home before you settle the bill? It's a common sales tactic called upselling. When you're buying curriculum supplies, agents will often try to upsell an additional item for you to purchase. While some are obviously unnecessary and easy to turn down, some may seem vital to your success in the program (even when they're not), and some seem downright mandatory.

At one point in our homeschooling adventure, I thought I had found the one and only wonder box that might actually meet the needs of our entire family. It was from a very small subcategory of homeschooling called "Enki education." I adore the teaching philosophy, but I had never experienced a comprehensive Enki education for myself. After doing some research and talking to a dear friend who used it and loved it, I felt compelled to buy their entire second grade kit. I went to their website and purchased the very pricey wonder box.

A few hours later, I received an e-mail stating that they would only sell me the second grade kit if I also purchased the kindergarten and first grade kits. Their explanation was that the second grade material wouldn't be accessible to learners who hadn't gone through the other two previous levels. Using concern over my children's educational wellbeing as a pretense, the company tried to convince me to buy three years of wonder boxes when I only wanted one. To me, this was an epic scam. I replied with a critical e-mail, explaining how genuinely disappointed I was to find that a company with such a nurturing and down to earth educational philosophy was trying to blatantly upsell me items I didn't need or want. My complaint turned into an e-mail battle, with the author of the curriculum even stepping in. She explained that it wasn't a scam and that it was disappointing that I'd let something as "minor" as money ($600— not small change!) stand in the way of giving my children the best education they could get.

While that kind of sales tactic is easy for any savvy parent to recognize, there are other, more subtle cases of upselling that curriculum companies try to get away with. When shopping at some company websites, you may find that additional materials are automatically added to your shopping cart. Sometimes, the online shopping system won't let you opt out of buying them. If this happens, call the company and have them remove the unwanted items from the cart. After all, most reasonable businesses would rather have some of your money than none at all.

A common product that curriculum sales agents may try to sell you is the teacher manual, an instructional guide for parents on how to teach a particular subject or topic. Some teacher manuals are an absolute necessity, but most manuals on topics like handwriting or phonics, aren't, in my opinion. You know how to read and write, and even if you aren't formally trained in the instructional methods, there's enough information on the student books to help you along. You don't need to spend more on additional guides to remind you that you should tell your child during a handwriting lesson to start the letter 'O' at the top of the line.

So, feel confident in turning down those extras that are foisted on you. If you're wondering if those extra items are really necessary, always say, "I'll call you back," and check around online to see if other families have anything to say on the matter. If you get several honest endorsements about the extras, then consider them. Also, as always, refer to your support communities at your trusted online forums. Homeschooling parents are generally very vocal about the non-necessities that companies will try to sell you. Until you've done your research, remember: *Buyer, beware*.

Buying software that isn't compatible: Be aware of the computer-based programs you buy. Make sure that your computer and its operating system is compatible with the programs you want to purchase. I wanted to get all of the kids their own tablet computers, but it turns out that their online classes aren't supported by any of the tablet operating systems we shopped for. I've got my eye on the horizon as new tablets come out, but it would have been easy to assume that, of course, the latest and greatest technology would be compatible with our regular programs. If you're not careful, getting stuck with software or online courses that aren't compatible with your computers can be money down the drain.

Giving in to the impulse buy: Before you enter your credit card number and click submit, slow down, walk away from your choices, and come back a day or so later and reassess your wants and needs. It can be easy to get swept up in the hype of a well-designed sales site or by the rave reviews from a slew of parents. To maintain a better perspective, do your research and order your curriculum on different days.

First, before you make your purchases, take some time to sit down and look at your schedule and the curricula that you've decided upon again. I assume you took the time to do this as you were making your short list, but review your completed worksheets to get a feel for how the day will flow with the specific combination of curricula at home. You might ask yourself: Does everything fit and flow together? Have you chosen a social studies program that will work as a Friday-only subject if that's what you've scheduled? Is the math program you are choosing going to work on a three-days-a-week schedule like you wanted?

Don't try to force-fit your materials into the education plan you designed. You may have to reimagine your schedule to use your dream curriculum. Be prepared to compromise, but compromise wisely without giving up something that's central to your values and goals.

Second, consider the curricula you're looking to buy with regards to your children's temperaments and learning styles: Will you have to take breaks during the intense science program to allow your students to get up and move around? Is this particular program much too text-focused for your spatial child? The curriculum got good reviews, but do your children's unique needs fit with the approach?

Third, let's review the methodology that best complements your own innate information delivery style and that meshes best with your new understanding of how children learn. Check your choices and see if they make sense: Did you find yourself drawn to the Charlotte Mason approach, but have chosen a science program that utilizes textbooks and a Q&A format for assessment? Were you drawn to the Trivium method for its wide array of factual information, but have chosen a social studies plan that only takes up a small portion of your school week?

Once you're confident that you've made the absolute best choice, only then should you make your investment. Before that, walk away and think through your decisions. Look at your completed worksheets a few more times. Talk to your spouse and your children about what you see for the future of the family's schooling and what curricula you're considering, and give them a chance to put in their two cents. Homeschooling spending decisions should never be made on impulse.

Evaluating Your Costs

Homeschooling is a financial investment, and like any financial decision you make, you need to consider costs and quality. You care about getting the best deal, right? I'm sure you also care very much about quality—especially when it comes to your child's education. I'm going to briefly go over some of the nitpicky points of evaluating the cost of a curriculum. Most of these points I learned through experience, and not always the good kind. I've made mistakes every way you can, and hopefully my experiences can spare you the ordeal.

Evaluating Curriculum Costs:
- Cost isn't always the best measure of quality.
- Always check what you get for the price.
- You don't need to buy the latest tech tools.
- "High quality, Fast, Cheap"

Here's what you should know about evaluating curriculum costs:

Cost isn't always the best measure of quality. Don't be fooled into thinking that just because a program is affordable that you're sacrificing quality. Educational publishing isn't always a "you get what you pay for" industry. The homeschooling business has an unusual mix of players. On one end of the spectrum, you have the big publishing houses that are just looking to make money. That's not always a bad thing. If they're business savvy, they realize that the best way to make money is to offer the best product. In fact, the very same companies that publish materials for public schools also realize the value of publishing content geared towards home education. Then on the other end, you have small businesses made up of homeschooling parents who found a really unique way to present a concept and want to make it available to anyone who wants to use it for a more than reasonable profit. These small-time players can often give the big boys a run for their money.

An example of this notion of "less being more" is my experience shopping around for a phonics program. After reading the "part-whole" section in Chapter 8, you're probably very clear on my opinions about the necessity of a solid phonics foundation. Seeing firsthand in the schools where I taught the negative impacts of the "whole language" method in teaching reading, I've always been really careful about my selections for phonics programs for my own children.

After doing my research and going through the educational planning steps I discussed earlier, such as reading countless reviews and talking to other homeschoolers about their experiences with particular curricula, I narrowed my short list to two programs. The first one was pricey and came from a notable company that I was familiar with from my stint as a first grade classroom teacher. Using the company's materials, the students in that class (and the whole school for that matter) seemed to excel in whatever reading they approached, so I took comfort in knowing that this program option on my short list was from the same publishing group that my beloved Paideia school had chosen.

The second program on my short list was a ridiculously cheap workbook system with a goofy, nonacademic sounding name. It sported workbooks with ugly, obnoxious illustrations on the covers. But it was getting rave reviews from parents who seemed to have my same zeal for phonics and my same general approach to homeschooling. Could it really hold up?

After careful evaluation, I opted for the cheaper, second option. Spending a whopping $7, I bought the first workbook. Because the financial risk was low, I told myself that it was a sort of trial subscription. If it was a flop, it was less than a week's worth of diaper money down the drain. After a few days, the workbook arrived in all its humble glory, thinner than I had expected and more ugly than any web photo could convey. I swallowed my pride and tried to act excited about it when I called in Hannah Jane to begin our lessons. Are you ready for this? She loved it. I loved it. It was the most amazingly simple yet effective method for teaching phonics that I had ever encountered. How could it be that this cheap, little workbook could harness her imagination and interest while teaching fundamental skills as well, if not better, than the $200-plus curriculum?

Well, I still can't explain it, though I can say that the simple, basics-first approach really did the trick. Homeschool magic, perhaps. *Lesson learned:* Never discount budget options and equate quality with price. All of my children have found success with this ugly duckling of a series, and we've never turned back.

Always check what you get for the price. When shopping around for programs, carefully look at what you're getting for the price and what amount of time it should take to complete. A curriculum's astronomical sticker price will make more sense when you realize it covers four years worth of learning, compared to a "cheaper" competitor whose materials only cover a single year or even just a single unit. It's not unlike savvy grocery shopping where you check the "unit price" to make sure you're not fooled by seemingly low prices.

While many educational companies won't give you their unit price in an obvious way, there are ways to figure it out on your own. For example, a math program you're considering may offer a "lesson per day," so you can easily calculate the total number of days of schooling you're getting for your money. Social studies programs, however, aren't as easy to calculate, and you'll end up with a ballpark timeframe. Some companies sell by the unit, semester, quarter, or year. Ask the sales agents if you're unsure.

Some programs, like Tapestry of Grace that utilizes a Trivium-inspired, spiraling style curriculum, sell you a comprehensive set of materials that includes a packet, notebook, and even a CD set that contains all of the materials in digital, printable format. Tapestry of Grace curricula can be bought by the unit or by the year (for a total of four units). If you recall, in the Trivium method (Chapter 5) your child will revisit different time periods (e.g., Ancient times, the Middle Ages, the Renaissance and Age of Exploration, and modern history) each at the elementary, middle, and high school levels. Tapestry of Grace is unique in that it's set up so that the whole family, regardless of age, can study the same topic together—but at their age appropriate level. Each unit comes with a sort of buffet of literature, art projects, writing assignments, and discussion topics for elementary, middle, and high school students. This means that if you buy it when your eldest is studying Ancient history at the elementary school level, you can use it again later, when he or she spirals back to the time period at the middle school level, and again at the high school level.

So, even though buying this curriculum program feels like a big, initial investment, after purchasing each of the four time periods from them, you can advance all the way through high school never having to purchase curriculum for that subject again. In addition to the curriculum package (notebook or CD), their website has links to additional digital resources related to each unit, as well as extensive forums for parents to ask questions and trade ideas. When you consider how much you're getting out of the program and the longevity of the materials, the hefty price tag feels like a steal.

A caveat: This type of long-term arrangement works best if you find a curriculum or program you and your children really love and can accept using for many years. Be aware, though, that just as your children's tastes in clothes, hobbies, and friends may change over time, so may their schooling tastes as they get older and mature. If you've made a large upfront investment in school materials, intending to use them for multiple years, you might feel less inclined to follow your children's lead when they desire something new.

You don't need to buy the latest tech tools. Some homeschooling families feel pressured to buy the latest computers and tablets for their children because that's what they've come to expect when they see computer labs and iPads in the classroom at the local institutional schools. Sure, a computer can be indispensible. There have been times when about half of my daughter's subjects required the computer. Having a few family computers around worked fine until the boys were old enough to have computer-based courses. Then, we were all taking turns on two computers, one of which I needed for writing this very book. We had to very carefully schedule every moment of the day, so that everyone had a chance to complete their courses on the computer, and I still had time to work on my own projects.

Sometimes, the answer is to mix up paper-based work with computer-based work (unless you have the resources to buy a personal computer for each of your students, of course). For many of the exercises and activities you do, good, old-fashioned pencil and paper works just fine, especially in the early years—and you don't need to buy expensive software updates every couple of years.

"High quality, Fast, Cheap": Finally, with regards to cost, I'd like to share with you this handy visual I came across. Imagine, if you will, a triangle, and at each point is a word: *high quality, fast,* and *cheap.*[3] You'll notice that each side of the triangle can only touch two points, meaning you can generally only meet two criteria at a time:

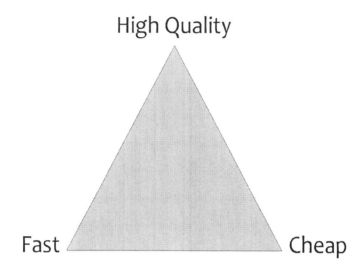

High Quality

Fast   Cheap

This simple, unassuming visual explains three likely scenarios every parent faces when it comes to learning materials:

1. You can create your own curriculum cheaply and end up with high quality material, but you won't be able to do it in a fast way. In fact, it will be very time-consuming to do all the necessary research and work.

2. You can buy a packaged curriculum (remember those wonder boxes?) and end up with high quality material, quickly delivered to your door, but it won't be cheap.

3. Finally, you can make your own materials cheaply and quickly, but it probably won't be of high quality.

As you can see, your materials can meet two of the criteria, but rarely all three.

At different times, I've had more time than money, so I've opted to spend hours after the kids go to bed making my own fantastic school activities and mapping out lesson plans. At other times, I've found that my time is more valuable, and I decided I'd rather spend the money to have all of the work done for me.

It's about priorities. The choice is yours—but realize that it's a rare thing to have educational materials that meet all three criteria.

HERE'S THE FINAL takeaway as you continue to put together your educational plan: As a homeschooler, you're no longer bound by the traditional. You can be as creative with your educational plan as you feel meets the needs of your children.

While your idea of goals, schedules, lessons, instructional styles, and curricula might be inspired by what you know of the institutional school day and the skilled way in which classically trained educators schedule their classes, use those conventions as loose guides. While those systems are designed to cater to the educational needs of large groups of students, your homeschooling efforts are focused on catering to the unique needs of your family.

TWELVE:
Designing Your
Homeschooling Environment

The classroom should be an entrance into the world, not an escape from it.

- John Ciardi, poet and teacher

OVER the years, much research has been done on the best way to structure the physical learning environment for children at various ages. Attributes of the physical environment, such as size, layout, open versus closed floor plans, air pollution, color, student density in a defined space, and others, have been studied to find any possible links to student and teacher experience. Researchers from the University of Georgia, among others, have conducted extensive research on the subject of the school environment as it relates to student achievement. Some studies claim to have found concrete evidence that certain elements of the environment, such as the type of lighting or wall color, have a direct impact on student achievement, while others maintain that nothing in the environment is as influential to student achievement as quality instruction.

Ironically, while research abounds, very little actually makes its way to the practitioners—the educators and teachers who work with children— in a way that they can use. In my education classes in college, complete courses on the subject of creating optimal learning environments were rarely offered. In fact, few universities address it in their teacher education coursework. The reason why is pretty clear: Most teachers usually don't have control over their classroom environments anyway. When teachers are hired to teach at a school, they inherit their classrooms from the teacher who had the room before them. School districts also allocate very little money by way of a "classroom budget" for teachers to use to design their ideal learning environment. Sometimes teachers will luck out and parents may volunteer to paint the room or donate plants or furniture to make it nicer, but in general, the environment is fixed before teachers ever get there.

As a teacher, I'm fascinated by the detailed body of research that is available. I'd be lying if I didn't admit to being wildly interested in the topic. As a parent, I'm bothered by the lack of definitive consensus among the experts, so I believe it's best to let common sense rule.

As a homeschooler, you have a lot more say in designing your learning environment, so you may also be interested in the research. But while many of these studies are fascinating, few of them actually matter with respect to the homeschool environment. Most families are unlikely to alter the physical structure of a portion of their house based on a study done on public schools. They may go so far as to install bookcases, or to change the wall color, but they're unlikely to knock out a wall because a study claims their child will learn better in a bigger space. Still, I can't help but recall families who have done just that; they knocked down walls or changed their normal-size windows to long, narrow windows that rise up to the ceiling to maximize favorable spectrums of light. However, I suspect that those families aren't the norm.

> No matter your space limitations, there are innumerable ways to maximize any area's potential for your homeschooling needs.

In my home, we converted a small room that the former occupants had used as a sewing room. Touring the house before we bought it, I remember thinking, "Gosh! This is too small to be billed as a bedroom, but with a wall of bookcases, this would be a surefire schoolroom!"

I admit we are lucky in that we have a designated space that functions as our schoolroom. Most families, however, probably won't have a room devoted to schooling at all. In truth, a kitchen table and a storage space for books and supplies is all you really need. Our schoolroom is a luxury, but it's by no means a requirement for a wonderful homeschooling environment. To be honest, there are months that go by where the schoolroom gathers dust and the kitchen table acts as the preferred hub of our school lives. No matter your space limitations, there are innumerable ways to maximize any area's potential for your homeschooling needs.

Furniture: From Reading Trees to Work Nooks

Don't feel limited to doing a typical desk-chair set-up. At most schools, classrooms are outfitted with desks and chairs, so it's natural that the desk-chair set-up is what we come to expect for a proper learning environment for children. We've become so used to what we see in institutional settings that homeschoolers seem almost conditioned to recreate something similar at home. Most parents are unaware that classroom design has undergone its own evolution over the years. In the 1960s and 1970s, designers pushed to create more comfortable classrooms. Children were given pillows and even beanbag chairs to lounge in during instructional time. (Not really all that shocking for the sixties, is it?) In the past decade, the classrooms for special education students or those with attention disorders, received makeovers. Stationary bikes and standing desks were installed, which allowed students to lean and swing their legs around while they listened to class lectures. Many students showed improvements in retention (further evidence to support physical activity breaks, if you ask me).

In our home, we started our homeschooling adventures around a wobbly red table that we found at a yard sale. Eventually, the kids began asking me about "real school," and launched their own campaign for us to be more school-ish. At that point, I began rummaging around at thrift stores where I found some old-style college chairs with the fold-down desks. They turned out to be much too big and uneven. During activities, pencils and crayons would roll off the slanted desktops and fall into their laps. No good.

Then, to our great fortune, my neighbor, Ginger, called me one day and said that the school district was having a yard sale and selling off tiny desks and chairs for a buck a piece! Before long, she had pulled into my driveway and unloaded the goodies! I'll admit that it's fun to have the traditional school space—but it's totally unnecessary. Most families don't realize what a broad spectrum exists for setting up your homeschool. I've seen kids comfortably getting their lessons at kitchen tables, hammocks, and picnic tables. In other countries, it's not uncommon to see children sitting in groups on the floor.

Use the selected curricula and your children's learning style as your design guide. The curricula you choose and your children's learning styles should play a primary role in what furniture you select for your home classroom. If you have a child who needs to change topics frequently, or if you've chosen a curriculum that utilizes several workstations or learning centers, you may find it beneficial to buy smaller desks or tables. If you have those conditions, but no room space for multiple tables, try using crates or baskets to store materials for different subjects, which can be swapped out quickly when you finish up one topic and move on to the next. Keeping your children's work spots mobile or altering their learning environment in some way can be an invaluable way to help students with short attention spans focus better.

Make sure the furniture is comfy. As a teacher, I never could understand why students were forced to sit in rock-hard chairs all day long, while the teachers got cushy, ergonomic swivel chairs. In our homeschooling classroom, I've set up a different kind of space. My own work area in the schoolroom is unconventional. While my kids do most of their work at desks, we also have a study nook that I call our "reading tree." The "tree" is actually a mural painting of a leafy tree set in one corner of the room. At the base of the tree is a comfy nook made out of a bunch of throw pillows. My children often go there to read, and I often make good use of it myself. My husband makes fun of the amount of time I spend lounging under our reading tree when I'm working on my laptop.

One evening as I was preparing several weeks of lesson plans and printing out lapbook templates, I decided I'd try one of my children's desk chairs. After an hour of sitting, my rear end was sore! How could I have made them endure these horrible chairs? Still, my kids loved their little school chairs so much that they wouldn't part with them. As a compromise, I made cushioned seat covers for each of their desk chairs.

I've also found that setting up comfy little nooks around the house encourages reading, so I make them wherever I see the possibility. My son got new curtains for his room, so the old camouflage curtain panels that once adorned his windows became a little tent off the side of some storage drawers. I put some pillows in the space under the curtain, and without me even pointing it out, my daughter just naturally grabbed a book and crawled inside. Other odd places, like behind a giant flower pot in the sunroom or under the computer desk, have at one time or another served as impromptu reading nooks. All that's needed for a nook is a pile of pillows in a small space; no furniture necessary!

Color: Anything but Institutional Off-White

We all know that color can change the mood of a space. For your homeschooling classroom, you may be tempted to paint your walls different colors to create a livelier environment. There's nothing like a splash of color to brighten a space. So, what colors should you use?

While personal preference will guide much of your design decisions on color, there are a few guidelines that may be helpful:

Avoid bland colors and décor. Your schoolroom is a learning environment; use color to stimulate your young minds. Educator Edward B. Nuhfer, who's written about classroom design, recommends a palette of shades rather than your usual plain, white walls:[1]

> ... light yellow-orange, beige, pale or light green, or blue-green are good choices for three of the four wall surfaces. Pastel oranges promote cheerful, lively and sociable moods that are desirable in a college classroom. Pastel yellow has a similar cheerful effect. Greens and blue-greens in pastels are calming and provide a good background color suited to relaxation in tasks that require concentration. Deep or loud tones are appropriate for trim...

As you can see, you have a flexible palette to work with and there are many hues appropriate for your schoolroom. In general, colors best suited to classroom use are those that reduce agitation and promote a sense of wellbeing. Even without knowing anything about color theory, we'd expect that softer colors are better for soothing children, while glaring colors might trigger irritability. Nuhfer recommends against "deep reds, browns (excluding natural wood finish, which is good) and dark blues," calling them "particularly detrimental."[2] Traditional white and off-white walls and ceilings, while seemingly neutral can have a potentially negative effect on vision, but only if combined with partial spectrum, fluorescent lighting that's common in institutional spaces like offices, hospitals, and public schools.

Our own schoolroom was painted with colors that were purchased for a particular room and then deemed not quite right, or that we had left over after painting other rooms. The room is light green, from a color we used in my son's safari-themed room, accented with some of that pumpkin orange color from the paint we used in the hallways.

Adding a colorful mural of a painted reading tree (see below) surrounded by paths and shrubs and a little bunny peeking over the top on one wall sets the tone of the room as a place that's pleasant but also academically focused.

It's a quiet moment of reading under the reading tree.
(Left to right: Hunter, Hannah Jane, and Haven)

Lighting: Light Bulbs and Happy Lamps

I don't have to tell you that good lighting is essential for a good learning environment. Most parents think that lighting is all about having enough illumination to see, but there's more to lighting than just the amount of light needed to read a book or do an activity.

Opt for broad-spectrum, natural lighting. In the traditional classroom setting, fluorescent lighting is most common but that's changing. Emerging research suggests that the common fluorescent bulbs emit more yellow and red light than pure white. This artificial lighting can cause stress on the eyes and even affect student mood. Broad-spectrum bulbs that emit a more pure white or blue light mimic natural light and can have a calming affect.

Seasonal Affective Disorder (SAD) is a documented condition among people who lack adequate exposure to natural light due to the local climate or the season, such as during the winter months. Those affected by SAD can become moody and more depressed. A common treatment for this disorder is time under special lighting that mimics natural sunlight. During my six years living in Eugene, Oregon, a town with weather similar to Seattle in terms of overcast and dreary winter days, I learned that the university where my husband worked had quite an arsenal of what we lovingly referred to as "happy lamps." Students suffering from SAD, or who felt they were being adversely affected by the lack of sunshine, could sign up to sit under the special, broad-spectrum lamps for short periods each day. Even if your child isn't suffering from SAD, it's clear that there are emotional and psychological benefits to having ample, natural sunlight.

Set up your classroom in a room that gets natural sunlight, if possible. With all that in mind, you may want to be a bit choosy when it comes to lighting for your schooling area. Most children function better in spaces illuminated with natural light. If your schoolroom has natural sunlight streaming in through big windows, consider yourself lucky. We like to place our little desks right by the windows on the south side of our house, and forget the overhead lights completely for the months that we can. Increased energy costs are an often-overlooked expense associated with homeschooling. Taking advantage of natural sunlight can cut your expenses while saving the eyesight and mood of your children.

If this topic is of particular interest to you and you have the resources to adjust your home's lighting scheme, browse the Web for builder resources that discuss optimal window placement for achieving the best sunlight exposure for different seasons, and explore your local hardware store's lighting section for bulbs that mimic natural light.

Floors: More than Just Hard and Soft

While there is little research to suggest one floor type or covering is preferable to another in the school setting, there is much for the family to weigh when deciding on floor surfaces for their homeschooling area.

Watch out for potential allergens from carpeted surfaces. While you'll find scant academic research in the area of floor coverings and the impact on learning environments, research is abundant on the effect of carpets on allergies. Chemicals in carpet fibers have been found to cause respiratory issues for some sensitive children, and many families with certain health problems opt out of carpet for that reason. Carpets can trap common household airborne allergens and dirt more than hard surfaces, and are harder to clean. If you anticipate a lot of spills and accidents, carpeted surfaces may end up being a housekeeping nuisance.

Aside from allergies, there are also other risks. Perfluorinated chemicals (PFCs) are synthetic chemicals designed to repel grease and water and found in most products that claim to be stain resistant, including carpets. Research shows that these chemicals pose harmful effects to the human body. Even if your children haven't shown any signs of allergies, the chemicals often present in stain-resistant carpets could be a risk to them if they're spending much of their time on the floor. If your children tend to read or write lying down on their stomachs much of the day (though for posture and writing mechanics reasons, I advise against regularly writing on the floor instead of at a desk or a table), it might be worth investigating what kind of chemicals are used in your carpet.

Softer, carpeted surfaces act as noise dampeners and feel more comfy. One advantage that carpet has over hard surface flooring is that carpet can absorb sound waves, resulting in a more quiet and relaxing environment. It's also much warmer and more comfy underfoot. Unlike their peers enrolled at institutional settings, your children will likely spend a great deal of time barefoot while schooling at home, so carpet or rugs can add an element of warmth to their day. Carpet is also more inviting for playtime and for activities that involve sitting in groups on the floor.

One solution that many families with delicate allergy issues find works for them is covering hard floors with area rugs. Unlike wall-to-wall carpeting, rugs can be frequently washed and dried on a high heat setting to eliminate allergy-causing mites or animal hair. It can also be more affordable to buy a smaller area rug made of special low-chemical fibers than to cover an entire home with specialized carpeting.

Minimizing Distractions

As a teacher, I found that school buildings were full of distractions, depending on the location of the room within the building. Horrifyingly enough, my SLC (structured learning center) classroom for special education students, many of whom had difficulties concentrating, was located right next to the school's playground. For the better part of the day, balls would bounce against the external door and classroom walls, kids on the playground would crowd around the windows to gawk rudely at the "special kids," and the general buzz from the playground activity would seep in through the walls. Suffice it to say it wasn't a good arrangement. I've also taught in classrooms that bordered the school parking lot, and by the end of the day, students would become so preoccupied with whose parents had just pulled up outside that they couldn't concentrate.

The most horrifically distracting school building I've ever been in was actually the school where my son received speech therapy for a time. Every single classroom in the entire building had one glass wall that separated it from the hallway. I don't know if it was designed this way so that all classroom activities could be monitored easily by passersby, or so that kids walking down the hallway always felt a watchful eye on them, but it was evident that it was a source of distraction. Every time someone walked through the halls, classrooms full of kids would all turn their heads to see who was passing through. I don't know what the architects or designers were thinking, but it was clearly a case where aesthetics superseded concerns regarding an optimal learning environment.

Designate separate spaces for school and for play. At home, it's both easier and harder for homeschoolers to control distractions. Just as my SLC students had difficulty doing their school work while they were in such close proximity to kids indulging in blissful, carefree play outside, you can expect any child who's "doing school" to have difficulty performing his or her best with a sibling playing video games in the next room, or with a parent chatting on the phone down the hall.

When setting up your homeschooling space, make sure it's a space designated for academic pursuits only. If you don't have a clear separation between the schoolroom and the rest of the house, designate quiet zones while "school is in session." Always keep a clear separation between recreational and learning activities. Make sure *everyone* is done with school work before letting play spill over into your learning space.

Play background music only at certain times. Some families work well with music or gentle background noise filling the void of a silent room, while other families are much more sensitive to sound and can be easily distracted. I know friends who can't write while listening to music that contains lyrics, and often find themselves inadvertently writing the words to the song. Others claim they can't work without a little background noise. As I get older, I find it hard to even write my own name if there's too much noise in the room!

As a student teacher, I once taught in a classroom where the teacher played classical music in the background all day. It was meant to be soothing, but unfortunately it distracted the fire out of me. The music made it so difficult for me to concentrate that I had trouble filling out simple administrative forms in that room. Yet looking around, I saw that the students actually enjoyed the background music, many claiming to feel mellow and calm as a result.

The jury is still out on the question of the appropriateness of music during periods of study. While newer research shows a slight improvement in cognitive retention among students who listen to quiet, slow tempo, lyric-free music, older studies report the opposite. So, what's going on?

Here's my take on interpreting the research so far: More than ever before, we've seen a marked increase in incidences of attention disorders among elementary-age children. According to the Eastern Virginia Medical School and Children's Hospital of the King's Daughters, there was a 700% increase in psychostimulant use among children in the 1990s.[3] A very common assumption about the underlying cause of conditions that required these medications was environmental: Children were experiencing a decrease in quiet time and an increase in stimulation, contributing to a rise in attention disorders.

In theory, in environments full of distraction, young developing brains can become dependent on stimuli and experiences. Over-stimulation may work like a drug that the brain becomes addicted to, and then later can't function without. Prescribed psychostimulants, a professor once explained to me, create a sort of "white noise" in the brain that mimics the constant stimulation that the brain has come to need.

While these are just working theories at this point, parents, especially homeschoolers, should take note. The evidence that overstimulation can lead to attention disorders tells me that the wise thing to do is to avoid playing music during activities that require focus and to minimize as many distractions as possible during study time.

Do I play music during the day in my home? I certainly do. We have a variety of instrumental music that we play during various other activities. When we do art projects, we listen to music from the culture whose art we're studying or replicating. When we stretch together in the mornings, we have a soothing relaxation track we enjoy. We even have a clean-up song we play when doing chores or putting things away. So yes, we play a lot of music, but never while we're studying or when I'm giving the children a focused lesson.

THERE IS MUCH to consider when designing your homeschool environment. From lighting to colors, floor covering to furniture, there are endless possibilities before you. Be patient and take time to observe your young students as they study, and to consider ways that you could make their physical learning environment more conducive to focused learning and creative play.

A FINAL WORD:
Your Homeschooling
Adventure – It's Just Started

AFTER reading this book, I hope you now have a basic understanding of the core methods and approaches to teaching that can illuminate your own homeschooling curriculum. You've now learned how to assess your children's different intelligences, learning styles, and temperaments, and know which methods and strategies may work best to complement them. You now also have the basic tools and frameworks to figure out how best to plan and adapt your learning environment at home.

I've said it before throughout the book and will say it again: "Homeschooling is an adventure." Make this your mantra.

As you work your way down this priceless path, remember that life is about growing and changing, about joy and love, and that the road you're on right now has the potential to increase all of that. Get ready to learn things you never knew. Right alongside your children, you'll experience the wonder of the world through their eyes. You'll have more time than you ever dreamed of with your family, learning who they are and who they want to be; more time to giggle and laugh together and to bathe them in love and acceptance.

So many good things are coming your way as a homeschooler. Get ready to enjoy the ride.

RESOURCES

Here you'll find some of my handpicked resources for crafting the ideal homeschool experience for your family. For even more ideas, thoughts, and resources, you can always visit my website, At Home with Momma Skyla (athomewithmommaskyla.blogspot.com), where I'm always adding new content.

Books

- *Form Drawing for Beginners* (offered by Christopherous Homeschool Resources)
- *Soul Development Through Handwriting: The Waldorf Approach to the Vimala Alphabet* by Jennifer Crebbin
- *The Well Trained Mind* by Susan Wise Bauer (welltrainedmind.com)
- *Teach Your Child to Read in 100 Easy Lessons* by Siegfried Engelmann, Phyllis Haddox, and Elaine Brunner
- *The Teenage Liberation Handbook: How to Quit School and Get a Real Life and Education* by Grace Llewellyn

Online

Lectures, Lessons, and More

- Brain Pop (brainpop.com)
- Cozy English Grammar (splashesfromtheriver.com)
- Donna Young Homeschool Resources (donnayoung.org/index.htm)
- Exploratorium (exploratorium.edu)
- K-12 (k12.com)

- Khan Academy (khanacademy.org)
- Reflex Math (reflexmath.com)
- RSA Animate lecture series (comment.rsablogs.org.uk/videos/)
- Starfall (more.starfall.com)
- Teacher Tube (teachertube.com)
- Vi Hart Math Videos (vihart.com)
- WatchKnowLearn (watchknowlearn.org)
- X-tra Math (xtramath.org)
- Homeschool Buyer (homeschoolbuyersco-op.org/homeschool-id)

Montessori

- Montessori Outlet (montessorioutlet.com)
- Montessori Print Shop (montessoriprintshop.com)
- YouTube channels: myworksmontessori, AtHomeMontessori, InfoMontessori, unitedmontessori, and montessoritraining
- Brilliant Minds Montessori (an actual brick and mortar school that also sells comprehensive math and reading kits on Amazon)

Waldorf

- Waldorf Books (waldorfbooks.com)
- Waldorf Curriculum (waldorfcurriculum.com)
- A Little Garden Flower (waldorfjourney.typepad.com)
- Over in the Meadow (overinthemeadow.wordpress.com)
- Ancient Hearth (ancienthearth2.blogspot.com)

Trivium

- Classical Scholar (classicalscholar.com)
- Trivium Academy (triviumacademy.blogspot.com)
- Trivium Pursuits (triviumpursuit.com)
- Classical Conversations (classicalconversations.com)

Charlotte Mason

- Ambleside Online (amblesideonline.org)
- Simply Charlotte Mason (simplycharlottemason.com)
- The Tanglewood School (tanglewoodeducation.com)
- Living Books Curriculum (livingbookscurriculum.com)
- A Charlotte Mason blog summary (blogcarnival.com/bc/cprof_2378.html)
- The Handbook of Nature Study blog (handbookofnaturestudy.blogspot.com)
- Harmony Art Mom (harmonyartmom.blogspot.com)
- Practical Pages (practicalpages.wordpress.com)

Unschooling

- Sandra Dodd's site (sandradodd.com)
- Unschooling Ruminations (unschoolingblog.com)
- Christian Unschoolers (christianunschooling.com)
- John Holt's Growing Without Schooling (holtgws.com)

Curricula Reviews

- Homeschool Reviews (homeschoolreviews.com)
- Homeschool Curriculum Reviews (homeschool-curriculum-reviews.com)
- Yahoo Groups Homeschool Reviews (groups.yahoo.com/group/o-homeschoolreviews)

Forums, Groups, and Networks

- Homeschool World Forum (home-school.com/forums)
- Homeschool.com (homeschool.com/forum)
- Yahoo Groups (groups.yahoo.com) - Search to find a relevant forum related to homeschooling

Tools

- Screenr (screenr.com)
- GoView (goview.com)
- Microsoft Visio (visio.microsoft.com)
- Gliffy (gliffy.com)
- Houghton Mifflin Harcourt's Education Place (eduplace.com/graphicorganizer)

Planning Worksheets

Over the next few pages, I've included several worksheets to help you take what you've learned and start planning and devising your homeschooling adventure.

- Worksheet 1: Financial Planning
- Worksheet 2: My Homeschooling Vision and Mission
- Worksheet 3: My Homeschooling Goals, By Subject
- Worksheet 4: School Day Schedule
- Worksheet 5: Weekly Activities Calendar
- Worksheet 6: Student Assessment
- Worksheet 7: Curricula Comparison

Make copies of the forms printed in the book or download printable PDF versions at www.nightowlspress.com/e-book-store/home-field-advantage/ under the "For Parents" tab. Feel free to create new forms based on these worksheets as you discover and rediscover what works best for you and your family.

Worksheet 1: FINANCIAL PLANNING

Complete the following lists to start planning your homeschooling budget. Homeschooling is more affordable than you think.

List	Your Assessment
Family priorities: *Make a list of everything you value and want most for your family.*	
Time accounting: *Make an honest assessment of where your time is spent. If you're like most families, you'll see more time than you'd like spent on television, random web surfing, and commuting in the car.*	

List	Your Assessment
Expenses:	
List your monthly spending. Include what you spend on housing, utilities, auto/transport, food, dining out, insurance, entertainment/ recreation, clothing, medical/dental, and debt (student loans, bank loans).	

Worksheet 2: MY HOMESCHOOLING VISION AND MISSION

How do you define an education? What do you hope your children will take away from class time? What are your educational goals for them?

Homeschooling Vision and Mission

Homeschooling Vision and Mission

Worksheet 3: MY HOMESCHOOLING GOALS, BY SUBJECT

For each subject: How much time do you want to devote? What type of approach appeals to you and will be best suited for each child's learning style? What sort of activities will you engage in? How will you approach those less desirable subjects?

Subject	Goals
Language Arts:	
Math:	

Subject	Goals
History/ Social Studies:	
Science:	

Subject	Goals
Other:	
Other:	

Subject	Goals
Other:	
Notes:	

Worksheet 4: SCHOOL DAY SCHEDULE

Use this schedule to spread out a typical, school-only day for each of your children. This schedule will help you stagger the high-need and independent subjects, allowing you to give your children your undivided attention when they need it the most. Don't work in co-op sessions or extracurricular lessons unless those are everyday activities.

	Child's Name:	Child's Name:	Child's Name:	Child's Name:
7:00-7:30				
7:30-8:00				
8:00-8:30				
8:30-9:00				
9:00-9:30				

	Child's Name:	Child's Name:	Child's Name:	Child's Name:
9:30-10:00				
10:00-10:30				
10:30-11:00				
11:00-11:30				
11:30-12:00n				
12:00n-12:30				

	Child's Name:	Child's Name:	Child's Name:	Child's Name:
12:30-1:00				
1:00-1:30				
1:30-2:00				
2:00-2:30				
2:30-3:00				
3:00-3:30				
3:30-4:00				

Use this area for notes on your school day schedule.

Notes:

Worksheet 5: WEEKLY ACTIVITIES CALENDAR

This is the place to consider your weekly obligations that don't occur everyday, but are regular and predictable. Once you've filled in those regular activities, you can begin to write in other subjects around those activities for days that aren't going to be school-only. Don't forget to account for travel time to and from activities.

	MON	TUE	WED	THU	FRI
7:00-8:00					
8:00-9:00					

	MON	TUE	WED	THU	FRI
9:00-10:00					
10:00-11:00					
11:00-12:00n					

	MON	TUE	WED	THU	FRI
12:00n-1:00					
1:00-2:00					
2:00-3:00					

	MON	TUE	WED	THU	FRI
3:00-4:00					
4:00-5:00					
5:00-6:00					

	MON	TUE	WED	THU	FRI
6:00-7:00					
8:00-9:00					
9:00-10:00					

Use this area for notes on your weekly activities.

Notes:

Worksheet 6: STUDENT ASSESSMENT

Make copies of the following worksheet for each child and consider each child as an individual as you fill in the spaces. This is the first step towards individualizing your educational plan to meet the needs of each student in your home.

	Your Assessment
Child's Name:	
Grade level:	
Aptitudes: *List the subjects your child will study. Which areas does he/she excel in and where does he/she need extra TLC or tutoring?*	

	Your Assessment
Learning style(s): *Is your child an auditory, visual, or tactile learner?*	
Temperament(s): *What is your child's general temperament (sanguine, melancholic, choleric, or phlegmatic)?*	

	Your Assessment
Special needs or accommodations: *How does he/she react to rewards and discipline? Do you need to set up learning stations or break up teaching sessions?*	
Scheduling considerations: *How will you stagger group work and individual work with your child?*	

Your Assessment

Notes:

Worksheet 7: CURRICULA COMPARISON

This is the time to make copious notes about your options for each subject. Take your time here. Even when you take the plunge and make a purchase, keep these notes; down the line, you may find that your needs change and your thoughts in the past may help you change course while staying true to your vision.

	Curriculum:	Curriculum:	Curriculum:	Curriculum:
Price/cost:				
Primary educational method used: (E.g., Waldorf, Charlotte Mason, Trivium, etc.?)				
Company reputation:				

	Curriculum:	Curriculum:	Curriculum:	Curriculum:
Customer or technical support: Y/N?				
Lesson plan support: Y/N?				
Trial period or sample units: Y/N? Duration of trial period?				
Money back guarantee or other policies:				
Community networks Y/N?				

	Curriculum:	Curriculum:	Curriculum:	Curriculum:
Noteworthy customer reviews (positive or negative):				

Use this area for notes on your curriculum research.

Notes:

GLOSSARY

Attention Deficit Disorder (ADD): a syndrome typically diagnosed in childhood and characterized by a persistent pattern of impulsiveness and short attention span that interferes with normal functioning at school, work, or home.

Attention Deficit Hyperactivity Disorder (ADHD): Attention Deficit Disorder with the added component of hyperactivity.

Advanced Placement (AP): a program that offers college level courses at high schools across the U.S., and provides testing that may allow students to skip basic freshman courses in college.

Adler, Mortimer: American philosopher and educator who wrote extensively on a variety of topics; author of the Paideia Proposal, which provided a classical style framework for the public education system in the U.S.

Anthroposophy: a philosophy expounded by Austrian-born Rudolph Steiner that explores the existence of an objective, intellectually comprehensible spiritual world accessible by individuals through direct experience and inner development.

Asperger's Syndrome: a disorder on the high functioning end of the autism spectrum; characterized by uneasy social interactions, often characterized as robotic, repetitive patterns of behavior, and obsessive interest.

Bodily-kinesthetic: an area of intelligence, as proposed by educational philosopher Howard Gardner, characterized by excellent motor control, skillful bodily movements, and the ability to choose and develop reflex-like motions.

Charlotte Mason: British educator who committed her life to improving the quality of education and to training mothers and governesses to respond more thoughtfully to the needs of their children.

Choleric: one of the four temperaments outlined in the area of proto-psychology known as humorism, and later expounded upon by Rudolph Steiner. Choleric individuals are characterized by having high energy, passion, aggression, and leadership abilities.

Classical Education: originally the foundation of liberal arts education in medieval universities, it is composed of the trivium and quadrivium. In modern times, it has evolved into a highly rigorous and academically focused style of education, often used by homeschoolers and revamped for the public education system by Mortimer Adler under the name, Paideia Proposal.

Curricula: the defined courses of study that a student will undertake in a year. This may be a complete educational plan that outlines the topics to be studied and resources to be used, or it may be a set of scripted lesson plans. Sometimes a curriculum covers all areas of schooling for a period of time, or a parent may choose different curricula for different subjects and execute each of the different curricula daily.

Democratic Schools (free schools): schools that participate in a worldwide movement that advocates for students to have equal shares in decision making for all aspects of their school along with the faculty and staff. Popular models for democratic schools are the Summerhill School and the Sudbury School.

Eurythmy: a form of expressive performance art used primarily in Waldorf schools; considered to have both educational and therapeutic value for students. It was created jointly by Rudolph Steiner and Marie von Sivers.

Free Schools: see "Democratic Schools."

Gardner, Howard: American developmental psychologist and professor of Cognition and Education who pioneered the new theory of intelligence known as "multiple intelligences" that claims that, in addition to having multiple learning styles, human beings manifest intelligence in different ways. His theories offered an alternative to the historically accepted "general intelligence factor" or the "intelligence quotient" as a measure of intelligence and aptitude.

Graphic Organizers: any visual set-up or layout to organize information on paper. Examples of popular graphic organizers include: brain storming bubbles, Venn diagrams, story webs, concept maps, KWL tables, and Ishikawa diagrams (herring bone diagrams).

Informal Learning: any learning that occurs outside of instructor-led courses, commonly used in language and cultural studies because most typically functioning individuals acquire these skills without taking formal classes. In more loose terms, informal learning may also apply to self-led learning such as independent research outside of formal classwork.

Lapbook: a form of recordkeeping akin to academic scrapbooking in which students keep a notebook or set of folded file folders. The lapbook is generally filled with smaller "mini books" that contain related content about the subject of the lapbook; it will often open to a display of many elaborately folded and decorated pieces of paper that can be lifted or opened in some way to reveal more in-depth information. Lapbooks can be made from scratch or templates may be downloaded or purchased.

Learning Style: an individual's identifiable best method for absorbing and processing new information. Individuals may be visual, auditory, or tactile learners, but are most often a combination of two or all three.

Lesson Plan: a step-by-step guide to teaching a concept. Lesson plans may be scripted, with answers for the teacher to give for various responses or questions from students, or they may present the sequence of activities that need to be followed. Lesson plans differ from curricula in that a lesson plan is what will be covered in one day and one subject; a curricula may include lesson plans, but generally covers a subject or subjects over the span of a unit, semester, or year.

Manipulatives: anything that a student can physically manipulate in order to better grasp an otherwise abstract concept. Popular manipulatives include linking cubes, base-ten blocks, tangrams, Cuisenaire rods, and counting bears, though any physical items provided to students for the purpose of helping them understand an academic concept may be considered manipulatives.

Maslow, Abraham: American professor who created what is now called Maslow's Hierarchy of Needs, a pyramid-shaped visual representation of human kind's physical and emotional needs. Needs are arranged in successive order, from broad physical needs like food and shelter at the base of the pyramid, to higher, emotional and intellectual needs like creativity, a sense of community, and personal fulfillment at the top. Basic needs at the lower levels must be met or fulfilled before higher needs can be accessed and reached.

Melancholic: one of the four temperaments outlined in the area of proto-psychology known as humorism, and later expounded upon by Rudolph Steiner. Melancholic individuals are characterized as being introverted, thoughtful, worrisome, and creative.

Montessori, Maria: Italian physician and educator who worked extensively in special education and early childhood, developing highly specialized materials and methods for teaching children. She is the founder and namesake of the popular Montessori school movement and method that emphasized child-led, individualistic forms of learning.

Multiple intelligences: theory originated by Howard Gardner, an American developmental psychologist and professor, which claims that in addition to having multiple learning styles, human beings manifest intelligence in different ways. The theory offered an alternative to the historically accepted "general intelligence factor" or the "intelligence quotient" as a measure of intelligence and aptitude.

Paideia Proposal: a plan for institutional school reform proposed by Mortimer Adler; it is loosely based on classical education (the trivium and quadrivium) and advocated that all children can be educated.

Part to Whole: a lesson progression in which the small details or individual parts of a concept or topic are examined before the overall, whole picture of how the parts all fit together.

Phlegmatic: one of the four temperaments outlined in the area of proto-psychology known as humorism, and later expounded upon by Rudolph

Steiner. Phlegmatic individuals are characterized by a calm demeanor, self-acceptance, and are often quiet and possibly shy. Phlegmatics tend to appreciate routine and predictability.

Quadrivium: The higher order of studies in Medieval and Renaissance times, consisting of arithmetic, geometry, astronomy, and music. These subjects were only studied after the trivium courses of grammar, logic, and rhetoric had been mastered.

Sanguine: one of the four temperaments outlined in the area of proto-psychology known as humorism, and later expounded upon by Rudolph Steiner. Sanguine individuals are characterized as being impulsive, highly social, pleasure-seekers who often make strong leaders.

Steiner, Rudolph: Austrian philosopher and educator who began what are now known as Waldorf schools or Steiner schools; his educational philosophies placed great emphasis on the social dynamics and creative aspects of education.

Structured Learning Center (SLC): a classroom set-up for small group learning, typically utilized by students with behavioral or cognitive processing difficulties. SLCs generally have a much lower student to teacher ratio, while still allowing students to interact and progress with same-age peers. Its purpose is to help with the reintegration of these students into mainstream classrooms.

Temperament: a psychological term referring to those aspects of an individual's personality that are innate rather than learned. Initially discussed as part of the area of proto-psychology known as humorism, the concept of temperaments has been reinterpreted over time to include many nuanced aspects of personality and behavior. Temperaments were also a large part of Rudolph Steiner's work with children, though his theories are less accepted by the broader medical and educational communities.

Trivium: an introductory curriculum at medieval universities involving the study of grammar, rhetoric, and logic.

Unschooling: a conscious decision not to provide formal education for a child, usually based upon the belief that children will learn what they need to learn from everyday living.

Waldorf: refers to a style of schooling started by Rudolph Steiner that has a strong emphasis on the artistic and social aspects of learning.

Whole Child approach: a way of viewing the child as a complex, multifaceted being with unique social, emotional, and intellectual needs.

Whole to Part: a lesson progression that first looks at the big picture and then moves towards teaching the component parts in increasingly refined detail.

Wonder Box: a box set that contains a full school year of curriculum materials usually produced by a single company and that uses a single educational method or framework for all subjects.

ACKNOWLEDGMENTS

This book owes its existence to so many of my family members, friends, and kind strangers that I could never mention them all. It all began because a handful of persistent blog readers and friends had endless questions about homeschooling and somehow decided that I had the answers.

Over time, I decided that the answers to all of those questions asked in desperation should reside in a single place—a book that I could hand to the next, nervous, new homeschooler I met that would set them down a clearer path.

And here it is. So, my first thank you really must go to the moms who were brave enough to ask a million questions. Your determination and drive for excellence have inspired me.

To my dear family who tolerated my endless typing, researching, and interviewing even as the laundry piled higher and the dinners were served later—thank you. This project has grown to be so special to me, and I couldn't have done it had you not been so supportive. So thanks for the extra chores, for making your own lunches, and for allowing me the time to realize this little dream of mine! I love you all!

Thanks a thousand times over to my mom friends who didn't laugh when I told them I was writing a book, who celebrated when I signed a publishing contract, who watched my children when I went to conduct interviews, and who never ever forgot to ask how the project was going and what they could do to make my life easier while my workload was heavier. I don't know what I would do without my girls!

Finally, thank you to all of the moms, dads, and young people, strangers and friends, who responded to questionnaires, who invited me into your homes, who met me in bistros and coffee shops to chat about schooling methods and motivation. Thank you for your honesty, for your courage, and for sharing a small part of your lives with me. My hope is that through this book, your stories will get to inspire even more families.

NOTES

Chapter 1: The Case for Homeschooling

[1] Brian Ray, *A Nationwide Study of Home Education: Family Characteristics, Legal Matters, and Student Achievement* (Salem, OR: National Home Education Research Institute, 1990), 53.

[2] In addition to legal services, Homeschool Legal Defense Association (HSLDA) conducts research and advocacy work on homeschooling. For more information, visit http://www.hslda.org/.

[3] Chris Klicka, "Can Homeschoolers Participate In Public School Programs?" *Practical Homeschooling* 33 (2000), http://www.home-school.com/Articles/can-homeschoolers-participate-in-public-school-programs.php (accessed June 18, 2012).

[4] Ibid.

[5] See Runyon v. McCrary, 427 U.S. 160 (1976), FindLaw Legal Database.

[6] See Wisconsin v. Yoder, 406 U.S. 205 (1972), Cornell University Law School.

[7] As cited in Kristin Kloberdanz, "California Resists Homeschool Ruling," *Time,* March 12, 2008, http://www.time.com/time/nation/article/0,8599,1721703,00.html (accessed June 18, 2012).

[8] Walter Croskey quoted in *Christian Examiner*, "Justices Rule Homeschooling in California Illegal," March 2008, https://www.christianexaminer.com/Articles/Articles%20Mar08/Art_Mar08_19.html (accessed June 18, 2012).

[9] National Center for Education Statistics, "Fast Facts," http://nces.ed.gov/fastfacts/display.asp?id=65 (accessed May 7, 2012).

[10] Yetunde Ijaiya, "Effects of Over-Crowded Classrooms on Teacher-Student Interactions," *Llorin Journal of Education* 17, 1 (1997).

[11] Sarah Sparks, "Class Sizes Show Sign of Growing," *Educational Week*, November 24, 2010, http://www.edweek.org/ew/articles/2010/11/24/13size_ep.h30.html (accessed May 7, 2012).

[12] Ibid.

[13] *Education Week*, "High School Reform," Edweek.com, August 4, 2004, http://www.edweek.org/ew/issues/high-school-reform/ (accessed May 7, 2012).

[14] Ken Robinson, "Bring on the Learning Revolution," SirKenRobinson.com, http://sirkenrobinson.com/skr/bring-on-the-learning-revolution#more-25 (accessed May 8, 2012).

[15] National Academy of Education, "Standards, Assessments, and Accountability," http://www.naeducation.org/Standards_Assessments_Accountability_White_Paper.pdf (accessed May 8, 2012).

[16] Ibid.

[17] Ken Robinson, "RSA Animate – Changing Education Paradigms," SirKenRobinson.com, http://sirkenrobinson.com/skr/rsa-animate-changing-education-paradigms (accessed June 2, 2011).

[18] Abraham H. Maslow, "A Theory of Human Motivation," *Psychological Review* 50, 4 (1943): 370-96.

[19] Wikimedia Commons, "Maslow's Hierarchy of Needs," June 18, 2009 (accessed October 9, 2012).

[20] Brian D. Ray, *Home Educated and Now Adults: Their Community and Civic Involvement, Views about Homeschooling, and Other Traits* (Salem, OR: National Home Education Research Institute, 2004).

[21] Homeschool Legal Defense Association, "Homeschooling Thru High School," HSLDA.org, http://www.hslda.org/highschool/college.asp (accessed July 12, 2012).

[22] Daniel Golden, "Home-Schooled Kids Defy Stereotypes, Ace SAT Test," *The Wall Street Journal*, February 11, 2000.

[23] Christopher Klicka, "Homeschooled Students Excel in College," *Homeschool Legal Defense Association: Current Issue Analysis* 1 (2006): 1.

[24] "Q. and A.: College Admissions," *The New York Times* blog, December 17, 2008, http://questions.blogs.nytimes.com/2008/12/17/qa-college-admissions/#homeschool (accessed July 12, 2012).

[25] Bruce Walker and Jeff Brenzel quoted in "Q. and A.: College Admissions," *The New York Times* blog, December 17, 2008, http://questions.blogs.nytimes.com/2008/12/17/qa-college-admissions/ (accessed June 13, 2012).

[26] Daniel Golden, "Home-Schooled Kids Defy Stereotypes, Ace SAT Test," *The Wall Street Journal*, February 11, 2000.

[27] Homeschool College Counselor, "*Should a Homeschooler take the GED?*" December 21, 2010, http://homeschoolcollegecounselor.com/academics/should-a-homeschooler-take-the-ged/#comments (accessed June 13, 2012).

[28] From the Drug Enforcement Agency Congressional Testimony, Hearing before the Committee on Education and the Workforce: Subcommittee on Early Childhood, Youth and Families, 106th Congress (2000). Testimony of Terrance Woodworth, http://www.justice.gov/dea/pubs/cngrtest/ct051600.htm (accessed June 18, 2012).

[29] Lawrence H. Diller quoted in Dianne Dunne, "Statistics Confirm Rise in Childhood ADHD and Medication Use," *Education World*,

http://www.educationworld.com/a_issues/issues148a.shtml
(accessed June 18, 2012).

Chapter 2: Educational Methods and Approaches 101

[1] Emma Goldman, *My Disillusionment in Russia* (Mineola, NY: Dover Publications, 2003), 260.

[2] The classic text on statistical fallacies is Darrell Huff's book, *How to Lie with Statistics* (New York: Penguin, 1993).

Chapter 3: Montessori Method

[1] Maria Montessori quoted in Don Jennings, "Montessori Teachers Collective," Montessori Quotes, February 1, 2001, http://www.moteaco.com/quotes.html (accessed April 20, 2012).

[2] Maria Montessori quoted in Montessori Synergies: Integral Visions for Education, "Doctor Montessori on the Prepared Environment," July 22, 2010, http://www.montessorisynergies.com/synergies/the-prepared-environment/the-environment-quotes-by-maria-montessori/ (accessed April 20, 2012).

[3] Maria Montessori quoted in Okemos Public Montessori at Central, "Quotes," December 9, 2009, http://www.okemosschools.net/education/components/scrapbook/default.php?sectiondetailid=9823&PHPSESSID=1f662fdebbf8e6b31b772bd930b3cfe8 (accessed April 20, 2012).

[4] Maria Montessori quoted in Montessori Institute of San Diego, Teacher Training Center, "Montessori Graduate Program," March 31, 2010, http://www.misdami.org/misd-trainingcenter/graduate-program-loyola.html (accessed April 20, 2012).

[5] Maria Montessori quoted in Patrick F. Basset, "Utopian Schools," National Association of Independent Schools, June 1, 2005,

http://www.nais.org/Magazines-Newsletters/ISMagazine/Pages/Utopian-Schools.aspx (accessed April 20, 2012).

[6] Maria Montessori quoted in Thomas C. Tiller and Anne Marshall Huston, Eds., *Education: Ends and Means* (Lanham, MD: University Press of America, 1997), 322.

[7] Maria Montessori quoted in North Shore Montessori, "Montessori Philosophy," January 11, 2010, http://www.northshoremontessori.com/index.php/about-us/montessori-philosophy (accessed April 20, 2012).

Chapter 4: Waldorf Education

[1] Rudolf Steiner, *Intuitive Thinking As a Spiritual Path: Philosophy of Freedom* (Hudson, NY: Anthroposophic Press, 1995).

[2] Rudolf Steiner and George Adams, *Anthroposophical Leading Thoughts: Anthroposophy As a Path of Knowledge* (London: Rudolf Steiner Press, 1973), 13.

[3] Rudolph Steiner quoted in Steve Talbot, "Why Not Globalization?" The Nature Institute, March 1, 2001, http://www.natureinstitute.org/pub/ic/ic5/global.htm (accessed April 20, 2012).

[4] Rudolph Steiner, *The Crossing Point: Selected Talks and Writings,* Mary Caroline Richards, Ed. (Hanover, NH: Wesleyan University Press, 1966), 210.

[5] Roy Wilkinson, *The Temperaments in Education* (Fair Oaks, CA: Rudolph Steiner College Press, 1997).

[6] Ibid.

[7] David Vawter, "Block Scheduling Research," Winthrop University,

http://coe.winthrop.edu/vawterd/block/research/research.html
(accessed June 13, 2012).

[8] Rudolph Steiner and Ita Wegman, *Reader's Journal: Extending Practical Medicine* (London: Rudolph Steiner Press, 1925), 63.

[9] Peter Staudenmaier, "Bibliography on the Applicability of 'Occultism' as a Description of Anthroposophy," Waldorf Critics, http://www.waldorfcritics.org/articles/occultism_bibliography.html (accessed June 18, 2012).

[10] Jon Reyhner, "The Reading Wars: Phonics versus Whole Language," North Arizona University, http://jan.ucc.nau.edu/~jar/Reading_Wars.html (accessed June 13, 2012).

Chapter 5: Trivium

[1] Dorothy Sayers, *Recovering the Lost Tools of Learning: An Approach to Distinctly Christian Education* (Irvine, CA: Fieldstead Institute, 1991).

Chapter 6: Charlotte Mason Education

[1] Charlotte Mason, "Out-of-Door Life for the Children," *Home Education* 1 (1906): 67. Available at: http://www.amblesideonline.org/CM/1_2_01to08.html (accessed June 18, 2012).

[2] Essex Cholmondeley, *The Story of Charlotte Mason* (London: Dent, 1960).

[3] Household, "Letters Addressed to Charlotte Mason, 1923-51," Charlotte Mason Archive, Armitt Library and Museum.

[4] Ibid.

[5] Charlotte Mason, "In Memorium," Parents' National Educational Union, 1923.

[6] Elaine Cooper, *When Children Love to Learn: A Practical Application of Charlotte Mason's Philosophy for Today* (Wheaton: Crossway Books, 2004).

[7] Charlotte Mason, "Habit is Ten Natures," *Home Education* 1 (1906): 113. Available at: http://www.amblesideonline.org/CM/1_3.html (accessed June 18, 2012).

[8] As cited in Cathryn Delude, "Brain Researchers Explain Why Old Habits Die Hard," Massachusetts Institute of Technology, 2005, http://web.mit.edu/newsoffice/2005/habit.html (accessed June 13, 2012).

[9] Charlotte Mason, *An Essay Towards a Philosophy of Education: A Liberal Education for All* (London: Dent, 1925).

[10] Charlotte Mason, "Lessons as Instruments in Education," *Home Education* 1 (1906): 280. Available at: http://www.amblesideonline.org/CM/1_5d.html (accessed June 18, 2012).

[11] Ibid.

[12] Charlotte Mason, "Out-of-Door Life for the Children," *Home Education* 1 (1906): 61. Available at: http://www.amblesideonline.org/CM/1_2_01to08.html (accessed June 18, 2012).

Chapter 7: unschooling

[1] Neill Alexander Sutherland, *Summerhill: A Radical Approach to Education* (London: V. Gollancz, 1969), 24.

[2] Ibid., 26.

[3] Anna Craft, "An Analysis of Research and Literature on Creativity in Education," Qualifications and Curriculum Authority, 2001, http://www.euvonal.hu/images/creativity_report.pdf (accessed June 18, 2012).

[4] Mark Twain, "The Facts Concerning the Recent Resignation," *Sketches, New and Old* (Hartford, CT: American Publishing Company, 1875).

[5] Good Morning America, "Extreme Homeschooling: No Tests, No Books, No Classes, No Curriculums," ABC Television, April 19, 2010, http://abcnews.go.com/GMA/Parenting/unschooling-homeschooling-book-tests-classes/story?id=10410867#.UIoaQoU-J3M (accessed June 18, 2012).

[6] Sandra Dodd, "Unschooling: You'll See it When You Believe it," SandraDodd.com, http://sandradodd.com/seeingit (accessed May 12, 2012).

Chapter 8: Whole and Part Instructional Techniques

[1] Jon Reyhner, "The Reading Wars: Phonics versus Whole Language," North Arizona University, http://jan.ucc.nau.edu/~jar/Reading_Wars.html (accessed June 13, 2012).

[2] Ibid.

[3] Brian Mackenzie, "Teaching Methods," Brian Mac Sports Coach, http://www.brianmac.co.uk/teaching.htm (accessed 13 June, 2012).

Chapter 9: Different Kids, Different Smarts and Learning Styles

[1] Shannon Houston, "The Positive Effects Performing Arts Has On Participating Youth," The Community Unity Music Program,

http://communityunity.cfsites.org/custom.php?pageid=1161 (accessed June 13, 2012).

[2] Allan Miller and Dorita Coen, "The Case for Music in the Schools," *Phi Delta Kappan* 75, 6 (1994): 459-61.

[3] Originally, there were only seven intelligences. After presenting those seven, two additional areas were submitted for intelligence status: naturalistic intelligence and spiritual intelligence. While naturalistic intelligence passed the strict criteria, spiritual intelligence did not. Spiritual did not hold up to the strict criteria, regardless of how much some people felt that spirituality must be an intelligence. The distinct features of a separate intelligence for spiritual aptitude could not be convincingly identified.

[4] For more information on Open Culture, see http://www.openculture.com/; on Khan Academy, see https://www.khanacademy.org/; and on NPR Podcasts, see http://www.npr.org/rss/podcast/podcast_directory.php.

[5] For more information about the Movement Matters program, see http://library.usask.ca/theses/available/etd-03182011-205031/.

[6] As cited in ScienceDaily, "Physical Activity May Strengthen Children's Ability To Pay Attention," April 1, 2009, http://www.sciencedaily.com/releases/2009/03/090331183800.htm (accessed May 18, 2012).

[7] Ibid.

[8] As cited in John Cloud, "Kids with ADHD May Learn Better by Fidgeting," *Time*, March 25, 2009, http://www.time.com/time/magazine/article/0,9171,1889178,00.html (accessed June 13, 2012).

[9] Ibid.

Chapter 10: Personality and Learning

[1] As cited in David K. Osborn, Greek Medicine, "Hippocrates," http://www.greekmedicine.net/whos_who/Hippocrates.html (accessed May 18, 2012).

[2] Research on the "serial position effect" and its impact on recall and trust abound. See: Adrian Furnham, "The Robustness of the Recency Effect: Studies Using Legal Evidence," *The Journal of General Psychology* 113, 4 (1986): 351-357; Donald E. Broadbent and Margaret H. P. Broadbent, "Recency Effects in Visual Memory," *The Quarterly Journal of Experimental Psychology Section* 33A (1981): 1-15; and Bennet B. Murdock Jr., "The Serial Position Effect of Free Recall," *Journal of Experimental Psychology* 64, 5 (1962): 482-488.

[3] Hermann Ebbinghaus, *Memory: A Contribution to Experimental Psychology* (New York, NY: Teachers College, Columbia University, 1913).

[4] Ibid.

[5] Thomas S. Critchfield and Michael A. Magoon, "Research in Progress on the Differential Impact of Positive and Negative Reinforcement," *Experimental Analysis of Human Behavior Bulletin* 19, 1 (2001): 16-18.

[6] Shirley King, "Criticism's Harmful Effects," Parent.net, http://www.parent.net/article/archive/criticis.shtml (accessed June 19, 2012).

Chapter 11: Designing and Planning a Tailored Home Education

[1] As cited in Brian Ray, *Strengths of Their Own: Homeschoolers Across America* (Salem, OR: National Home Education Research Institute, 1997).

[2] Ibid.

---

[3] This visual is also known as the "project management triangle." For more information, see http://en.wikipedia.org/wiki/Project_management_triangle.

Chapter 12: Designing Your Homeschooling Environment

[1] Edward B. Nuhfer, "Some Aspects of an Ideal Classroom: Color, Carpet, Light and Furniture." Presented for Idaho State University's Council for Teaching and Learning, 2004. Available at: http://profcamp.tripod.com/ClassroomDesign/IdealClass.html (accessed June 18, 2012).

[2] Ibid.

[3] As cited in D.F. Connor, "ADHD Among American Schoolchildren: Evidence of Overdiagnosis and Overuse of Medication," *Scientific Review of Mental Health Practice* 2 (2003): 49-60.

ABOUT THE AUTHOR

SKYLA-KING CHRISTISON has been teaching for over 10 years. She has a bachelor's degree in education and has given lectures to college students, taught in elementary, middle school, and special education classrooms in both Tennessee and Oregon. After all of that, she turned a sharp corner in her teaching career. Choosing not to send her own kids to school, Skyla teaches her three children their full range of studies right in their own home, using the skills that she developed in both the university and classroom setting to tailor lessons to meet the distinct needs of each of her children.

When she's not teaching or lesson planning, Skyla maintains a popular blog, At Home with Momma Skyla (athomewithmommaskyla.blogspot.com), where parents from around the world visit to read stories from her daily life and get tips for blending the roles of teacher and parent. There, she shares lesson ideas, discusses challenges unique to homeschooling, and answers questions from other parents in addition to musing about the goings on of daily life. She also teaches classes for groups of homeschooling children in her town, nestled in the Rocky Mountains of Northern Utah.

Home Field Advantage: A Guide to Choosing Teaching Methods for Your Homeschooling Champions is her first book.

ABOUT THE PUBLISHER

NIGHT OWLS PRESS (nightowlspress.com) is a small, independent press that publishes nonfiction books that challenge and re-imagine prevailing conventions about business, work, and life. Covering topics on entrepreneurship, education, innovation, and social responsibility, its focus is to turn big ideas into great books that inform and inspire.

Find out more about Night Owls Press books at www.nightowlspress.com/e-book-store/. For special or bulk orders, contact admin@nightowlspress.com.

Made in the USA
Lexington, KY
10 March 2013